D1201635

James K. Humphrey
and the
Sabbath-Day Adventists

James K. Humphrey

AND THE

Sabbath-Day Adventists

R. Clifford Jones

UNIVERSITY PRESS OF MISSISSIPPI

JACKSON

www.upress.state.ms.us

The University Press of Mississippi is a member of the Association of
American University Presses.

First edition 2006

∞

Library of Congress Cataloging-in-Publication Data

Jones, R. Clifford.
  James K. Humphrey and the Sabbath-Day Adventists / R. Clifford
  Jones.— 1st ed.
        p. cm.
  Includes bibliographical references (p.   ) and index.
  ISBN-13: 978-1-57806-891-3 (cloth : alk. paper)
  ISBN-10: 1-57806-891-6 (cloth : alk. paper) 1. Humphrey, James K.
(James Kemuel), 1877–1952. 2. Seventh-day Adventists—Clergy—
Biography. 3. African Americans—New York (State)—New York—
Religion. 4. Harlem (New York, N.Y.)—Church history. I. Title.
  BX6193.H88J66 2006
  286.7'092—dc22

                                               2006002268

British Library Cataloging-in-Publication Data available

CONTENTS

James K. Humphrey
and the
Sabbath-Day Adventists

INTRODUCTION

"I have determined, my friends, that like the apostle Paul, I shall allow nothing to separate me from the love of God—nothing! . . . In 1905, a brother came to my house and urged me to cut loose from this denomination. . . . I refused then to do it, and I refuse now to do it."[1] Uttering these words with conviction and clarity, James Kemuel Humphrey, pastor of the First Harlem Seventh-day Adventist Church in New York City, clutched the pulpit and did all he could to prevent tears from flowing down his face. The occasion was the Fortieth Session of the General Conference of Seventh-day Adventists, and Humphrey was delivering the evening sermon on May 23, 1922. Preaching about suffering, Humphrey let his listeners know that he would never disassociate himself from the Seventh-day Adventist church in spite of calls by other Black pastors for him to do just that. Yet, less than ten years later, James Kemuel Humphrey would leave the Seventh-day Adventist church and establish his own religious organization, the United Sabbath-Day Adventists. What brought about the turnaround in Humphrey's thinking? How could a pastor so bent on staying the course with one religious group change his opinion in a matter of years?

The history of people of African descent in the New World is one of struggle for freedom, empowerment, and self-determination. Their humanity initially challenged by European traders who viewed them as heathenistic and a notch or two above animals in terms of their physiognomy, theirs was an unending quest to prove their humanity and to claim their equality. In the course of their sojourn in Western society, people of African descent have been subjected to "scientific" experiments that sought to ascertain their physical, moral, and intellectual constitution.[2] What African Americans[3] found particularly disturbing was the treatment they received at the hands of White[4] Christians, who, ostensibly, had introduced them to Christianity.[5] Refusing to accept the discriminatory practices of Whites, some of these Blacks left predominantly

White denominations and founded their own independent Black religious organizations.

This study is the account of one such religious group. It is the portrayal of how the United Sabbath-Day Adventists came into existence and of its founding pastor, James Kemuel Humphrey, a Jamaican expatriate who pastored in Harlem during the first half of the twentieth century. By no means institutional history, it is an account of Humphrey's tenure as a Seventh-day Adventist minister and a Sabbath-Day Adventist religious leader, and of the events and conditions that shaped his ministry with both groups. It recounts the circumstances that led to his break with the Seventh-day Adventist denomination, surveys the history of the independent religious organization Humphrey established and led for the first twenty years of its existence, and assesses Humphrey's role and impact as a bold agent of change.

James Kemuel Humphrey was born in the parish of St. Elizabeth, Jamaica, on March 7, 1877. He attended elementary school in the parish and graduated from Colbar College, where he distinguished himself as an exceptional student and eloquent speaker. On December 19, 1900, he married Viola (Roseanne) Anderson of Kingston, Jamaica, embarking shortly thereafter on a career as a Baptist minister. Always painfully aware of the plight of people of African descent in the "New World," Humphrey left Jamaica in 1901 to visit Africa. On his way there he stopped off in New York City, where he was converted to Adventism by a Seventh-day Adventist layman named J. H. Carroll. A former Catholic, Carroll had been converted to Adventism by Stephen Haskell, an Adventist pioneer, and was facilitating meetings in his home in Brooklyn, New York, when Humphrey entered one day. The encounter altered Humphrey's plans and changed his life. Struck by the simplicity and logic of what he heard, Humphrey joined the Seventh-day Adventist church, walking away from the Baptist ministry, itself a significant step. He aborted his trip to Africa, deciding to remain in New York City, where his wife joined him the following year.[6]

In 1903 Humphrey, not Carroll, was chosen to lead the small group of Adventists that had grown out of Carroll's labors, a testament to Humphrey's extraordinary organizational and leadership skills. A gifted musician and reputable scholar, Humphrey had innate charisma, a quality that contributed in no small way to the almost hypnotic effect his presence and words had on people. Humphrey stood over six feet tall and was lean all his life. His lithe frame, however, was not his most distinguishing feature, but the way he grew and styled his hair. Parted to the left and heaped up to the right, Humphrey's hair was snow white from his late forties onward, and Humphrey also had a thick moustache that was hooked upward on both sides. Humphrey's hair and moustache captured and kept the attention of people, exerting somewhat of a mystical pull on some of them, especially in his later years when his hair was completely white. Though he shunned the ostentatiousness and flamboyance of other notable Harlem ministers of his era, Humphrey was an impeccable dresser whose wardrobe was tasteful and conservative, as were his manners. Courteous almost to a fault, Humphrey would nod to people as he walked the streets of Harlem, gracefully acknowledging their presence and cultivating the society of those he encountered.[7]

When Humphrey assumed the leadership of Carroll's group in 1903, it consisted of ten people. The following year, Humphrey began to function as a licensed missionary with the Greater New York Conference of Seventh-day Adventists,[8] and he was ordained as a Seventh-day Adventist minister in 1907. That year, he was invited to serve on the Executive Committee of the Greater New York Conference and on the Executive Committee of the Atlantic Union Conference some time later. When the North American Negro Department of the General Conference of Seventh-day Adventists was established in 1909, Humphrey was appointed as one of the members of its Executive Committee.[9] Humphrey generally approved of the establishment of this department, though he was not necessarily pleased with its White leadership, saying that the church should be intentional in its efforts to win Blacks in the North as it had been to do so in the South.[10]

Humphrey's meteoric rise in the Adventist Church continued through the 1910s. He was chosen as a delegate from the Atlantic Union to the General Conference Session in 1913, the first of the many times he would serve in this capacity. He found the experience enlightening and educational, as meeting and interacting with church leaders from around the world helped him to understand the global mission and impact of his church. Yet Humphrey could not lose sight of the challenges the race issue presented the Seventh-day Adventist denomination. When a recommendation was introduced at the Session to drop the words "North American" from the name of the Negro Department, Humphrey spoke out against it, claiming that he was afraid the racial conditions then permeating North America would spread to the West Indies. Obviously, Humphrey, not unlike some other West Indians, believed that the region from which he hailed had rid itself of racism and was basking in racial enlightenment.[11]

As 1913 drew to a close, the Atlantic Union of Seventh-day Adventists boasted over two hundred Black members, many of whom were members in the churches of the Greater New York Conference. Humphrey, a gifted evangelist, continued holding tent revivals in New York City, especially in the borough of Manhattan, and the result was that by 1920 the membership of the First Harlem Church, where Humphrey was serving as pastor, was about six hundred. At the Greater New York Conference Session of 1920, Humphrey was appointed a member of the Conference's Credentials and Licenses Committee and reappointed to the Conference's Executive Committee. Humphrey tendered the report of the Colored Department of the Conference, which in 1920 consisted of three churches—First Harlem, Brooklyn Number Two, and White Plains. At the Session, Humphrey's wife was voted to the Medical Missions and Sabbath School subcommittees of the Conference, receiving a missionary license along the way. When a resolution calling for the training of suitable individuals for foreign missionary work was introduced, Humphrey gave it his wholehearted endorsement, saying that many unproven and ill-trained individuals had gone forth to labor and that the resolution was long overdue. It was Humphrey who made the motion to adjourn the Conference Session.[12]

Two years later, at the Seventeenth Session of the Greater New York Conference, Humphrey offered the opening prayer of the first meeting. No sooner had the first business meeting of the Session started than he took to the floor to explain why a group of Black Adventists meeting in New Rochelle should be accepted into the sisterhood of churches in the Conference.[13] During the summer of 1921, Percy Brownie, a member of Humphrey's Harlem congregation, had collaborated with a few members from the White Plains, New York, church in an outreach initiative that resulted in five baptisms. Along with eleven members from White Plains and two transferees from Kingston, Jamaica, a church of eighteen had been started and was by the time of the Session returning appreciable tithes and contributing liberal offerings. Humphrey's motion that the delegates the group had sent to the Session be seated and that the congregation be accepted into the sisterhood of churches was overwhelmingly accepted. Thus, by the end of 1922, four Black churches were in the Greater New York Conference, all of them under the supervision of Humphrey.[14]

At the Seventeenth Session of the Greater New York Conference, Humphrey was appointed to the Conference's Pastoral Committee, the Committee on Nominations, the Plans Committee, the Constitution and By-Laws Committee, and the Executive Committee. Black delegates to the Session totaled fifty-nine, with the majority—forty-eight—coming from Humphrey's Harlem congregation, as well as six from Brooklyn Number Two, three from New Rochelle, and two from White Plains. First Harlem had the largest number of delegates of any church in the Conference. As the Session was about to adjourn, Humphrey joined the Greater New York Conference and Atlantic Union presidents in thanking God and the assembled delegates for the harmonious way in which the Conference had moved forward.[15] At the following Session of the Conference, Humphrey served in the key role of secretary of the Session.[16]

Part of the reason for Humphrey's success as a minister was that he was both available and approachable. Often, he opened up his home to his members, welcoming them there for fun, food, and fellowship with his family. These social engagements had the additional benefit of fostering the faith of the members, who generally were always on the lookout for environments beyond the church's precincts that were conducive to the strengthening of their faith. With most of Humphrey's membership having migrated to New York City from the South and Caribbean, members were truly pilgrims in a strange land. Humphrey cultivated community and reciprocity among his members, encouraging them to band together and to be supportive of each other.[17]

First Harlem continued growing so well that no building in Harlem was large enough to accommodate the burgeoning congregation. Consequently, in consultation with Atlantic Union and General Conference officials, the group's leaders made a decision to start a new congregation in Harlem. On January 1, 1924, Harlem Number Two was launched with 108 members, and Matthew C. Strachan was called up from Florida to lead the new congregation.

At his installation, Strachan spoke glowingly of Humphrey's twenty-four years of labor and leadership in the New York City area. By the time Harlem Number Two was voted a part of the Greater New York Conference at the Conference's Eighteenth Session held on March 12–14 that year, the membership of the church had grown to 125. Harlem Number Two fielded six delegates and three alternates to the Session.[18]

Humphrey could not stop influencing the spawning of new churches, which made for a widening of his sphere of influence. Three years after Harlem Number Two was organized, the First Jamaica Colored Church was founded in Jamaica, New York. In 1925, a lay preacher, Sidney Armstrong, had started to work the area. Organized in 1927 with a few additional members from Second Brooklyn joining those Armstrong had led to Christ, the Jamaica congregation was already making a significant contribution by 1928 in tithes and offerings to the mission field and the Harvest Ingathering[19] program of the denomination, and when it was voted into the sisterhood of churches in 1928, its membership was twenty-five.

At the Twentieth Session of the Greater New York Conference, Humphrey was moved to propose that his groups be recognized, that their delegates be seated, and that the rest of the delegates be fully informed about the progress of Seventh-day Adventist efforts in the African American community. Humphrey superintended the work in the African American community with vigilance and diligence, yet his influence transcended the African American community. Humphrey opened sessions of the Greater New York Conference with prayer, moved to adjourn meetings, spoke to critical resolutions, served on several important committees, and influenced many actions of the organization.[20]

As early as 1924, Humphrey appeared to be giving in to a certain kind of megalomania. As he tendered his report of Adventist ministry in the African American community to the delegates at the Eighteenth Session of the Greater New York Conference that year, Humphrey lamented his physical condition, which he claimed had curtailed his evangelistic activities in Harlem the previous year. He explained that his burden then was not to raise money but to see his membership grow and that membership growth was his lifelong ambition. Yet Humphrey held up the giving totals—$22,224 in tithes and $18,388 in foreign missions—of the previous year for analysis, arguing that, given their limited economic resources, Blacks were giving more than other groups proportionally. In his report, Humphrey expressed hope for the time when he would be asked to evangelize not only in New York City but in Philadelphia and Chicago as well.[21]

It appears that Humphrey wanted to leave New York City, twice petitioning church leaders to be relocated. On both occasions he was turned down, ostensibly because the church in New York City was thriving under his leadership. Humphrey never offered reasons for wanting to leave New York City, though they are evident. Humphrey's association with, and tenure within, the Seventh-day Adventist church was marked with emotional stress over the race issue and his perception of the way people of color were treated in the denomination. In 1905, one year after he began working as a licensed missionary, Humphrey was accosted by an individual twenty years his senior who was about to cut ties with the denomination over the race issue and asked to do the same.[22] Obviously, Humphrey was disenchanted with the Seventh-day Adventist church, and his displeasure was known. However, Humphrey "flatly refused" to disassociate himself from the denomination at that time, saying that he had never come across a precedent in God's word for anyone rejecting "God's organized plan of work" and succeeding.[23]

Humphrey chose the General Conference Session of 1922 to share this information, the occasion a high point in his ministry. Asked to preach at the Session, Humphrey chose suffering and "The Divine Program" as the theme and title of his sermon. Basing his sermon on 1 Peter 5:10, Humphrey lifted up and expanded on the theme of suffering, asserting that it was God's wonderful program for Christians, who must all suffer in this world.[24] Suffering being the will of a sovereign God, Christians have no control over it and must accept it as submissive children of a God who knows what is in their best interests and what serves their greatest good. Suffering puts people on an equal footing, uniting them in a community of shared sympathy, and leading them to a state of perfection. In fact, suffering is one of the means through which perfection is realized. For Humphrey, suffering liberates and sanctifies, grounding Christians in the truth, and is but a fleeting reality caused by the temporal nature of the universe. This being the case, Humphrey, like most Christians, was eager for the return of Jesus Christ, and he urged his fellow pilgrims to hold on until the climatic event.[25]

Humphrey's General Conference sermon on the evening of May 23, 1922, did not occur in a vacuum. More personal testimony than the exposition of a particular biblical passage, the sermon revealed a man with a heavy heart, a person struggling to come to grips with some unresolved issues.[26] After asserting that, like the apostle Paul, he would allow nothing to drive a wedge between his love for God and himself, Humphrey, at that time supervising four congregations in the metropolitan New York City area, related the incident about the brother who years before had encouraged him to leave the Seventh-day Adventist church. Humphrey claimed that independent churches, such as the one the brother wanted him to start, only appealed to recalcitrants and individuals who had grown lukewarm in their commitment to the church. He stated that those who love truth as it is found in Jesus Christ do not lower the bar of truth.[27]

Humphrey informed his listeners that he was often asked about his plans for the future, implying that there was a measure of interest, if not uncertainty, about his tenure in the Seventh-day Adventist church. His intention then was to remain in the word, he claimed, elaborating that "the cause of Jesus is greater than men, greater than plans, greater than organization." Of supreme importance to Humphrey were the salvation of his own soul, the glorification of God, and the salvation of all whom God had entrusted to his care.[28]

Humphrey continued ministering as a Seventh-day Adventist minister in Harlem throughout the 1920s, baptizing over three hundred persons between 1920 and 1927.[29] By 1925, Harlem, with a population of approximately 250,000, presented Humphrey with some unique challenges, made more daunting by the fact that there were only two Black Seventh-day Adventist pastors and no Bible worker laboring in Harlem.[30] Humphrey and his colleague, Matthew C. Strachan, had been unable to engage in tent evangelism because of the difficulty of procuring a vacant lot between 125th and 145th streets in Harlem on which to have the meetings. In spite of the setback, the First Harlem church had grown, becoming the largest in the Greater New York Conference during that time and remaining so even after dropping some missing members midway through the 1920s.[31] In 1925, Humphrey was asked to provide pastoral leadership for the Brooklyn Number Two congregation, established that year as the result of a tent effort that netted nine baptisms.[32]

Humphrey had been a Baptist minister when he was introduced to the teachings of the Seventh-day Adventist church by an Adventist layman at the start of the twentieth century. At that time, a stream of Blacks was beginning to flood the urban communities of the North from the South and the Caribbean, making the period one of change and volatility in New York City. One area in New York City that was being settled by Blacks was the Harlem section of the borough of Manhattan, and during the 1920s people said that Harlem was in vogue. By the end of the decade, Harlem was the "Black capital of the world" and home to most New York City Black organizations as well as its Black social and political leaders. In spite of the egalitarian claims of the Progressivism that characterized the politics of the first two decades of the twentieth century, however, African Americans remained locked in a struggle for their civil and human rights.[33] Amid calls from political leaders for restrictive measures to deal with the burgeoning urban Black population, African Americans fought to achieve legitimacy and relevancy in the broader community.

The gospel Humphrey preached was social as well as theological.[34] Humphrey wanted Black people to be empowered economically and spiritually, and he began to promote a program he thought would lead to greater self-determination for Blacks. Yet his program was also a way of dealing with the discrimination Humphrey believed Blacks were experiencing in the Seventh-day Adventist denomination, treatment that had led at least a couple of outstanding Black pastors to disassociate themselves from the denomination and establish their own religious groups.

Humphrey's self-enhancement program, called the Utopia Park Benevolent Association project, did not sit too well with Adventist church leadership—it was in violation of Adventist church policy, and Adventist church leaders learned about the project in a roundabout way because Humphrey failed to fully brief them on the project up front. When church leaders sought to get full details of the project from Humphrey, he balked, and when he refused to alter his plans at the request of church leaders, Humphrey was stripped of his ministerial credentials. Humphrey's Harlem congregation, which almost unanimously stood in solidarity with him, shortly thereafter was expelled from the Seventh-day Adventist denomination. Subsequently, Humphrey established an independent Black religious organization, the United Sabbath-Day Adventists, which was comprised of most of his former members.

No research on independent Black Seventh-day Adventist churches has been attempted to date, and James Kemuel Humphrey and the United Sabbath-Day Adventists are not much known in Seventh-day Adventist history. They constitute instead a passing footnote and are often spoken of with disdain in some Seventh-day Adventist circles. Humphrey is considered a recalcitrant who used his charisma and leadership skills to exploit gullible African Americans during a difficult period in this nation's history, when Black people were on a painful journey toward acceptance by the broader American society. To put it bluntly, Humphrey became a largely unknown and miscast figure, and the telling of his story is a critical matter.

Humphrey's break with the Seventh-day Adventist church starkly reveals the tenuous state of African Americans in the Seventh-day Adventist denomination in the early twentieth century and sets the stage for the creation of the separate administrative structure for Blacks known as "regional conferences," established by the denomination in 1945.[35] To be sure, the independent Adventist group Humphrey established never rivaled the congregation he left in terms of membership or influence in the Harlem community. Yet, Humphrey's split with the institutional Seventh-day Adventist church had a fundamentally significant impact on Black-White relations within the denomination and has shaped the course of Black-White working relationships in the denomination since. Sabbath-Day Adventists believe that African American Seventh-day Adventists owe much to James K. Humphrey and the United Sabbath-Day Adventists.

This study will fill a gap in the history of the Seventh-day Adventist church and allow a fuller understanding of how race relations have been experienced and developed in the denomination. This understanding should aid in how present realities are addressed. To understand Humphrey's experience, it must be examined in relation to those of other Black leaders who founded independent Black religious organizations as well as some who continued to minister in largely White denominations. These Black prophetic voices, antecedent to and contemporaneous with Humphrey, include Francis J. Grimke and Richard Allen and find a resounding and effective echo in Humphrey. Humphrey and the United Sabbath-Day Adventists constitute a significant link in the larger African American religious community, with Humphrey standing in solidarity with that community, which reflected his appreciation for self-determination and independence over marginalization.

Even though in this study Humphrey is compared to some significant Black religious leaders, the Sabbath-Day Adventists are not compared to other well-established and influential Black religious groups such as the African American Baptists and the African Methodist Episcopals. Because Humphrey and the United Sabbath-Day Adventists operated in the tradition of Black urban cults, Humphrey was viewed more like a Marcus Garvey, Father Divine, Prophet Jones, or Daddy Grace. To be sure, Humphrey was somewhat different in appearance and in his methods of operating, yet he operated in a community and context similar to those of these cultic Black religious leaders, who were dubbed "Black Gods of the Metropolis."

In telling the story of James Kemuel Humphrey and the United Sabbath-Day Adventists, cultural history and ethnohistory are utilized as methodologies. Twentieth-century American history as well as twentieth-century African American history and biography are also accessed and engaged to place James K. Humphrey and the United Sabbath-Day Adventists in their sociopolitical context—twentieth-century Black New York, particularly Harlem, New York City.

In Chapters 1 and 2, I examine the Utopia Park project, which was the spark that led to Humphrey's break with the Seventh-day Adventist church and the establishment of the Sabbath-Day Adventists. For Humphrey, Utopia Park was an attempt to achieve self-determination for Blacks in the Seventh-day Adventist church.

To fully appreciate Humphrey's struggles and actions, it is vital to understand the tenor of his times. Chapter 3 contains an overview of early twentieth-century Harlem at a time when it was said to be in vogue. The area offered newly arrived Blacks from the South and the West Indies a refuge from the strange, alien conditions they encountered in New York City. Harlem was not an African American community in a vacuum, but one that came of age in the context of unique developments in patterns of race relations in the United States. More important, beneath the veneer of "good times" and optimism that characterized early twentieth-century Harlem, disturbing realities were revealed during the Great Depression.

In Chapter 3, I also examine the West Indian community in Harlem. Humphrey, a Jamaican expatriate, was part of a generation of ambitious West Indian men and women who streamed into Harlem from the turn of the century to 1924, when a change in the immigration laws of the United States slowed their entrance into the country. I investigate the myth of West Indian superiority, focusing on the foundation of the myth. I discuss whether West Indian immigrants were the "cream of the crop" and what the radicalness of the immigration experience suggests about the West Indians who came to America. I also explore the interactions between West Indian and indigenous African Americans and show that West Indians and American Blacks, though tension did exist between them, contributed to each other's growth and progress in the United States. West Indians were victims of warring impulses, torn between a larger Anglo-American culture and a unique West Indian American identity.

In Chapter 4, I trace the African American experience in the Seventh-day Adventist denomination. Like most Christian organizations, Seventh-day Adventists espouse a theological doctrine of community, inclusion, and affirmation. Adventists place a premium on the worth and dignity of all people, whom Adventists believe were created in the image of God.[36] Yet, from its inception, the denomination has struggled with the issue of race as it relates to people of African descent and on occasion has reflected the contradictory racial tendencies and practices of the American society in which it was born and has grown.

In Chapter 5, I survey the church history of the United Sabbath-Day Adventists and offer an oral history retrospective of James K. Humphrey. I review the church-planting activities of the infant organization, explore the early struggles of the group, and investigate the General Conference Sessions the denomination conducted. Also, I conduct a comparative analysis of the Seventh-day Adventists and the Seventh-Day Baptists.

In Chapter 6, I review the attempts made to reconcile the Sabbath-Day Adventists with the Seventh-day Adventists, examine the social and religious context in which the Sabbath-Day Adventist church was born and grew, and evaluate the Sabbath-Day Adventists before summarizing and drawing some conclusions.

Chapter 1

The Utopia Park Affair

November 2, 1929, was a historic day for James Kemuel Humphrey and the members of the First Harlem Seventh-day Adventist church. That Sabbath, Humphrey preached his last sermon as pastor of the flagship congregation of the Greater New York Conference of Seventh-day Adventists. The title of his sermon, which was based on the first of the Ten Commandments recorded in Exodus 20, was "Thou Shalt Have No Other God," and for reasons that he never divulged or never became known, Humphrey cried throughout the sermon. It is unclear whether Adventist church leaders were present for the worship service at First Harlem that morning, though it is certain that they were in attendance at the business meeting of the church that evening. Among those present were the president and secretary of the General Conference of Seventh-day Adventists, W. A. Spicer and C. K. Meyers; the president of the Atlantic Union, E. K. Slade; and the president of the Greater New York Conference, Louis K. Dickson.

Alleging that the meeting had been requested by Humphrey, Greater New York Conference president Louis K. Dickson, reading from a prepared statement, stated that church leaders were at First Harlem to "talk over"[1] with the congregation "as brethren" a matter of great importance to the denomination and the "cause of God." He regretted the "much-to-be-deplored crisis" to which they had been brought by the actions and attitude of James K. Humphrey and went to great lengths to assure the church that church leaders had an abiding interest in their welfare and the future of Adventist efforts in the African American community in Harlem. Dickson characterized Humphrey as an individual of "large ability" whose work God had signally blessed with success. Yet Humphrey's speculative dealing in a real estate "promotion and colonization enterprise" was proof positive of his "disregard for the well-established policies and regulations of the denomination." Dickson then elaborated on the unity that he claimed was both a legacy and hallmark of the Seventh-day Adventist denomination, saying that unity was "one of our most sacred legacies and our most potent weapon against the assaults of the enemy of truth." Moreover, the success and prosperity of the church were directly tied to the loyalty of its members to the organization, and the disregard of the fundamental principles of church organization was tantamount to offering hospitality to Satan.[2]

Dickson then painstakingly delineated the evolution of the events that had brought the group to that point. He read in their entirety his letter of August 13 to Humphrey, in which he had appealed for information about Humphrey's Utopia Park venture, Humphrey's August 20 response, in which Humphrey claimed the project was "absolutely a problem for the colored people," and his follow-up letter to Humphrey, in which he expressed dissatisfaction with Humphrey's response. Dickson informed the congregation that Humphrey's uncooperative attitude had left him with no other alternative than that of taking the matter to the Executive Committee of the Greater New York Conference, which, with Humphrey present, had voted to accept the recommendation of the Executive Committee of the Atlantic Union Conference that Humphrey's ministerial credentials be revoked. Still, opportunity had been provided for Humphrey to acknowledge the error of his ways and to seek counsel from church officials. Not surprising, Humphrey had rebuffed all such overtures.[3]

Dickson informed First Harlem that their pastor, contrary to his claims that the denomination had failed to demonstrate care and concern for African Americans in general and Humphrey in particular, had spurned its efforts to resolve some Black-White issues in a collaborative way. Specifically, Humphrey, who had been appointed to a special committee impaneled at the 1929 Spring Council of world church leaders to study the feasibility of Black conferences, had failed to attend any of the meetings called by the group, on one occasion saying he was too sick to attend. Even though the church was already fractured, Dickson stressed the incongruity of members of an organization dividing and working independently of each other and appealed again for Humphrey to reconsider his position. The Conference president also appealed to church members, asking them "to take their stand as loyal supporters of order and organization in the church of Christ" and reminding them that their allegiance was "to God and to His church, and not to any individual."[4]

The November 2, 1929, meeting lasted five stormy hours, during which the First Harlem congregation, standing in almost unanimous solidarity with its pastor,[5] demanded the deed to its property and voted to splinter from the Greater New York Conference.[6] Later, in a report he prepared for the regular biennial session of the Conference held in January 1930, Dickson characterized the actions of First Harlem on the night of November 2 as "open rebellion" in support of Humphrey, whom, the president claimed, had reportedly cast himself as a present-day Moses intent on leading his people out of the slavery of disenfranchisement and White oppression into the proverbial promised land of liberation and empowerment. The president claimed that "the wild confusion and uproar" of church members on that fateful evening testified to their "disrespect of the presence, counsel and advice of the leaders of the denomination."[7]

On the night of November 2, Dickson had claimed that the Adventist denomination did not want to argue the "merits or demerits of any real estate enterprise," but to the delegates of the January 1930, Biennial Session he said that Utopia Park was a "speculative real estate scheme" and the "ill-conceived independent personal plan of Humphrey."[8] In addition, Dickson openly speculated then that Humphrey had had ambitions of replacing W. H. Green as secretary of the Negro Department of the General Conference and that when it had become clear to Humphrey that he would not be given the position, Humphrey began to poison the minds of his members toward the Adventist church.[9]

News of First Harlem's and Humphrey's difficulties with the Seventh-day Adventist denomination were not restricted to the Adventist community. New York City's Black weekly, the *New York Amsterdam News*, in a front page story covering the November 2 meeting that appeared in its November 6, 1929, issue, said that First Harlem's break with the Adventist organization was triggered by the racial discrimination Black Seventh-day Adventists faced in the denomination's schools, hospitals, and missions and that the governing bodies of the church were all composed of White men. The newspaper placed the number of people who attended the historic meeting at nine hundred, claiming that they all protested the attempted ousting of Humphrey, who had faithfully served the Harlem congregation for twenty-seven years.[10] One week later, the newspaper again carried a front-page story about the matter, saying that the irate members of First Harlem had been calmed by Humphrey, whose wise intervention had returned the meeting of November 2 to order. Humphrey informed the *New York Amsterdam News* that the denomination was trying to discredit him by having the District Attorney of New York City and the city's Welfare Department investigate Utopia Park, that in the previous ten years his congregation had contributed over $300,000 in tithes and offerings to the organization only to receive nothing in return, and that his congregation's request that the deed to its property be turned over to it had been made to bring an end to White domination.[11]

New York Age was more accusatory in its coverage of the story, asking in its front page issue of November 16, 1929, whether Humphrey was a second Marcus Garvey who was ambitious to accomplish something grand for his people but who allowed ambition to get the better of sound business judgment. It asked if Humphrey had been victimized by two White real estate developers, John L. Le Berthen and George D. Spalding, who had introduced the idea of Utopia Park to him. Allegedly, Berthen and Spalding had taken Humphrey to Wappingers Falls, New York, where they showed him 313 acres of land that included a lake they failed to explain was part of the Wappingers Falls water system. Later, when residents saw busloads of Blacks, whom Humphrey had started to take to the location on weekends, swimming in the lake, they rose up in protest, causing Humphrey to temporarily suspend the project. The project was then relocated to New Jersey. The newspaper also claimed that Humphrey may have misappropriated funds, depositing money for the project in a bank in his name.[12]

The local press continued to cover Humphrey's break with the Seventh-day Adventist church, informing readers a couple of weeks later that the district attorney of New York City, at the end of his investigation, had concluded that Humphrey had violated no state law in his promotion of Utopia Park. Even the solicitation of funds on the streets of New York City did not violate any city ordinance. The commissioner of the Department of Welfare also issued an emphatic denial that the department had ever intended to or had prosecuted Humphrey, a statement the embattled pastor claimed was both exoneration and vindication for him.[13]

Yet, the Greater New York Conference was not finished with Humphrey and the First Harlem Church. At a meeting of its Executive Committee held on January 14, 1930, two resolutions concerning First Harlem were adopted on the basis that the church had acted inconsistently with the teachings of the Adventist denomination and had failed to live up to its obligations to the Conference. The first resolution called for First Harlem to be dropped from the sisterhood of churches of the Greater New York Conference, and the second called for an arrangement to be made for the reorganization of the few members still loyal to the denomination into a new church. Another resolution was adopted, inviting First Harlem to send delegates to the upcoming Biennial Session of the Conference for the purpose of presenting facts in its defense. Officially,

First Harlem did not send any delegates to the Session, which voted unanimously to disfellowship the church.[14]

When the secretary of the Greater New York Conference informed the delegates at its Twenty-First Session that First Harlem had failed to field delegates to the Session, a group in the audience told him that there were indeed people from First Harlem present and that they desired to continue with the Adventist organization. The vice-president of the General Conference of Seventh-day Adventists, James L. McElhany, who was at the Session, moved that since there were people from First Harlem who "in heart and in spirit" wished to remain loyal to the Conference, that the president of the local conference, the "de facto" pastor of all the churches in the Conference, should meet with the group for the purpose of organizing them and bringing a recommendation to the entire body concerning the group's plans and intentions. Subsequently, three people from First Harlem were seated as delegates-at-large.[15]

Humphrey's struggles and break with the Seventh-day Adventist denomination was not covered in the *Advent Review and Sabbath Herald*, the general paper of the denomination. W. A. Spicer, General Conference president, writing in the December 19, 1929, issue of the periodical about Adventist efforts in New York at the time, chose to remind readers that the greater New York City area represented "pretty much all the world" and that what goes on in New York City impacts the rest of the world. Spicer, who had been at the historic November 2 meeting at First Harlem, said nothing about it, choosing instead to inform the world church of the three facilities that New York City congregations had acquired "for reaching the public and housing believers." One reason Spicer may have opted not to share news about Humphrey is that he may have viewed such news as unhelpful. Spicer's objective in the column was to share news with those "interested in everything that makes for progress and strength in the great cities of the world."[16] A couple of months later, F. C. Gilbert reported on revival and reformation efforts toward the end of 1929 in Brooklyn, New York, again saying nothing of Humphrey's or First Harlem's difficulties with the SDA denomination.[17]

In the March 13, 1930, issue of the *Advent Review and Sabbath Herald,* James L. McElhany, General Conference secretary, reported on the Greater New York Conference Session of January 27–28, 1930, at which were present Louis K. Dickson, Conference president; E. K. Slade, Atlantic Union president; and W. A. Spicer and James L. McElhany of the General Conference. According to McElhany, "the outstanding feature of the Session was the study and emphasis given to soul winning." He reported that the biennial term of 1928–1929 had seen 405 people baptized into the Adventist church. Two new churches had been added to the Conference, and Dickson shared thrilling news about the acquisition of church properties, news that was well received since the suitable housing of congregations was a "problem of untold difficulties" in New York City. Yet absolutely nothing about the disbanding of First Harlem and the subsequent reorganization of the handful of members still loyal to the Adventist denomination into the Ephesus SDA Church was mentioned.[18]

PRELUDE TO UTOPIA PARK

What was the Utopia Park Affair all about? What led up to it, and could it have been avoided? What, if anything, does the way it was handled by denominational leaders say about race relations in the Seventh-day Adventist church during this time period? What clues does it provide for the engagement of the race issue today? Was Utopia Park nothing more than self-promotion on Humphrey's part, as some detractors have alleged? Does it provide eloquent witness that Humphrey during the 1920s succumbed to a type of megalomania, using his body as a symbol with evangelical and public relations dimensions?

The United States Supreme Court's much-heralded maxim that separate is equal was not matched in the nation's cities, towns, and villages in the early twentieth century. On the contrary, segregation and inequality seemed synonymous, an almost axiomatic truth that was exacerbated by discrimination and oppression. On every hand, and by every measure, segregation militated against the attempts of Black people to get a fair crack at the proverbial "American Dream," leading to frustration and anger on their part. Christians in general, and the members of Humphrey's Harlem congregation in particular, were confused and distressed by the tacit endorsement and acceptance of segregation witnessed in the Christian community in the United States.

Throughout the 1920s, Humphrey had served the Seventh-day Adventist church with distinction and vision, leading First Harlem Seventh-day Adventist Church to a position of primacy and prominence in the Greater New York Conference of Seventh-day Adventists. In 1927, First Harlem was the largest Seventh-day Adventist church in New York City and the third largest in the United States. In spite of his successes, Humphrey was uncomfortable with the way the Adventist church treated people of color, and, more important,

Humphrey began to believe that the denomination, its lofty pronouncements of support of—and solidarity with—the Black cause notwithstanding, was not anxious to bring about substantive changes in the conditions faced by African Americans. For almost his entire tenure as a Seventh-day Adventist minister, Humphrey had kept the race issue before the denomination's leadership, agitating for change that would result in greater self-determination for African Americans, and Humphrey had waited patiently for the denomination to match its words of support with corresponding actions. As the 1920s drew to a close, Humphrey's patience began to wear thin.

Humphrey's disenchantment with race relations in the Seventh-day Adventist church was not unfounded. Among other things, he knew that W. H. Green, in 1918 the first Black to work at the General Conference, was banned from eating in the *Review and Herald* cafeteria, where the other General Conference workers ate. According to Delbert Baker, "segregation was the norm for the first half of the 1900s" in the Adventist church, with "White Adventist congregations and administrative leadership positions . . . rarely accessible to Blacks prior to the 1940s."[19]

James K. Humphrey was not the first African American pastor with whom the Seventh-day Adventist church had experienced difficulty over the treatment of Blacks in the church. That distinction belonged to Louis Sheafe, who from 1903 pastored the First Church of Seventh-day Adventists located at 324 Spruce Street, Washington, D.C., and later the People's Seventh-day Adventist church located at the corner of 10th and V streets in the nation's capital. Sheafe, a compelling preacher who often graced the pulpit at General Conference sessions of the Adventist church, occupied a propitious position among Seventh-day Adventist Church leaders and was viewed as a sort of de facto leader in the Black Adventist community. But Sheafe, like Humphrey after him and Charles Kinney before him, found it difficult to resonate with what he perceived as racial prejudice within the denomination and began to agitate for separation.[20] Sheafe's efforts received encouragement from Alonzo T. Jones, who in 1888 had brought the denomination to a turning point in its theological understandings by championing the notion of righteousness by faith.[21] Brilliant and charismatic, Jones vaulted into prominence in the Seventh-day Adventist church toward the end of the nineteenth century and just as quickly plummeted into ignominious disrepute as the first decade of the twentieth century was ending. Jones and Sheafe shared similar feelings of ill will toward the Seventh-day Adventist church, and Sheafe even allowed Jones to preach at the People's Church.[22]

In 1907, disagreements between the denomination and Sheafe made The People's Seventh-day Adventist church vote unanimously to sever its association with the Seventh-day Adventist denomination. Not surprising, denominational leadership cited other reasons for its rift with Sheafe and his congregation. The organization alleged that its problems with Sheafe were, at least in part, fueled and compounded by Sheafe's sympathy with the pantheistic beliefs of Dr. John Harvey Kellogg, the Battle Creek Adventist doctor and businessman who revolutionized the breakfast habits of Americans with the introduction of the breakfast cereal.[23]

Sheafe's disaffection with and subsequent withdrawal from the SDA Church were due to more than issues of race. To be sure, racism was the catalyst that propelled him to cut ties with the denomination, but congregationalism, spawned partly by the preponderance of the disenchantment that characterized Adventism at the start of the twentieth century, was then fomenting within the church, and the phenomenon found ready acceptance by individuals like Sheafe.[24]

The departure of the People's Church from the Seventh-day Adventist sisterhood of churches may have contributed to the establishment of the North American Negro Department of the General Conference, the administrative arm of the denomination created in 1909 to foster and promote the spread of the gospel among African Americans. At the time of the creation of the Negro Department, the Seventh-day Adventist denomination had already instituted ethnic entities to facilitate the grafting of European immigrant groups into the American and Adventist culture. Yet the North American Negro Department differed from the departments that catered to the needs of German-Americans, Danish-Americans, and others in fundamentally different ways. Foremost among the ways was the fact that the Negro Department did not have the integration of Blacks into the life and mission of the church as one of its paramount objectives.[25]

Was the establishment of the North American Negro Department tantamount to the institutionalization of racism within the Seventh-day Adventist church? Or was the denomination simply reflecting the tone of Black-White relations in the broader American society, legitimized and standardized in the United States by the Supreme Court's *Plessy v. Ferguson* ruling that separate but equal was an ethical and legal notion? Credible answers to these questions are made difficult by the fact that the North American Negro Department was not run by Blacks for the first ten years of its existence. Indeed, Blacks were in a minority in the department, serving mostly on its Advisory Committee and leaving most of the formulation and execution of the department's plans to Whites. Still, if nothing else, the establishment of the department is proof that "separate but equal" had in 1909 made its way into the Seventh-day Adventist church.[26]

Fewer than a thousand people of African descent were in the Seventh-day Adventist Church when the North American Negro Department was established, leading some observers to question the move. Officially, the Department was to promulgate Adventist efforts in the Black community. General Conference president A. G. Daniells, noting the unprecedented number of "colored ministers" participating in the 1909 General Conference Session, said the creation of the Negro Department was "a step in the right direction" that would help the denomination "have one solid, systematized, concerted effort to push this important branch of the work." Included in those efforts were the publication and marketing of Christian literature uniquely geared to meet the special needs of the African American community.[27] In addition, the department was "a movement for the betterment and uplifting of a people."[28]

Yet the creation of the Department did not completely satisfy or quiet the misgivings of some in the African American Adventist community. Sydney Scott, for example, objected to the Department being called the "North American Negro Department," arguing that the term was misleading and that "Afro-American" should be used instead. Scott also stated that, while the idea of such a department was sound, he could only endorse the concept if "just and fair representation" in the Department "from the local mission clear to the head" was a reality. W. A. Wentworth, of the Southeastern Union, interpreted the launch of the Department as the creation of a foreign mission station. M. C. Strachan, who later pastored Harlem Number Two and the Ephesus Seventh-day Adventist congregation that grew out of First Harlem, saw the Department as a necessary expediency, and James K. Humphrey stated at its creation that the Department would be in his prayers.[29]

Humphrey was asked by General Conference leadership if he were "thoroughly convinced" about the name the denomination had anticipated calling the Department, answering, "I am convinced so. The term 'colored' is not definite in fact.... But we are the Negro race. I am not ashamed at all to acknowledge that."[30] Humphrey also noted that the denomination had set about and executed the task of evangelizing other White ethnic groups with intentionality and resolve, and he bemoaned the lack of both when it came to the evangelization of people of African descent. Yet his support of the creation of the Negro Department, which General Conference president A. G. Daniells had called for as early as 1905, can be said to have been strong.[31]

Accepting neither the way the Negro Department was constituted nor the way it was operated, African Americans continued to agitate for change, arguing among other things that only one of their own could run the Department with the sensitivity to their unique needs for which conditions in society and the Seventh-day Adventist denomination called. As long as Whites continued to control the department, they believed, their cause would be hurt. In 1918, their lobbying efforts paid off with the appointment of William H. Green as the first African American director of the Department. Yet the appointment of Green did little to acquit the denomination of the charges of racism leveled against it. On the contrary, it provided evidence to sustain the charge, because in spite of the fact that his three predecessors had maintained and worked out of offices at the denomination's world headquarters in Washington, D.C., Green was not allowed to do so. Four years after he assumed the leadership of the North American Negro Department, the official yearbook of the SDA denomination listed the director as having two addresses—one at its world headquarters and the other in Detroit, Michigan, where Green resided.[32] The fact is that Green was working out of his suitcase.

In 1920, as James K. Humphrey was expanding his efforts in Harlem, a Black Seventh-day Adventist minister in Savannah, Georgia, had run afoul of denominational policies. J. W. Manns, like Humphrey a leader of uncommon homiletic ability who possessed an extensive knowledge of Seventh-day Adventist doctrine and policy, had pioneered in the establishment of several Adventist congregations in the South. Included in the network of churches he had established was the Savannah congregation, where it was rumored that he had baptized approximately 160 people.[33] In violation of denominational policy, Manns led his Savannah congregation to retain the deed to its property. When pressed by denominational leadership to return it, he refused to reverse his decision, arguing that the denomination's demands were racist and discriminatory. Consequently the Savannah congregation was dismissed in late 1920.[34]

Manns did not view his leaving the Seventh-day Adventist denomination as church leaders did. He claimed that he bolted from the denomination because he chose to stand upon the principle demonstrated by Abraham, which calls for the separation of people when methods of reconciliation and rapproachement have failed. For Manns, separations are of a necessity "in order to safeguard the interests of all concerned," and he claimed that "bigoted white leaders among Seventh-day Adventists" were the cause of many "intelligent Negro ministers" leaving the denomination, many of whom had done so in utter disgust. Worse, Manns asserted, many Black ministers had given up on Christianity altogether, choosing to find solace in "the cold world, from which there can be no peace of mind." Yet, Manns, an evangelist and pastor, vowed that he would allow nothing to separate him from the love of Christ, demonstrating that as far as Manns was concerned, the independent religious group he launched was not to be construed as a descent into apostasy.[35]

Manns viewed his separation from the Seventh-day Adventist denomination as in keeping with the command of the angel of Revelation 18:4 for the true of heart to separate themselves from that which is at variance with the truth of God. He noted that Protestant reformers such as Martin Luther and John Wesley had done just that, bequeathing to all Christians a legacy of "freedom of conscience and religious liberty," which he desired to be the bedrock of the Free Seventh-day Adventists, the group he launched. Manns bewailed the fact that many Black Seventh-day Adventists, in remaining with the denomination, had placed the denomination above what he considered a just cause, and he called them "weak-kneed." Moreover, he alleged that in staying in the Adventist church, these Blacks had made the organization their hope of salvation.[36]

Manns and his followers admitted that the early Seventh-day Adventist efforts to reach Blacks were well-intentioned and purposeful and that Blacks and Whites initially "experienced little or no difficulty in the North and West in equal enjoyment of religious rights and privileges." Yet the cordial, positive relations between the two races changed as more and more Blacks joined the ranks of Adventism. As Manns put it, denominational leadership started "in a most deceptive and un-Christian way" to initiate segregation in all Adventist churches in North America, a policy that stood in stark contrast to the denomination's "former teachings and profession." Manns asserted that "this unscriptural course," consisting of "base acts of prejudice and proscription," was found to be acceptable by the "more intelligent negroes."[37]

A gifted strategist and charismatic leader, Manns believed that there was more racism in the Seventh-day Adventist church than in any other religious organization "under heaven" and that the "prejudice existing in this professed commandment keeping church would shame the Papacy and make the devil blush." He characterized as a "lie of their own manufacturing" the statements by Adventist leaders that the denomination's position on the race issue was intended so as not to stir up "the prejudice of the unconverted white people against our denomination," and he was neither alarmed nor disappointed that he had lost his job as a minister in the Seventh-day Adventist church for speaking out against its discriminatory practices. He firmly believed that, even though his name had been dropped from the denomination's records, it had not been erased from the "Lamb's Book of Life."[38]

The goal of Manns and his followers was not social equality in the Adventist church but only "a fair deal." They desired, fundamentally, to be treated as others were being treated, not any better, and certainly not any worse. Having been denied the basic rights and courtesies extended to others, and, worse, having been excoriated when they had asked for and contended for those rights, African Americans had no option other than that of standing in solidarity as a people and looking out for their own interests. Free Seventh-day Adventists resonated with all the "fundamental principles of the doctrines as were taught by the founders of the Seventh-day Adventist denomination" and chose to call themselves "Free"[39] because they believed it was wrong for Christians to judge people based on externals and race.[40] In clarifying the move to establish the Free Seventh-day Adventists, Manns stressed that it was not an attempt "at reformation of corrupt Christianity" but instead "a noble effort to secure for ourselves and our race religious privileges which we could not, nor ever would be able to enjoy among our **WHITE BRETHREN-SEVENTH-DAY ADVENTISTS.**"[41]

It is unclear how much the *Advent Review and Sabbath Herald* reported on Manns's defection from the Seventh-day Adventist denomination, though it is clear that the general periodical of the denomination contained no information about the Free Seventh-day Adventists. Arthur L. White, secretary of the Ellen G. White Estate at the General Conference of Seventh-day Adventists, responding to an inquiring for information about the group in 1972, said that he had found "no reference to this group in the Review and Herald" and that "we would hardly expect to." White stated that he was "totally in the dark in regard to this group of people" and as such could give "no information along this line."[42]

Fortuitously, a collection of Ellen White's counsels on the race issue fell into the hands of Manns and his congregation just before they opted to go their separate ways.[43] Their reading of White's counsels could not have occurred at a less convenient time. In the book, White advises against the erection and perpetuation of barriers between American Adventists and their newly arrived European cousins, asserting that the unity of a Christian body provides convincing proof that the Godhead is one and reminding her readers that the principle of heaven is oneness.[44] Yet Ellen White admonished African Americans to refrain from agitating for change for fear of stirring up ill will among Whites, to labor for and among their own race, and to seek separate church facilities since it was not in the best interests of Whites and Blacks to worship together.[45]

More perplexing to Blacks was Ellen White's counsel that African Americans accept their second class citizenship and submit to hardship for Christ's sake. Moreover, she wrote that they should not press for an equal footing with Whites and should not forget the altogether important principle that sometimes expediency is a higher value than legality. Yet White's most confusing statement was her implicit endorsement of a higher morality among Whites, albeit one that had come about because "Northern people have lived in a clearer, purer moral atmosphere than have the colored people of the South."[46] Undoubtedly, most Blacks in Ellen White's day occupied the lowest rung of the social ladder in American society, yet it is a leap to conclude that, based on these and similar statements, Ellen White believed people of color were innately or inherently inferior to Whites.

African Americans received White's counsels with a mixture of reservation and bewilderment. Given their subordinate status in the American society and with the vestiges of slavery and Jim Crowism making a mockery of the freedoms they were said to have acquired with the signing of the Emancipation Proclamation, they had hoped to find spiritual and social salvation in the Seventh-day Adventist church, which wore its uniqueness as God's special end-time people as a badge of honor. At a loss to comprehend White's statements, which seem at variance with others in which she called for unity among God's people, many Black Adventists rejected them outright, and others used them to argue against her authenticity as a contemporary prophetess.

In 1905, Ellen White had received "light" indicating that separate organizations to address ethnic and national issues would bring about divisiveness, not coherence and unity, in the church. Were separate organizations to be implemented, they would reflect to the world human thinking, not God's, and God could never bestow a blessing on such an arrangement. Indeed, all such arrangements would dishonor God, who desires that Christians practice the principles of heaven, which "is one grand meeting place." One compelling reason Ellen White in 1905 looked with disfavor on the separation of people based on nationality or language was because of the deleterious impact it would have on the mind. White believed that narrow provincial thinking was bound to happen as a result of people becoming locked in only with those of their kind. God's ideal was for a "harmonious blending of a variety of talents." Moreover, wrote White, "each nationality should labor earnestly for every other nationality."[47]

In spite of Ellen G. White's call in 1905 for each nationality to labor earnestly for every other nationality, a few years later she was admonishing Blacks to "prepare to give the truth to their own race." She stated that among Blacks were those of "talent and ability" who were to be trained for ministry among their kind.[48]

J. W. Manns firmly believed that Ellen G. White was God's inspired prophet, though the evangelist was quick to point out that not everything she spoke or wrote was inspired "anymore than everything said or act done or written by other prophets was inspired." Manns argued that when White's early statements on the race issue, which he believed could "stand the test of the Bible," were juxtaposed with those of later years, any "candid, fair-minded person" would see the later statements for what they truly were. Manns believed that volume 9 of the *Testimonies,* which contained the material on Black-White relations just referenced, was not White's work but the product of Adventist leaders, who, knowing the penchant of African Americans to accept White as an authentic, inspired prophet, were confident Blacks would embrace it wholesale. For Manns, the two chapters specifically addressing the Black man's plight were intended by church leaders to provide support for prejudice that could not be found in Scripture.[49]

Manns characterized the two chapters as "ROT" and "garbled." He claimed they were "junk," written with the intention of keeping "the Negro ministry and membership in a proscribed place in the denomination with a permanent bar fixed to Negro leadership." Manns was especially disturbed by the purported statement of Ellen White that even though in the South "many wise, Christian colored men" would enter into Adventist ministry, "for several reasons white men must be chosen as leaders." He was quick to note that the statement recognizes and admits that many of those entering ministry would be people of ability, knowledge, and intelligence. Moreover, they would be Christians who would be disqualified for leadership solely on the basis of their race. Because the Holy Scripture "knows no caste or color," viewing and accepting all human beings as equal, Manns found the statement palpably absurd and patently unacceptable. He cited Jethro's instruction to Moses that men of ability be tapped to lead as convincing proof that God looks to people of "ability and character, and not white and black, red or brown," to lead.[50]

Ellen White's counsel on the race issue, when read out of context, is indeed troubling. Yet, when viewed in the scheme of the times, they make sense and reflect that White was cognizant of the shift that had taken place in race relations in the nation at large. In the last decade of the nineteenth century, White had encouraged Blacks and Whites to worship together, and the arrangement was held up as the way God would have it. Then, in the first decade of the twentieth century, White advocated separate worship services "in order that the progress of the truth may be advanced."[51] Thus, according to George Knight, "separation was far from God's ideal but was necessary for mission in a troubled racial atmosphere." Knight believes that, for White, the suggested arrangement "was pragmatic and missiological and had importance."[52]

Issue may have been made about whether White's counsels were authentic or not but hardly with the everyday treatment of African Americans within the Adventist church. Undeniably, a practice of discrimination in Adventist institutions and organizations was the norm in the early twentieth century. For example, in 1919, J. E. Jervis applied to Union College, one of the twelve union colleges owned and operated by the Adventist church in North America at the time, for admission to pursue a degree in theology. Jervis wanted to become a Seventh-day Adventist minister and, not unlike some Blacks of his era, desired to attend an integrated school instead of all-Black Oakwood College in Huntsville, Alabama. To his surprise and chagrin, Jervis was not accepted at Union, receiving a letter signed by the school's president, Harvey A. Morrison, that informed him that it was not the institution's policy to accept Blacks from outside its territory[53] and that under normal circumstances and conditions the institution did not have Black students.[54] Ten years later, as the First Harlem SDA Church was becoming embroiled in the Utopia Park Affair, Jervis was serving the congregation as its associate pastor.

The denomination's attitude and policies toward educating Blacks in its educational institutions did not change much between 1919 and 1929, the year a member of First Harlem applied for admission to the nursing program of the denomination's only institution for medical training in the United States. Mrs. Beryl Holness received word from the College of Medical Evangelists in California, now Loma Lina University, that her request for admission had been denied on the ground of her "nationality." That Holness, from a well-known Black family, was turned down in the midst of Humphrey's struggles with the Greater New York Conference fueled the controversy all the more.[55]

The Seventh-day Adventist church was not blind to the plight of African Americans. At the 1929 Autumn Council of the General Conference Committee, held in Columbus, Ohio, from September 24 to October 2, much time was devoted to studying the needs of the "good and growing work" executed by Blacks in North America. The previous year, W. H. Green, who had led the Negro Department for almost ten years, had died, creating a vacuum in the Black work.[56] Prior to the Autumn Council, a commission appointed at the spring meeting of world church leaders had met, and, through the Plans Committee, had tendered a slate of recommendations concerning work among Blacks. Among the recommendations was one calling for serious study of the feasibility of establishing a school for Blacks in the North. Also, that Blacks be encouraged to enter the colporteur field so as to win souls and secure scholarships to Christian schools; and that Adventist sanitariums, where possible, accept Blacks into their nursing programs. No mention was made about training Blacks to become medical doctors. Yet the actions that may have struck Humphrey the hardest were the ones calling for the office of the secretary of the Negro Department to be located at the church's world headquarters in Washington, D.C. and the recommendation that George E. Peters be appointed secretary of the North American Negro Department.[57] A gifted speaker with a commanding presence and impressive bearing, Peters, like Humphrey, was a West Indian.

Before becoming secretary of the Negro Department, Peters, who was Antiguan by birth and spoke with an unmistakable accent, had ministered in Chicago for seven years. When he arrived there, the Black church had a membership of 250 and was worshiping in small quarters on Prairie Avenue. But Peters, an effective evangelist, conducted evangelistic meetings almost every year, with the result that the membership of his church burgeoned and the group had to find larger quarters. By 1930, the membership had more than doubled, making Shiloh one of the largest Black congregations in the country. Peters had partnered with C. E. Mosely to raise up a church in Evanston, Illinois, and pioneered in establishing another Black church in Morgan Park. He was largely responsible for the appreciable growth in tithe receipts of these congregations, which in 1929 represented 12 percent of the tithe receipts of the local Conference. More important, Peters had a reputation for being a team player who contributed immeasurably to the solving of knotty issues "not only for the colored work, but in the conference generally."[58]

In early 1929, at the spring meeting of the world church held in Washington, D.C., the Black Caucus had passed a resolution calling for the creation of regional conferences to replace the nebulous, ineffective Negro Department.[59] Stressing that regional conferences would relate to the General Conference in much the same way as other conferences, the resolution nonetheless stated that with regional conferences African Americans would control and administer their own funds, hire and terminate their own workers, negotiate for the acquisition and disposal of real property, and cast and pursue the vision for the Black work. In sum, the regional conference idea was an attempt on the part of Blacks in the Seventh-day Adventist church for self-determination. The request of Black church leaders, as they saw it, would bring concretization and legitimization to the "separate but equal" condition that existed in the Seventh-day Adventist church.[60]

Humphrey was at the forefront of the call for regional conferences for African Americans, and his argument was based on the plight of Blacks within the Seventh-day Adventist church. As he and fellow Black leaders saw it, the denomination's attitude, policies, and actions toward Blacks left them feeling powerless and unappreciated. The North American Negro Department, its high objectives notwithstanding, had done little to assuage the situation of Blacks within the church, in part because even when the Department was finally led by an African American, it had no clout. Humphrey and other Black leaders knew that African Americans in the Adventist church lacked credible, tenable constituent representation at the higher levels of the organization, a situation they found unacceptable given their financial contributions and the number of baptisms they had amassed.[61]

The General Conference leaders responded to the request for regional conferences by empaneling a committee to study the issue. The committee consisted of eighteen individuals, eleven of whom were White. Not surprising, Humphrey was among the six Blacks asked to serve on the committee. Outnumbered two to one, the Blacks on the committee were powerless to stop the body from "emphatically and absolutely" voting down the idea of regional conferences. Yet, what particularly distressed them was the committee's statement that "Black Conferences are out of the question. Don't ever ask for a Black Conference again."[62]

The Utopia Park Health Benevolent Association

Sometime after the 1929 spring meeting of Adventist world church leaders, Humphrey began to promote the idea of an all-Black commune among his members. The project was called Utopia Park, and Humphrey had grand goals and objectives for it. To be owned, operated, and occupied by people of color, Utopia Park was to be completely nonsectarian. It would provide Blacks with an environment conducive to their physical, social, and psychological well-being, as well as provide them with employment opportunities. Initially, Utopia Park was to be located in Wappingers Falls, New York, a small town about seven miles from Poughkeepsie and about an hour and a half car ride from New York City. Yet problems with that property caused Humphrey and his group to settle for an estate in Atlantic Highlands, New Jersey. Humphrey believed that divine providence led them to the New Jersey location.

Touted and billed as the "Fortune Spot of America for Colored People," Utopia Park was said to consist of rolling hills, sixteen acres of gardens and lawns, plants and flowers too numerous to list, a main lake three acres wide that could accommodate five thousand swimmers, three smaller lakes uniquely suited for ice skating in the winter, and a high point from which the New York City boroughs of Manhattan and Brooklyn could be seen on a clear day. Accessible from New York City by boat, rail, or automobile, the property was fanned by ocean breezes that supposedly helped the physically and emotionally ill to regain their health and was dominated by a twenty-eight-room mansion that sat amid floral gardens. Plans called for the mansion to be converted into a community center, and recreational activities running the gamut from tennis to canoeing were planned for the old and young alike.

The property's main building had a seating capacity of one thousand and housed one of the park's main attractions—a twenty-thousand-dollar custom-built organ that came with an organist. A Black master musician, William E. Batson was said to be able to thrill his brothers and sisters, a respite they would need after working in the farming and dairy industries, as well as in the polytechnic school, that were planned for Utopia Park. It was alleged that already there had been inquiries from Black entrepreneurs about the prospects of establishing manufacturing plants and other businesses there.

Utopia Park was said to be the brainchild of Pastor James K. Humphrey, who, allegedly, had conceived of it after several years of introspection and reflection. Dubbed an "intelligent, earnest and indefatigable worker," Humphrey was compared favorably to a modern-day Aladdin. A Promotion Committee of twenty-two men and a Ladies Committee of twenty-five, which included two teenagers and a young girl, served as overseers of the project. Lots measuring twenty-five feet by one hundred feet were offered only to Blacks of good moral standing; resident lots went for $600, corner lots for $650, and business lots for $750. A mere 10 percent down procured a residence lot, for which $3.50 was the weekly installment. All communications about Utopia Park were to be addressed to Utopia Park, Inc., located at 141 West 131st Street, the exact address of the First Harlem Seventh-day Adventist church, and the promotional materials listed Pastor James K. Humphrey as director general of Utopia Park.[63] To market Utopia Park, a song, replete with shades of Ethiopianism and to be sung to the tune of "My Motherland," was written. The words of the song were:

> Utopia, Utopia
> Sweet Land of Ethiopia
> I look away across the Sea,
> A mansion there now waits for me.
> CHORUS
> View that golden, sunny shore,
> My dream, my home, that I adore
> Utopia, Utopia;
> Sweet land of Ethiopia.
>   II
> Utopia, Utopia;
> Sweet land of Ethiopia;
> I'm waiting for thy great command
> To go to the promised land.
> CHORUS
> View that golden, sunny shore
> My dream, my home, that I adore;
> Utopia, Utopia;
> Sweet land of Ethiopia[64]

Members of Humphrey's First Harlem congregation embarked on an aggressive fund-raising campaign to acquire the money for the project. They took to the streets of Harlem, soliciting money in cans like those used in the Seventh-day Adventist denomination's Harvest Ingathering annual drive. They also sponsored a dinner that netted several thousand dollars. Allegedly, these funds were deposited in a Harlem bank in Humphrey's name.[65]

Humphrey's dream of establishing a commune where African Americans could achieve and experience a measure of self-reliance and independence in their social, economic, and political lives through a program of education, training, and practical experience approximated the philosophy and objectives of the utopian communities of pre–Civil War North America. In those societies leadership was derived from within and was almost always Black. Governing bodies were self-contained, and rules and regulations, which were strict, covered all facets of life in the community. The utopian communities were communitarian in structure, philosophy, and mission, providing a context of permanence for those who desired it. In short, these communities were all about equipping Blacks for life in a hostile society, while providing them with succor in the process. As training and support devices, their utility, significance, and purpose cannot be overstated.[66]

Its promotional and fund-raising activities for Utopia Park at full steam, Harlem Number One was envisaging a successful campaign, even though the church knew it was operating outside of denominational policies. Yet the church's chances of success dramatically changed when the president of the Greater New York Conference began to receive information of what Humphrey was doing at First Harlem. Earlier in 1929, the curiosity of the president of the Conference had been piqued by the visit to his office of five of First Harlem's leaders to explain the noticeable drop in the church's tithe and offering remittances. With that visit still fresh in his mind, Louis K. Dickson decided it was not in his best interests to delay asking for clarification about the news of Utopia Park that had reached his desk.

On August 13, 1929, Dickson dispatched a letter to Humphrey, affirming that he had received word Humphrey and his members were about to establish "a colored colony, sanitarium, and old people's home," a project of which he was "totally in the dark regarding the facts." Dickson requested of Humphrey information that would set him "straight on the matter."[67] To his credit, Humphrey did not keep Dickson waiting long for a reply, responding one week later that the news of the Utopia Park project that had reached the president was substantially true but informing him that the project was not a denominational issue. Humphrey thanked Dickson for his "expression of kindly interest" in the project and his "desire to cooperate in this good work" but informed him that Utopia Park was "absolutely a problem for the colored people."[68] Dickson found it difficult to understand and accept Humphrey's response. His follow-up letter, dated August 26, 1929, called upon Humphrey to remember his obligations as a Conference employee, which included counseling and conferring with Conference leadership on ventures such as Utopia Park. Characterizing

Humphrey's refusal to share details of his project "entirely unsatisfactory and disappointing," Dickson dispatched the follow-up letter to the pastor, again requesting vital information.[69]

Yet Humphrey would not be forthcoming, forcing Dickson to place the matter on the agenda of the September 5, 1929, meeting of the Executive Committee of the Greater New York Conference, of which Humphrey was a member. Given the opportunity to explain the project so that he could benefit from the "counsel of his associates in ministry," Humphrey made a few perfunctory remarks that left the Committee "as much in the dark as to the real status of the situation" as it had been before. Frustrated by Humphrey's uncooperative, if not recalcitrant, attitude, Dickson felt constrained to refer the matter to the next level of the administrative structure of the Adventist organization, the Atlantic Union Conference, whose president, E. K. Slade, was present at the September 5 meeting of the Greater New York Conference Executive Committee. Dickson believed that Humphrey, also a member of the Executive Committee of the Atlantic Union Conference, might be more forthcoming with details of Utopia Park before that body.[70]

Events were occurring at a rapid pace. Convinced that delay would compound the problem, church leaders decided to waste no time in tackling the issues surrounding Humphrey and Utopia Park, as challenging and thorny as the issues were. Humphrey and Utopia Park were placed on the agenda of the October 27, 1929, meeting of the Executive Committee of the Atlantic Union Conference. Before that meeting was convened, however, a development occurred that had a profoundly negative impact on the situation.

As it had done the previous two years, the Greater New York Conference sent a representative down to the commissioner of Public Welfare that fall to apply for a permit to solicit funds on the streets of New York City during the Christmas holidays. Asked by the commissioner if he knew a "Rev. J. K. Humphrey,"[71] who was promoting a project up in Wappingers Falls, New York, and shown a stack of material advertising the project with Humphrey's picture conspicuously displayed on it, the Greater New York Conference employee demurred, opting instead to let Conference leadership handle what he thought was an extremely sensitive matter with possibly legal implications.

The very next day, Louis Dickson met with the commissioner, who laid before the surprised president twenty-seven pages of material produced as the result of a hearing his department had conducted on the Utopia Park Health Benevolent Association. Dickson could tell that the commissioner was nonplused by the fact that the denomination knew nothing about Humphrey's venture. Embarrassed and feeling compromised before the public official, the president could think of no other recourse than that of sharing the new development with the Executive Committee of the Atlantic Union Conference at its October 27 meeting.[72]

Humphrey chose not to attend the October 27 meeting, during which "careful and sympathetic study" that took "all angles into consideration" was given to Humphrey and the Utopia Park project. The result was a unanimous vote recommending to the Greater New York Conference Executive Committee that Humphrey's ministerial credentials be revoked "until such time as he shall straighten out this situation in a way that will remove the reproach" that his actions had caused. The Union Committee based its recommendation on the fact that Humphrey was engaged in a "sideline" contrary to the established policies of the Seventh-day Adventist denomination, that he had consistently refused to apprise church leaders of his activities at their request, that he had absented himself from meetings where the matter was up for discussion and deliberation, and that his enterprise exposed the denomination to litigation of a "serious nature." For these and other reasons, the Atlantic Union Executive Committee placed upon Humphrey and the Utopia Park project its "unqualified disapproval."[73]

The Greater New York Conference gave Humphrey another chance to enter into dialogue. On October 31, its Executive Committee, with Humphrey in attendance, convened. Also present were two individuals (one of whom was Atlantic Union conference president, E. K. Slade) whom the Atlantic Union Committee had suggested meet with the Greater New York Conference. The purpose of the meeting was "to help Elder Humphrey to see his mistake and to let him know that . . . his brethren would do all . . . to help him if he would but turn from the course he has taken." When strong pleas of the group failed to move Humphrey, the committee then informed Humphrey that his credentials would be revoked. So that Humphrey fully understood what that meant, the Committee explained to him that he could no longer serve as the pastor of First Harlem or represent the denomination and that he was no longer a member of either the Executive Committee of the Greater New York Conference or the Atlantic Union Conference.[74]

Chapter 2

Assessing the
Utopia Park Affair

The revocation of the ministerial credentials of James K. Humphrey and the expulsion of First Harlem Seventh-day Adventist from the Greater New York Conference were unfortunate occurrences bemoaned by all who were involved in the events that led up to them. Certainly, Humphrey and his loyalists would have preferred to remain a part of the Seventh-day Adventist organization in spite of what they saw as its shortcomings and pitfalls relative to the race issue. The tears that seasoned Humphrey's sermon on November 2, 1929, officially his last day as pastor of First Harlem, indicate that at the very least Humphrey was troubled with the way events were unfolding. Yet how much church leaders empathized with and understood the position of the members of First Harlem and their pastor, as well as Humphrey's culpability in the matter, are issues that call for analysis.

There is no evidence that officials of the Greater New York Conference responded in any coherent, meaningful way to the five members from First Harlem who visited their offices in the summer of 1929 to explain the reasons for the significant drop in the church's financial remittances to the Conference. In addition, it appears that Humphrey's broad and deep support at the church, as starkly evident by the vote of November 2, had little, if any, impact on Conference leadership, leading one to conclude that Adventist leadership may have belittled the church's membership. The only time it is sure that denominational leadership visited First Harlem was on the evening of November 2 to inform church members that their beloved pastor of over twenty years had been defrocked for promoting a project that, as far as church members were concerned, would benefit them. It is not certain that denominational leaders were at First Harlem for the worship service of November 2, though it appears that they were not. One wonders how events would have played out that night had the members of First Harlem seen church leaders worshiping in their midst that day. Had the two groups interacted in the context of worship, their encounter that evening might have been stripped of the suspicion, anger, and hurt that characterized the historic meeting.

Given the assemblage at First Harlem on November 2 of personnel from the General Conference, the Atlantic Union, and the Greater New York Conference of Seventh-day Adventists, the absence of George E. Peters, the newly appointed secretary of the Negro Department of the General Conference, from the meetings that considered and deliberated on Humphrey and Utopia Park is noteworthy. It is unknown whether Peters's counsel or recommendations were sought or whether he was even aware of the controversy swirling around in New York City. Still, given the size and strategic significance of the First Harlem congregation and the official purpose for the existence of the Negro Department, the absence of Peters at these meetings, especially the crucial meeting of November 2, is inexplicable. As the highest ranking Black in the Seventh-day Adventist denomination at the time, Peters should have been present, and his involvement almost certainly would have had a telling impact on the many proceedings, if not their outcome.

Yet the absence of Peters may have been part of the strategic plan of church leaders, for when First Harlem was reorganized as the Ephesus Seventh-day Adventist Church, George E. Peters was assigned as its first pastor. A gifted speaker, Peters, a West Indian from Antigua, spoke with an accent familiar to many Harlemites. Undoubtedly, his assignment was an intentional move by church leaders to appeal to the large West Indian constituency among Seventh-day Adventists in New York City. In addition, the assignment of Peters was meant to convey the message that church leaders considered the removal of Humphrey from First Harlem so important a matter that it was willing to reassign its highest ranking Black employee to assume the responsibilities of pastoral leadership in the area.

Church leaders informed the members of First Harlem on November 2 that they were there at the invitation of the church "to talk over with you as brethren" a matter of great importance. Yet they quickly revealed the reason for their being at First Harlem that night. Humphrey's recalcitrant attitude toward "supremely important and vital principles" of church organization and leadership had driven them to take "decided action," which they had come "to announce" to the church. Thus, church leadership was not at First Harlem on November 2 to dialogue or listen but to announce a decision that had been already made without any input from church members.[1]

One reason the Utopia Park affair ultimately resulted in the revocation of Humphrey's ministerial credentials and the expulsion of First Harlem from the Adventist organization was the Anglo leadership's woeful ignorance of the fundamentally significant role African American religious leaders play in the Black community.[2] It is because of this key role that it is far from surprising that on the night of November 2 Humphrey won near unanimous endorsement for his course of action and attitude. Further, the support Humphrey received from his parishioners was not due to a gullible childlikeness that could easily be exploited by shrewd manipulators masquerading as religious leaders but to the profound love and admiration Black congregants have for their pastors.[3]

Adventist leaders also misread the social and political dynamics at play in the African American community during the 1920s, a decade that was fraught with vestiges of Pan-Africanism and Ethiopianism, two elements of the Black nationalism that had dominated African American life from 1850 to 1925. Complex and often elusive, Black American nationalism encapsulated and "expressed a people's desire for self-determination, for progress, and for the essential and indispensable rights and privileges of free humanity," and during the late nineteenth century the phenomenon was a paradox that simultaneously facilitated values that seemed incongruent in the African American community.[4] Notwithstanding its Afrocentric orientation and emphasis, Black nationalism[5] never caught on among middle-class Blacks as well as it did among the working class. Middle-class Blacks, in spite of the odds stacked against them, tended to believe that progress was being made in race relations and "the hallmark of the middle class was optimism." Among lower working-class Blacks were many who resonated with the ambitions, and perhaps the achievements, of middle-class Blacks, and though it is difficult to gauge the number of Blacks who supported returning to Africa as a viable, tenable Black nationalist goal, it is reasonable to assume that more of them supported the policy than actually acted on it. In the end, Black nationalism succeeded in instilling in Blacks race pride and raising their consciousness level to the conditions in American society that circumscribed them.[6]

Humphrey's drive for self-determination for Blacks was not based on a Messiah complex or Moses syndrome but was anchored in the broader African

American community's quest for increased autonomy and power during the 1920s, and no Black social or political organization better exploited that quest than the Universal Negro Improvement Association (UNIA). Founded in 1917 by a charismatic Jamaican immigrant named Marcus Garvey, the UNIA piqued the curiosity and fancy of not a few of the West Indians and Southerners who streamed into Harlem after World War I, and when the organization held its first convention in the summer of 1920, it claimed an international following of over two million. By 1922, it was alleging a worldwide membership of six million.[7]

Garvey was born in Jamaica, where he had heard and studied about Booker T. Washington's philosophy of Black uplift and self-empowerment and where he had put his words into action with the formation of the Jamaican Improvement Association. Coming to America by way of England, the diminutive Jamaican of stocky build and penetrating eyes arrived in Harlem in 1917, a couple of years shy of his thirtieth birthday. Garvey was appalled to see that Harlem's masses were under the rule of Whites, and he immediately set out to correct this state of affairs by establishing a Black state within the United States. His rise to prominence began one day when he was afforded a few minutes to address the small crowd gathered around one of the soap boxes that were staples on Harlem's street corners at the time. On these makeshift platforms self-styled prophets and social commentators held court, informing their listeners of impending doom and articulating their panacea for the social ills and pathologies then plaguing the Black race. Initially dismissed as a West Indian carpetbagger,[8] Garvey ultimately succeeded in commanding the attention, if not the admiration, of the crowd, holding it spellbound with his imagination and rhetoric.

One reason Garvey came to America was because of the frustration he had experienced trying to motivate the peasantry in Jamaica to accept the notion of racial consciousness. Asserting that Blacks in his homeland were victims of a sociological hypocrisy that negated the consciousness of race, Garvey experienced greater hospitality for his views among Blacks in the United States, who were searching for a Black Moses at the time of his arrival in New York. Yet Garvey never intended to dabble in politics. When he launched the UNIA in Jamaica in 1914, he repudiated involvement in Jamaican politics, asserting that among the organization's primary objectives was the establishment of a humanitarianism that would serve as an antidote to the ills of society. The UNIA initially functioned as a fraternal organization, espousing and promoting mutual improvement and strategic benevolence, and covenanting to develop the physical and psychological powers of its members.[9] Ultimately, Garvey eschewed his repudiation of politics, a reversal that was triggered in part by the harsh realities of the race situation in America.[10] In time, Garvey began to elucidate a philosophy for the redemption of Africa.[11]

After landing in New York on March 23, 1916, Garvey first went on a cross-continental tour of the United States, visiting no less than thirty-eight states to survey the social conditions of African Americans. The tour took fifteen months, so that it was not until June 1917 that he arrived in Harlem. As the majority of West Indians who came to the United States between 1900 and 1920, Garvey was drawn to Harlem by the sheer mass of its Black population and by its notoriety, and his rise to prominence coincided with Harlem's ascent as the Black capital of the world. As Blacks poured into the area, they seemed intent on grasping the elements of success so long denied them, making Garvey's doctrine of self-help and success especially appealing and addictive. A self-made individual, Garvey seemed paranoid about lapsing into poverty and failure, and held himself up as an example of what vision, industry, and sacrifice could bring to the Black race.[12]

Garvey recruited from the radical fringe ringing Harlem for the launching of his UNIA in the United States. Headquartered in Harlem, the UNIA had as its major goal the economic emancipation and empowerment of the Black race. More specifically, it sought to consolidate Blacks of the diaspora into a cohesive, strong unit, liberate the African continent from European exploitation, create an infrastructure for the region that would see it blossom as a commercial superpower within a few years, and provide for the spiritual well-being of people of African descent through the establishment of churches. Garvey preached a gospel of the Black recapture of Africa, instilling in the Black masses a pride of race previously absent. His doctrine of race consciousness, like a drenching downpour, blanketed Harlem.[13]

Bent on casting off everything White, Garvey created his own political and national order, assuming the titular role of "Provisional President-General of Africa," a title that smacked of republicanism. His hierarchal ruling structure, though, was modeled after the English monarchy and was called the Court of Ethiopia. On his coterie of closest aides Garvey bestowed titles, and he established an African Legion, replete with commissioned officers, quarter masters, and commissariats. Leaving nothing to chance, Garvey had manuals on the social graces for his court personnel, as well as instruction booklets on an array of subjects that included Black history and military and self-defense tactics.[14] Yet Garvey's most presumptuous move was the creation of a Black religion. Raised a Roman Catholic, Garvey first had been offered hospitality and a forum to dispense his ideas in the United States by a Roman Catholic priest, and it was that denomination's theology, liturgy, and ritual from which his lieutenants borrowed heavily to form the foundation of his church—The African Orthodox Church. Garvey, of course, Africanized everything in his church. He preached a homespun theology that boasted a Black God, a Jesus Christ who was "the Black Man of Sorrow," and a Blessed Virgin Mary as a "Black Madonna." In time, Garvey himself came to be viewed as the "Black Moses."[15]

Garvey's brand of Black nationalism was a blend of intellectualism and emotionalism that appealed to the peasant population who saw in him a symbol of what it might become. That the African American intellectual had failed to assuage the deep misgivings the Black community had about the current and future state of race relations in the country made Garvey all the more appealing. Garvey refused to limit himself and the possibilities of his people, passionately intoning a vision that transcended time and the American frontier. He wanted to transform people of African descent from victims to victors, and he attempted to forge a sense of common identity from the various elements and segments of the Black community. Garvey correctly reminded all Blacks of their shared heritage and underscored their shared experience of oppression. He was able to galvanize broad Black support for his program of self-determination and empowerment.

Garvey and Garveyism provide a critical link in the attempts of Black people to obtain justice and to experience freedom in the United States. Before Marcus Garvey, the quest of Blacks for freedom and empowerment utilized a myriad of strategies and movements, resulting in a recognizable mode of Black reflection and action. Throughout their struggles, Blacks oscillated between disbelief and faith that change would come. Yet Garvey and Garveyism symbolized more than the historic Black struggle for freedom, representing the marriage of two complementary Black movements for freedom—one in the West Indies and the other in the United States of America.

More than any other African American civil rights organization, the UNIA provoked a broad and profound interest in the plight of people of African descent in this country and around the world. Before Garvey, the Black man's predicament was largely an American predicament addressed principally for the benefit of indigenous Blacks. In the aftermath of Garvey and Garveyism,

Black nationalism was conceived of in global terms. Garvey's "Back-to-Africa" movement succeeded in welding together two culturally different groups with a common ancestry, and, more fundamentally significant, a shared experience of oppression and discrimination. Yet the UNIA was more successful because it satisfied the aspirations of the masses for concrete symbols of success and meaning. To the thousands of West Indians and newly urbanized African Americans from the South, the UNIA was an asylum, an oasis where they were people of value and worth in an otherwise desert of disenfranchisement.

While it is uncertain whether Humphrey ever personally met Marcus Garvey, it is sure that Humphrey exhibited many of Garvey's Black nationalist tendencies. Like Garvey, Humphrey wanted people of color to rise up and fulfill their true destinies and to throw off the yoke of oppression that slowed their drive to self-determination. Moreover, Humphrey envisioned his church's struggle with the Greater New York Conference as part of a larger crusade, namely the Black struggle against White oppression.[16] So sure of this was Humphrey that in the promotional material for his Utopia Park project, he quoted from another Jamaican expatriate—Harlem Renaissance figure Claude McKay:

> So I would live in rich imperial growth,
> Touching the surface and the depth of things,
> Instinctively responsive to both,
> Tasting the sweets of being and the stings,
> Sensing the subtle spell of changing forms
> Like a strong tree against a thousand storms.[17]

In spite of the fact that Adventist leadership may have misread crucial phenomena permeating the African American community during the 1920s and may have displayed an insensitivity toward First Harlem's feeling about its pastor and his activities, church leaders did try to resolve their differences with Humphrey in a collaborative fashion. To be sure, meetings were convened in quick succession, calling into question the critical matter of due process, yet the conflict management measures church leaders utilized indicate attempts on their part to enter into meaningful dialogue with Humphrey.

Did friction or rivalry between James K. Humphrey and Louis K. Dickson, president of the Greater New York Conference, contribute to the controversy and its unfortunate outcome? Dickson was Humphrey's junior in many respects, including length of service in the Greater New York Conference. Humphrey had almost twenty years of service to his credit when Dickson joined the Conference in 1923, and when Dickson was elected president of the Conference in 1927, Dickson had been an ordained Seventh-day Adventist minister for only ten years. That Dickson shot past him to the presidency in such a short time may have troubled Humphrey, who was always painfully aware of the dearth of leadership opportunities available to people of color in the Adventist organization. Yet there is no hard evidence that a rivalry between Dickson and Humphrey contributed in any substantive way to the dramatic events of 1929 and 1930.

Humphrey did have his share of rivals and detractors, among whom was J. L. Moran, the principal of Harlem Academy in the late 1920s. Moran, who was appointed president of Oakwood College in 1932 after a student-led strike protesting discriminatory practices and conditions at the all-Black school, did not appreciate that Humphrey wielded so much influence and power among African Americans. Humphrey's popularity disturbed Moran immensely. Whether out of envy or because he favored organization over people, Moran kept the General Conference apprised of Humphrey's activities, and the principal, an indigenous African American, later banned the reading of Humphrey's periodical by his students. Whenever he could, Moran seized copies of the paper and forwarded them to the General Conference of Seventh-day Adventists.[18]

To what extent did Humphrey fail to provide his congregation with information and counsel that would have prevented it from being voted out of the Adventist organizational structure in January 1930? Did Humphrey put self before people? Did he allow resentment and anger to fester within him until they fomented a rebellion? How did Humphrey get to the point in 1929 where he could consciously facilitate and promulgate a break with the established Adventist church when less than a few years earlier he had declared in a sermon that nothing could drive a wedge between the Adventist church and him? Was Humphrey a person who played to the masses? Did he lack moral underpinnings on which to base his decisions, attitudes, and actions?

The answers to these and other attendant questions are not easily forthcoming. Yet one thing is certain, and that is that Humphrey was not without fault in the controversy that led to the revocation of his ministerial credentials and the expulsion of First Harlem from the Greater New York Conference. While it may be impossible to conduct a scientific psychological profile of Humphrey now, a reasonable inference may be made that the pastor was under stress throughout his tenure as a minister in the Seventh-day Adventist denomination. Humphrey comes across as a complex individual struggling to reconcile the denomination's biblical and theological positions with its beliefs about and treatment of people of color.

Humphrey's culpability in the controversy included his refusal to attend some of the meetings called by the organization to deliberate on the matter, his disregard for clearly outlined denominational policies and procedures, and his refusal to communicate substantively with denomination leadership when requested to do so. These acts have left him open to charges of recalcitrance and the exploitation of his power and influence.

That Utopia Park had been touted as a completely nonsectarian venture must have struck Seventh-day Adventist church leaders as significant. Adventist leaders of the early twentieth century strongly opposed such projects, their refusal to accept them dating back to the denomination's struggles with J. H. Kellogg, the colorful doctor and entrepreneur who, throughout his life, had his share of admirers and detractors. By 1929, Seventh-day Adventist church leaders had a history of resisting private ventures, making the mere mention of Utopia Park as such an enterprise a red flag to them. It is highly probable, therefore, that Utopia Park presented Seventh-day Adventist church leadership with issues that transcended race. More important, perhaps issues of control were involved as well.

The Official Seventh-day Adventist Explanation of the Utopia Park Affair

Shortly after the revocation of Humphrey's ministerial credentials and the expulsion of First Harlem Seventh-day Adventist Church from the sisterhood of churches of the Greater New York Conference, the denomination published a lengthy detailed account of the activities that led up to the unfortunate events. Undoubtedly, the publication of the document was intended to convey the gravity of the actions taken by the denomination, as well as their implications and ramifications both within and outside the organization. Humphrey wielded an influence that extended well beyond the precincts of his local parish. His ministerial career within the denomination up to the events of 1929 had been unblemished and illustrious, and his prominence precluded anyone from dismissing his ideas as irrelevant. In an ironic twist, the president of the General Conference of Seventh-day Adventists in 1945 and the person who was most instrumental in swinging denominational support behind the idea of regional conferences was James L. McElhany, the author of the organization's official explanation.[19]

One of the themes McElhany painstakingly emphasized in his official explanation is the notion of unity, the maintenance of which church leaders considered a matter of supreme importance. Again and again, church unity is mentioned by McElhany as a critical need of the church, with loyalty to the denomination apparently its identical twin. No comment is made by McElhany about Humphrey's allegations of racism and discrimination within the church.

Yet the denomination did not treat Humphrey's charges of racism and discrimination with benign neglect. In an attempt to rebut them, A. R. Ogden, president of the Antillian Union Conference of Seventh-day Adventists with headquarters in Puerto Rico, published an article in the *Jamaica Visitor*, at the time the denominational newsletter on the island of Jamaica, where, quite understandably, Humphrey had quite a following. Ogden professed that Seventh-day Adventists had manifestly showed its commitment to and love of all people by sending forth missionaries with the gospel to a languishing humanity. He claimed that the General Conference had allocated over $300,000 in aid to Africa in one year alone, and another $240,000 to the Inter-America region. "Outside of the small fees of the students," West Indies Training College, located in Mandeville, Jamaica, was being fully subsidized by the General Conference. Ogden asserted that "everyone who breaks rank today will soon see their mistake, and with sadness and shame because of their mistake, either seek re-admission to the remnant body, or give up in despair." For these and other reasons, Ogden appealed to Jamaicans not to fall prey to Humphrey's charges and characterizations.[20]

African Americans did not roll over and readily accept the official analysis and interpretation of the Utopia Park affair put out by the church. In a combative rebuttal to McElhany's *Statement Regarding the Present Standing of Elder J. K. Humphrey*, they laid blame for what had happened squarely in the lap of the church, which they claimed believed Black people were incapable of leading. Saying it was high time for the African American ministers of the denomination to "stand up like men with backbone and fight for their people," they dismissed the church's penchant for crying apostasy to such acts as nothing more than attempts to intimidate Blacks into complacency and acceptance of their second-class position in the church. They asserted that Adventist church leadership dealt with them only because of their ability to contribute to the coffers of the church, not because their White counterparts viewed or accepted them as true equals.[21]

Humphrey's supporters bewailed their treatment at the hands of Whites. They claimed that many of their congregations lacked buildings of their own, and as a result they paid exorbitant rents for the use of halls and other facilities that often barely met minimum building code standards. Moreover, some of these congregations lacked pastoral leadership, forcing them to utilize the services of lay personnel to keep their churches operating. Of particular distress to them was the contempt with which a small congregation called "Sharon" had been treated.[22] Having no ordained pastor, the group had petitioned that its elder, who was also a lay leader, be compensated for his services out of tithe funds.[23] The Conference had responded quickly, condemning the idea that the elder could be paid out of tithe funds and indicating that should the congregation elect to do so, it would be summarily dissolved.[24]

The authors of the rebuttal viewed the comments about Humphrey that had been made by the president of the Greater New York Conference as an attempt to discredit the veteran, if not venerable, pastor. They dismissed the charge that Humphrey was to be blamed for the decrease in the financial remittances to the Conference, explaining that the drop was due to a heightened awareness on the part of Blacks to their treatment in the church and to their decision to no longer support institutions that systematically discriminated against them. To the extent that Humphrey had taught them not to turn the proverbial other cheek any longer but to resist and to fight for their rights, he had done no wrong, and when Humphrey had refused to attend the meetings of the Negro Commission to study the feasibility of the denomination establishing regional conferences, it was because of the tactics of church leadership. Finally, the dismissal of Humphrey provided telling evidence of an unacceptable fact—the absence of any discernible and measurable benefits for their financial contributions.

The revocation of Humphrey's ministerial credentials and the expulsion of First Harlem from the Greater New York Conference did not slow or quiet Humphrey's call for more autonomy for and by Blacks within the Seventh-day Adventist church. Indeed, Humphrey's experience galvanized Seventh-day Adventist African Americans, providing them with a tangible issue around which they were able to focus their energies in their struggles for greater self-determination in the organization.[25] One year after Humphrey's expulsion from the Seventh-day Adventist denomination, students at all-Black Oakwood College rose up in protest against what they considered racist policies and practices at the school. A campus-wide, student-led strike brought the educational institution to a standstill and resulted in the installation of the college's first Black president, F. L. Moran. One of the student leaders of the strike, W. W. Fordham, was well aware of the events that had taken place in New York City the year before and believed that Humphrey's break with the denomination was the spark that ignited and fueled calls for regional conferences.[26]

The momentum gained, regional conferences were finally established fifteen years later after a couple of tragic incidents that underscored that the Seventh-day Adventist denomination was still mired in a quagmire of confusion and ambiguity over the race issue.[27] In one of the incidents, Lucy Baird, a Seventh-day Adventist light-skinned Black woman, was turned away from the denomination's hospital in Washington, D.C., because of her skin color. Hospital employees, thinking Baird was White, initially moved to attend to her but, on realizing she was Black, aborted their service. On her way across town to a Black hospital, Baird died. When regional conferences were finally organized in the spring of 1944, Humphrey was gleeful, telling Harlem's leading Black newspaper that he felt vindicated. Humphrey saw regional conferences as the "logical and proper thing" required "to manage and strengthen the work among colored people."[28]

Established with a view to fostering Adventist work among Blacks in the United States, regional conferences have brought about significant gains in evangelism, "new opportunities for training and experience in ministry, increased opportunities for leadership and service, and participation in church governance." Regional conferences have added vigor, vim, and vitality to the denomination's program,[29] yet questions about the viability and purpose of regional conferences persist. Calvin Rock, for example, believes that Seventh-day Adventist Christians will never achieve victory in the Christian journey while they "remain a psychologically and structurally divided people." Rock views "separate but equal" facilities and "segregated operations" as less than ideal, believing that Ellen White's call for the acceptance of separate operations "until the Lord shows us a better way" highlights that the ideal is not what Adventists currently have. That better way, Rock asserts, is "the way of open fellowship and complete desegregation by Seventh-day Adventists on all levels of communion, administration, and worship." Yet in 1970, forty years after Humphrey left the Adventist denomination and twenty-five years after the establishment of regional conferences, Rock contended that the Seventh-day

Adventist church was still not ready to usher in the age of "open fellowship and complete desegregation."[30]

Utopia Park provides eloquent evidence of the tenuousness of race relations in the Seventh-day Adventist Church in the early twentieth century and the fact that the race issue was not confined to the South. Previously, the denomination had focused its mission to Black America in the South, naively believing that the North was immune to the kinds of challenges it faced in attempting to reach African Americans with the gospel. Even the departure of Louis B. Sheafe and the People's Temple of Washington, D.C., and the establishment of the Free Seventh-day Adventists by J. W. Manns had failed to much alter denominational thinking on the race issue. It took Utopia Park to do so. No longer could the Seventh-day Adventist church deny that African Americans faced no difficulties in their drive for self-determination either in the northern United States or, for that matter, within the Seventh-day Adventist church.[31]

Chapter 3

THE TENOR OF THE TIMES

The first three decades of the twentieth century constituted a critical period in the history of people of African descent in the United States. During the era, thousands of African Americans abandoned the South for the urban centers of the North because of Jim Crow practices that made a mockery of their civil liberties. After World War I, America was a bonanza of optimism and hope, the feeling of euphoria permeating all of the nation's racial, ethnic, and socioeconomic groups. For some American Blacks, the war had provided opportunities for economic enhancement, as the wartime economy required labor previously provided by European immigrants. Yet racism was still rife in the South. The result of impatience with Southern racism, as well as the new opportunities opened by the war effort, was a wave of Black migration, with New York City receiving a significant share of the immigrants throughout the 1920s.

Of the first three decades of the twentieth century, the 1920s is by far the most celebrated.[1] Today the 1920s are referred to by many as the "Roaring Twenties," as a period of unparalleled and unprecedented fun and frivolity in New York City, and it is said that Harlem was in vogue then. Harlem was the quintessential American playground, providing New York City residents and all takers with art and entertainment. It was a city within a city, a safe haven for Blacks from the South and the West Indies, their center of empowerment and self-actualization in a desert of disenfranchisement and social and economic oppression. Yet Harlem during the 1920s was not without irony and contradiction. Craftily hidden beneath the veneer of "good times" were stresses and tensions that were glaringly exposed once the Depression set in at the end of the decade.

Harlem, New York, was not always the undisputed Black capital of the United States. Prior to the last quarter of the nineteenth century, Harlem had been an isolated village at the northern tip of Manhattan island inhabited by an overwhelming number of poor immigrants, many of whom were squatters. As the twentieth century dawned, New York City experienced an urban revolution marked by improvements in transportation, communication, sanitation, and, concomitantly, a population explosion that sent residents north in search of affordable housing. Land speculators capitalized in Harlem, and by the turn of the century a frantic building activity resulted in rows and rows of brownstones and luxurious apartment houses that were inhabited, for the most part, by middle-class Whites. Yet the glut of houses led, inevitably, to an alarming number of vacancies and a deflated real estate market that threatened New York City with financial ruin. Unwilling to face financial catastrophe, some White landlords began renting to Blacks at exorbitant, but traditionally high, prices. Thus began the mass movement of Blacks to Harlem.[2]

As the 1920s dawned, Harlem was still an overwhelmingly White community. In fact, the area around 125th Street would remain decidedly so until the middle of the decade.[3] But the African American migration to New York City in general, and Harlem in particular, increased significantly during the 1920s. Between 1920 and 1930, Black migration to New York City jumped over 100 percent, as both foreign-born and indigenous Blacks flocked to the city in search of the proverbial Promised Land. Most Harlemites during the period had at least one relative who was a newcomer to the area, and not a few of the old-timers provided temporary living quarters for the newly arrived.[4]

By 1925 Harlem had come to be viewed as another Statue of Liberty, and the migration of Blacks there was compared to the opening of the American Western frontier. It was the thrust toward democracy of African Americans, who were grasping for their destiny without giving much heed to the rest of New York. Harlem was not then a slum or ghetto, but neither was it a resort or colony. A little of all, it was the capital of the Black race, culturally and spiritually to African Americans what Dublin was to the New Irish and Prague was to New Czechoslovakians.[5] Atypical of many American cities, it was also unlike other Black enclaves in America in that it was not situated on the fringes or periphery of New York City. Rather, it was ensconced in the heart of the city, making it impossible for one to ignore it.[6]

Harlem became the nerve center of the Black community, the Mecca of the African American. In Harlem the pulse of Black America could be felt, and

Blacks there began to experience a "common consciousness" for the first time since being brought to the New World.[7] Blacks from around the world wanted to see, if not live in, Harlem. In "City of Refuge," a short story by Rudolph Fisher, one of the "New Negroes" of the Harlem Renaissance, King Solomon Gillis, the story's main character, emerges from the subway at the corner of 135th Street and Lenox Avenue exclaiming: "Done died and woke up in heaven." Gillis was stunned by the sea of Black faces swirling around him. As he put it, there were "Negroes at every turn . . . black ones, brown ones, yellow ones, men standing idly on the curb, women, bundle-laden, trudging reluctantly homeward, children rattle trapping about the sidewalks." Yet what really startled Gillis were the "cullud policemens" directing traffic, and to whom the occasional White person in sight paid full attention and obeyed.[8]

Gillis could have been the prototype of Langston Hughes, one of the key figures of the Harlem Renaissance. As a teenager spending the summer after his high school graduation in Mexico, where his father was living, Hughes incessantly dreamt of Harlem, for him the greatest city in the world, and the place he wanted to visit more than any European country. When Hughes moved to Harlem in 1921 as a nineteen-year-old freshman at Columbia University, it was still a racially mixed community, though it had already earned the moniker "Negro Capital of the World." Taking a room at the YMCA on 135th Street because of "overcrowding" at the Columbia dorm where he had been promised housing, Hughes was impressed and mesmerized by the glitter and glamour he saw. Seventh Avenue was Harlem's Broadway. A wide, spacious promenade lined with theaters, churches, restaurants, stores, and apartment buildings, it was a majestic thoroughfare into which the Black population poured daily in search of business and pleasure. At 132nd Street and Seventh Avenue stood the Lafayette Theater, where Black plays were running and where Hughes himself would later present many of his poems, and at 129th Street and Seventh Avenue stood the Metropolitan Baptist and Salem Methodist Episcopal churches, two of Harlem's prestigious Black churches, facing each other like proud sentinels. Of particular interest and delight to Hughes was the building at the corner of 135th Street and Lenox Avenue that housed the Schomburg Collection of Negro Literature and History. This branch of the New York Public Library was a resource Hughes utilized throughout his long and distinguished writing career.[9]

The Harlem of the 1920s was not just a city within a city, but, more important, a community that offered sanctuary to an oppressed people and acceptance and empowerment to those living on the margins of society. Thus,

Paul Robeson, the Black college football hero who later became a singer of world renown, found that in Harlem he was readily accepted even as the United States government was putting a mechanism in place to banish him to anonymity. The beleaguered Robeson, whose older brother was pastor of a Harlem African Methodist Episcopal (AME) congregation and lived in Harlem too, felt "at home among my people" in Harlem, where he met and married his wife, and where his career as an artist began and flourished.[10]

Economic Conditions

Despite the generally positive image Blacks had of Harlem during the 1920s, economic realities there were foreboding. In a groundbreaking study of twenty-four hundred African American families living in Harlem in the 1920s, Konrad Bercovici discovered that almost 50 percent who rented paid twice as much of their income on rent as Whites. Apartments for which Whites had paid forty dollars a month went to Blacks for one hundred or more dollars.[11] Ostensibly, it was all a matter of supply and demand. Furthermore, 25 percent of Blacks had at least one boarder, and an undetermined number of apartments were so cramped that dwellers had to sleep in shifts.[12] Many of the new arrivals to Harlem found temporary shelter at the Harlem Forum, which was almost always overcrowded with hungry, frightened, cold Blacks with hope in their eyes.[13] Adam Clayton Powell Sr., the venerable senior minister of the landmark Abyssinian Baptist Church, addressed the "stiff economic conditions" permeating Harlem in the first sermon he preached in his new church building there, saying that economic hardship was the cause of many dishonest lives. He stressed the improbability and impossibility of anybody earning fifteen dollars a week being able to pay rent of sixty dollars a month, saying that a poor widow with three children "looking up into her face crying for the necessities of life needs material help more than she needs spiritual comfort."[14]

Exorbitant rents and unscrupulous landlords conspired to create unsavory and unsanitary living conditions for the majority of Harlem's residents. Landlords were known to refuse to supply heat and hot water to tenants so that, frustrated, the tenants would move out, thereby giving the landlords an opportunity to increase rents.[15] Exacerbating matters was the fact that the majority of apartment buildings and brownstones housing the African American population had been built for people with family structures and lifestyles fundamentally different from those of the new inhabitants. Black Harlemites were given to dividing up their apartments into as many different spaces as possible, subletting the rooms to generate income to pay the rent. In the process, they made lodging and boarding legendary in 1920s Harlem.

Harlemites bemoaned the fact that Blacks in Harlem did not own much in the way of business enterprises. Langston Hughes, for example, decried having to go downtown to have his works published. He saw downtown as White and uptown as Black, with White downtown controlling everything in Harlem. African Americans could not even play the "numbers"[16] among themselves, he claimed, citing the kidnapping of Casper Holstein, the "numbers" kingpin, by Whites as proof that Harlem was controlled by Whites. Hughes also claimed that all the stores and businesses in Harlem were owned by Whites and that many of the businesses, even those located in the very heart of Harlem, did not even employ Black salespeople. Particularly distressing to him was the fact that almost all the policemen in Harlem were White.[17] Sounding a similar note, Claude McKay, the Jamaican poet and novelist, stated that the "saloons were run by the Irish, the restaurants by the Greeks, the ice and fruit stands by the Italians, the grocery and haberdashery stores by the Jews" and that the only African American businesses, except barber shops and hair stylists, were churches and carabets.[18]

Yet African Americans were not wholly absent from commerce in Harlem during the 1920s. As early as 1919 the Universal Negro Improvement Association (UNIA) was operating two restaurants, three grocery stores, and a laundry in Harlem. As the 1920s dawned, only one of the restaurants, the one located in Liberty Hall, was operating at a profit. Soon afterward, J. Raymond Jones, who had joined the UNIA in 1920, was handed the responsibility of operating the stores, wet-wash laundry, and restaurants. All operations were turning a profit within a couple of years. Toward the end of the decade, Jones launched an ice-vending business himself, servicing one of Harlem's major apartment complexes. Of course, the Black Star Line was the most ambitious attempt at a Black-owned and Black-operated business by the UNIA of the period. The failure of the Black Star Line resulted more from a lack of business sense than from chicanery and charlatanism on the part of the UNIA's head, Marcus Garvey.[19]

One industry that was not off limits to Blacks was the funeral industry, which did a brisk business laying Blacks to rest. Funeral directors advertised heavily in the Black newspapers and periodicals of the day, with one claiming to be able to provide a complete funeral with dignity for as little as $150.[20]

Low incomes and high unemployment put New York City Blacks in a precarious position during the period. When racism and discrimination were factored in, the ability of African Americans to mount a sustained effort at entrepreneurship and to be a reckoning force at the table of capitalism were all but erased. More consumers than producers, African Americans in Harlem still attempted to generate and control a local economy through the establishment of the North Harlem Community Council (1918), Harlem Stock Exchange (1920), Association of Trade and Commerce (1921), Harlem Economic Association (1924), Harlem's Businessmen's Club (1927), and the Housewives League (1930). In 1930 the National Negro Business League organized over one hundred Black-owned and Black-operated stores into the Colored Merchants' Association in order to buy cooperatively and sell at competitive prices. As part of its service to the merchants, the Association offered instruction in the rudiments of mercantilism. Over 130 merchants took advantage of the opportunity.[21]

Life in the Black community presented Black businesses with some unique challenges. One was that Black owners and consumers often were members of the same churches and civic organizations, which some consumers interpreted to mean easy credit and less-than-strident collection procedures. The granting of credit by Black merchants had an adverse impact on their cash flow. Unpaid accounts strained many a relationship and threatened some businesses with bankruptcy. The challenges did not end there. Black merchants often lamented that their clients were not as courteous with them as they were known to be with White merchants. On the other hand, Black customers were known to feel that they were doing Black merchants a huge favor by choosing them over White businesses. The net result was that Black merchants were caught in a no-win situation. At a time when African Americans were bemoaning the lack of economic opportunities available to them, they were less than enthusiastic about supporting their own.[22]

In addition to its legitimate entrepreneurs, 1920s Harlem bulged with a medley of merchants who peddled their commodities on its streets. Roots, herbs, powders, chains, cloths, and an assortment of products all intended to enhance the African American's chances of success in the big city could be found at any hour of the day and well into the evening. The recent immigrant was especially targeted by these street corner vendors, who did a brisk business despite the drawbacks and shortcomings of their products and their sales pitches. Yet the African American's greatest exploiter was still the landlord, who gouged and extorted huge sums from unsuspecting new arrivals, ostensibly because housing was at a premium.[23]

Educating children in Harlem during the first three decades of the twentieth century posed serious challenges. Less than a hundred children were graduating yearly from high school in the early 1920s because they had to work to help support their families. In fact, if the child labor laws on the books at the time had been enforced, many African American families would have been driven to starvation.[24] With Blacks from the South and the West Indies flooding the area prior to and especially during the 1920s, overcrowding in schools became a severe problem that necessitated, among other things, "double session classes," a phenomenon that contributed to lateness and truancy.

In 1916, a comprehensive study of Public School 89, the main elementary school serving Harlem, had shown that 1,736 of the 2,071 students were Black and revealed problems of attendance, overage students, delinquency, and health care. At that time, 34 percent of the students came from broken homes, and the study, conducted by the school's principal, revealed a direct relationship between retardation and those unfortunate home conditions. Seven out of eight children were overage, with some children being as far as four years behind in scholastic training and in ideals such as punctuality and conduct. Usually forty to fifty boys were on some kind of probation at any one time. The Board concluded that the influx of children from the South was to be blamed for the conditions and suggested that the erection of a new school building would help assuage the problems. In addition, the Board proposed the organization of smaller classrooms and the establishment of vocational training for overage students.[25]

The economic viability of Harlem was also influenced by health issues, a sore spot for Harlemites during the 1920s. The death rate for Blacks in 1923 was 20.85 percent, as compared to 11.25 for Whites. Ill-equipped to deal with the change in the climate, housing conditions, and other pathologies and social ills, Blacks paid a disproportionate toll for living in the city. In Harlem, Blacks were known to be exploited by poorly trained doctors, who often chose to work in the area because they knew they lacked the competencies to work elsewhere, and because they knew they could easily exploit the African American's lack of knowledge about medical matters. Harlem had doctors called podopractors, manopractors, and pedipractors. Charlatans from an array of medical schools preyed upon a naively hopeful Black community.[26] White doctors knew that Blacks had faith in them. This accounts for one telling a patient he was afflicted with "spider cancer," an incurable ailment the patient alleg-edly had contracted after a fall. Another doctor charged a patient six hundred dollars to relieve him of water, ostensibly because the procedure to correct a condition called pleurisy was major surgery.[27] In spite of their dealings with poorly trained doctors, African Americans still showed a 31 percent decline between 1911 and 1923 in the four childhood communicable diseases: measles, scarlet fever, whooping cough, and diphtheria.[28]

Harlem Hospital, the major provider of health care during the "Gilded Age," did not employ Black doctors until mid-decade, when it retained the services of five full-time Black physicians. This move occurred only after the National Association for the Advancement of Colored People (NAACP) challenged the monopoly White doctors had at Harlem Hospital. Working in tandem with Harlem Hospital to meet the health needs of the community was the Harlem Committee of the New York Tuberculosis and Health Association, which was organized in 1922 and served approximately thirteen hundred residents annu-ally. Located in the same building that housed the New York Urban League, the Harlem Committee endeavored to keep Harlem informed about getting and keeping well. An information service, dental clinic, health club, and nutrition classes were some of the services it provided, and its Institute for Physicians was immensely successful in mentoring young doctors.[29]

THE POLITICAL SCENE

Politics was an important activity in Harlem from the moment the area emerged as the premiere Black community in the country. As the twentieth century dawned, the Republican party still wielded a powerful influence upon Blacks. In 1905, Charles W. Anderson was appointed by the Republicans to the post of collector of internal revenue for the Second New York District. Anderson was born in 1866 in Oxford, Ohio, and moved to New York City when he was twenty years old. Beginning in 1893, he was appointed to a series of state jobs because the Republican party had little power in Democrat-controlled New York City. As the chief lieutenant of the Republican Party in New York City, Anderson worked assiduously to deliver the African American vote, going so far as organizing the Colored Republican Club in New York City in 1904 during the national presidential campaign. It was for his support of the re-election efforts of Theodore Roosevelt that Anderson was appointed collector of customs for the Second District of New York. He held the position well into the Democratic presidential administration of Woodrow Wilson, when Black patronage by the Republicans was eliminated.

The first African American to win elective office in New York City was Edward A. Johnson, a lawyer who in 1917 won the State Assembly seat for the Nineteenth Assembly District. Together with the Twenty-first District, the Nineteenth Assembly District covered Harlem. Johnson won re-election the following year, when John Clifford Hawkins, a Black Republican, won the seat for the Twenty-first Assembly District. For the next twelve years Blacks from both parties were elected to the State Assembly from both districts, with Hawkins himself winning re-election in 1919 and 1920.³⁰ Members of the New York State Assembly were elected annually. By 1920, two Blacks had also been elected to the city's Board of Aldermen: Charles H. Roberts, a dentist; and George W. Harris, a newspaper editor.³¹

Despite their activity at the polls, African Americas were treated as second-class citizens by the White leadership of both political parties, who almost always selected the Black district subleader themselves. Worse, Blacks were segregated in the political clubs. Even in the overwhelmingly Black Nineteenth Assembly District, the Black leader had to maintain a separate club for Blacks. A West Indian immigrant who eventually became a judge was initially sent away from one White district leader's club and became a member only after he refused to go away. The votes of African Americans may have been needed at the polls, but Blacks were not welcome at the district leaders' clubs. The Republicans were especially shrewd. They used intrigue and strategy to maintain their hold on power until 1929, when the Twenty-first Assembly of Upper Harlem, by then 70 percent Black, was divided by them into a White and Black district.³²

In spite of their involvement in politics African Americans never emerged as a political force in New York City in the early twentieth century because of their small numbers, their lack of economic clout, discrimination, the political alignments of the city and state, and because a significant number of them were still Republicans while most White New Yorkers were Democrats.³³ Early Black Democrats were considered traitors and shunned by fellow Blacks. Yet internal rifts and divisions also militated against Blacks winning elected offices and becoming a political force. Still, African Americans did vote, helping John F. Hylan, a Democrat, win the mayoral race in 1917. In that year Blacks constituted 27 percent of the Democratic vote. Four years later Hylan garnered

70 percent of the African American vote. In 1922, Alfred E. Smith, the Democratic candidate for governor, received about two-thirds of the Black vote.[34]

One quasi-political organization that dominated in Harlem during the early twentieth century was Marcus Garvey's Universal Negro Improvement Association (UNIA). Alert to the fact that Harlem was notorious for reveling in grand parades and colorful ceremonies, Garvey and the UNIA staged some of the biggest and brightest. Coverage of these and other UNIA events in the *Negro World* was usually couched in hyperbole.[35] "Monster" and "vast" audiences were always on hand to hear the Honorable Marcus Garvey, who often rode in the parades bedecked in attire that would have made a peacock blush and who was treated with the deference and decorum afforded monarchs and autocrats.[36] Adam Clayton Powell Jr., who succeeded his father as pastor of Abyssinian Baptist Church, recalled sitting as a youngster beside Garvey in his decked-out caravan as it wormed its way through the streets of Harlem, as well as sitting at Garvey's feet and being thrilled by his lectures.[37]

To summarily and scathingly dismiss Garvey as irrelevant, the UNIA as the "Ugliest Negroes in America," and Garvey's accomplishments as inexplicable aberrations of the times is to fail to sense and resonate with the temper of the era in Harlem. Garvey was infinitely more than a shrewd propagandist who skillfully exploited the uncertainty of the decade. The truth is that Garvey was able to tap into the latent, nascent nationalism then simmering in the African American community. A new African consciousness permeated Black America in the early twentieth century, and when Garvey arrived in Harlem in 1916, the cultural capital of Black America was a cauldron of bitterness and unresolved emotions that were later fueled by two fundamentally significant events. The first was the wholesale massacre of Blacks in East St. Louis in July 1917, which left a bitter taste in the collective mouth of the African American community, and the second was the treatment Harlem's Fifteenth Infantry Regiment received during World War I.

James Weldon Johnson, the respected senior statesman of the African American community and the executive secretary of the National Association for the Advancement of Colored People (NAACP) for most of the 1920s, refused to dismiss Garvey and his movement as irrelevant, calling Garvey instead a symbol and a symptom. Johnson claimed that anybody who was able to attract to himself the confidence and loyalty of four million persons, however gullible they might have been, and who could articulate his views in such a way that on calling an "international conference" he was able to get over forty foreign countries to send delegates to it, could not be dismissed as a joke. Johnson also reminded his readers that Garvey had been successful in getting the German government to send a petition to him asking that he use his influence against the deployment of Black troops on the Rhine, even though all parties involved knew that Garvey could do nothing about it.[38]

In a similar vein, A. F. Elmes, a contributing editor of *Opportunity* magazine, while disclaiming that he was ever a Garveyite, editorialized Garvey in the wake of the "tumult and shouting" that attended his last days in Harlem and subsequent imprisonment. Elmes believed that Garvey was not "fundamentally insincere" but "substantially in the main sincere." He opined that Garvey's mind was "short in analytic power and penetrating capacity," a drawback that made him miss the mark in "method and procedure," but that overall Garvey was a decent human being with a compelling vision for the African American community.[39]

THE RELIGIOUS CLIMATE

In 1896, the year the Populists exemplified the agrarian revolt in the United States, the United States Supreme Court ruled in *Plessy v. Ferguson* that separate was equal, giving legal sanction to the Jim Crow conditions that had settled over American society in the aftermath of the Civil War.[40] Blacks were systematically segregated from Whites in every area of life, including the church. Most political and religious leaders believed that, though not ideal, segregation was the most practical way of dealing with the complex race issue. Even President Woodrow Wilson, ostensibly a Progressive politician who was leader and architect of the New Freedom democratic platform, gave tacit endorsement to segregation in society when he allowed some branches of the federal government to be segregated.[41]

The influx of Blacks into Harlem was fueled and facilitated by the African American church, traditionally the most stable, influential and financially viable of all Black institutions. African American churches and religious groups either pioneered in the move to Harlem or followed their members and supporters there. Adam Clayton Powell Sr. had been smitten by the Harlem bug as early as 1911, when the area was still overwhelmingly White. Declaring that Harlem would be the final destination of the Abyssinian Baptist Church, Powell encouraged the members of his congregation not only to join the exodus there but to buy real estate in Harlem while the market was still depressed.[42] According to the leading national Black weekly newspaper of the day, the Abyssinian congregation cheered when its pastor announced at Easter services on April 4, 1920, that the church was moving to Harlem. Powell informed his congregants that the church would be buying six lots on 138th Street, and that the land would be used to erect a sanctuary with a seating capacity of two thousand, a "well-equipped gymnasium, reading room, employment agency, ladies' parlor, model kitchen and dining room, and a well-furnished home for teaching domestic science." Total cost of the building project was estimated at two hundred thousand dollars, and the church hoped to realize a large part of the figure from the sale of its West 40th Street property.[43]

Not all of Harlem's churches were large, institutional organizations. The area had many churches of the store-front variety that placed a premium on ecstasy, emotionalism, and the charismata. Not surprising, these congregations appealed to the less educated and sophisticated among the newly arrived Blacks. In the early twentieth century Harlem was fertile ground for the cultivation of religious thought, and just about any religious ideology or theology was offered a measure of hospitality there. Since its emergence as the Black capital of the United States, a steady succession of cult leaders had flowed through Harlem, leading groups with names as bizarre as their claims. Yet to dismiss these leaders, usually augmented by clairvoyants and herbologists, as transient charlatans who preyed upon the frustrations and fears of a vulnerable community is to miss the broader social and historical issues and themes of the era.

On the average, there was a church to each block in Harlem. Traditional and nontraditional religion were offered by these religious bodies, with worship services ranging from the austere, structured, high-church style of the Methodists and Presbyterians to the expressive, high-energy, loose, spontaneous emotionalism of the Baptists and Pentecostals. Musical instruments, especially drums and tambourines, were vital to the rhythm and flow of the services of the latter, although all types of religious services promised relief from the vicissitudes, vacillations, and voids of early twentieth century life in Harlem. Religious services were almost always well attended, and one enduring feature of religious life in Harlem then was the overwhelming support given churches by their congregants.[44]

Black churches in Harlem were more than religious sanctuaries where members assembled for worship. They were social centers that offered community, integration, and acceptance to a people reeling from the blows of oppression, disassociation, and discrimination. In addition, they were political centers in which African Americans enjoyed a measure of empowerment and self determination.[45] The churches were visible, concrete expressions of their congregants' struggle for power. Harlem, like most other Black communities, needed these churches to anchor and integrate African Americans into the broader community. Consequently, most Harlem churches remained open all day Sunday, offering their members a variety of activities that made their stay worthwhile. Fellowship or potluck meals assuaged the pangs of hunger that would inevitably set in after the morning's divine worship service, and the evening's evangelistic services were usually as packed as the morning services.[46]

In addition to religious services, the larger Black churches of Harlem provided ways for Harlemites to grow socially and educationally by organizing athletic and social clubs, and musical and literary organizations. Many of them sponsored a Sunday afternoon lyceum or forum that attracted overflow crowds. Discussions, always lively, focused on a wide range of issues, including the future of Blacks in such areas as politics, art, economics, and literature.[47]

Yet Harlem was criticized for the multiplicity and variety of its churches, it being said that at least 50 percent of them could have been closed and the community not suffer.[48] The proliferation of churches in Harlem did not escape the keen, analytical eye of James Weldon Johnson, who, as a contributing editor of the *New York Age*, at one time wrote a column addressing the issue with the hauntingly probing title, "The Question of Too Many Churches." Johnson argued that what Harlem needed was not more churches but better ones. He said that most of the churches operating at the time were "staggering under debt," "poorly pastored," and, as a consequence, inefficient and ineffective. Calling their operations and ministry a "waste of energy and money," he believed that the duplication of their efforts could be eradicated by "intelligent consolidation."[49]

The *New York Age* kept up the pressure on Black churches to give an accounting of their stewardship to the African American community. In a front page article under the caption, "What is Expected of the Churches," the newspaper bemoaned the fact that Harlem's Baptist and Methodist churches had failed to do "their whole duties by their constituencies" in that they had been making exorbitant and "continuous demand upon the time and money of their members without giving in return a reasonable and fair consideration in spiritual and material things."[50] In response, several pastors provided "concrete facts of work done" by their churches. Among the pastors who came forth was Adam Clayton Powell Sr., who spoke of the "helpful activities and noble sacrifices" of his congregation.[51]

Powell was a social activist who preached that Christianity is more than "preaching, praying, singing, and giving" and that preachers who only twice a week "ram the Bible down the throats of the people" are derelict in their responsibility to execute what he termed an "applied Christianity." He called on fellow pastors to "cease criticizing and abusing people for spending their evenings in questionable places" until they had provided "wholesome environments" for the people to socialize.[52] Powell's rallying cry, designed to address the personal and corporate issues with which African American were dealing, shows that Black religious leaders perceived the church as one of the principal weapons against the social, economic, and political challenges facing their community.

Powell's clarion call to fellow clergy to preach a holistic gospel was not without reason. During the 1920s the theology of most of Harlem's Black churches was a stifling fundamentalism that mostly denounced evil practices, such as going to the movies. Harlem's preachers loved to rail against the frivolous lifestyle that characterized the area and caused the era to be dubbed the "Roaring Twenties." Prohibition, a veritable bookend that marked the start of the period, had produced an underground liquor industry in Harlem, and the result was that liquor could be procured there at any hour of the day or night. Black preachers denounced liquor as the enemy of people in need of no more enemies, movie theaters as citadels of crime, clubs as crucibles of corruption, and several congregations collaborated in passing a resolution deploring these phenomena as placing the African American community in grave peril. Paradoxically, Harlem's preachers were not as quick to frown upon or censure numbers betting, the community's great game of chance, allegedly because they recognized that income from this source sustained several families and helped others contribute to their church's coffers.[53]

The Social Scene

The reputation Harlem acquired during the 1920s was that of a fun-loving, anything-goes place. Harlem was known for its laughter, which was one of the first things that struck White visitors to the area.[54] Harlem became known as a carnival of carabets and clubs and as the playground of New York's rich and famous. The area boasted seven neighborhood motion picture venues, six cinema palaces, and about twelve night clubs.[55]

As the 1920s dawned, so did the jazz age. Heretofore, ragtime had reigned supreme, capturing the antiwar sentiments and Black nationalist ferment of the late 1910s, albeit in subdued tones. With jazz, restraint and resignation were thrown to the wind, and spontaneity and improvisation took over. New Yorkers of every race, ethnicity, and socioeconomic status fell in love with jazz, heading to Harlem, the "city that woke up at night," to get their fill. The main thoroughfares of Harlem, always clogged during the day, exploded at nights with "lines of taxicabs and limousines standing under the sparkling lights of the entrances to the famous night clubs, the subway kiosks swallowing and disgorging crowds all night long."[56] The flurry of activity was another defining feature of 1920s Harlem, whose residents, "by nature a pleasure-loving people," did not hesitate to satisfy their appetite for enjoyment.[57]

Representative of the cultural revival that swept through Harlem beginning in the 1910s and continuing right on through the 1920s was the movement that came to be called the New Negro Renaissance and for which the period and place are best known. Dominated mostly by writers—poets, novelists, playwrights, and essayists—the artistic revolution got under way in 1917 with the publication of James Weldon Johnson's[58] book of poems, *Fifty Years and Other Poems*, and Claude McKay's sonnet, "The Harlem Dancer." A Jamaican by birth, McKay represented a shift away from the sanguine, tranquil style of earlier Black writers and initially was told that he would have to sanitize and tone down his bold references to the Black urban experience if his works were to sell.[59]

Four years after the appearance of McKay's watershed work, Langston Hughes, then a nineteen-year-old recent high school graduate, published "The Negro Speaks of Rivers" in the official organ of the NAACP, the *Crisis*. That same year, 1921, Johnson began work on an anthology of poetry by African Americans. Johnson's anthology, *The Book of American Negro Poetry*, was published early in 1922, the year in which McKay's immortal work, *Harlem Shadows*, hit the market. By then, the Negro literary movement was fully on.

The Harlem Renaissance substantively transformed the African Americans who were a part of it from creatures of condescension to people of decisive action. No longer were they inclined to a stifling conventionality and conservatism. Displaying a healthy, if not arrogant, self-confidence, they took their places beside others in the field, delving into hitherto unentered areas such as social injustice and intolerance. Harlem had come into its own as a throbbing cultural and artistic community by the end of the 1920s. It was the place many of the "New Negro" artists lived and worked and the focus of many of their works. More important, as the cultural and artistic Mecca of Black America, Harlem influenced the national culture in fundamentally significant ways.

The West Indian Community in New York, 1900–1930

James K. Humphrey lived and worked in Harlem during its ascendancy as the Black capital of the United States. He was a Jamaican who, like thousands of other West Indians, migrated to the United States and settled in Harlem in the years between 1900 and 1930. More significant, he was a West Indian who rose to leadership in his denomination. Humphrey was not the only West Indian leader in Harlem during this pivotal time but part of a generation of ambitious West Indian men who agitated and lobbied for the rights of people of African descent. Included in this group were Marcus Garvey, Claude McKay, and James Weldon Johnson, who, even though born in the United States, was of West Indian stock. West Indians were anything but the shy, retiring, shrinking individuals that immigrant groups are sometimes prone to be. In Harlem, at least, they were a visible ethnic group that refused to be ignored by either the indigenous African American population or the broader American society.

West Indian Life in Harlem

West Indians differed from their American counterparts in significant ways. One was their perspective on the family, for them a sacrosanct institution ruled by a father who worked hard to provide for his posterity. West Indian men worked hard, at times at two and three jobs, to make ends meet.[60] As the head of the home, fathers accepted no disrespect from their children, who married only after extended courtships and after they had received parental endorsement. Premarital sexual relations were frowned upon, and a person engaged in forbidden sexual relations at the peril of being disowned.

Issue may be made as to whether slavery made family dysfunctionality a defining feature of Black life, but issue may hardly be made with the fact that

West Indians had a different orientation and approach to religious life than native Blacks. From the days it existed as the "Invisible Institution" in the Antebellum South, the church of the indigenous African American functioned, among other things, as an agency of social reform that nurtured Black leadership. Its worship intentionally veered away from the formalism of the established church, choosing to demonstrate its freedom by being emotive and expressive. West Indians found African American worship difficult to resonate with, its liturgical spontaneity and energy offensive to their British formalism and ritualism. To be sure, that they opted to remain faithful to the pomp and rigor of their churches may have been due to the uncertainty and fluidity of their status in America. Yet, given the racism that was the portion of every person of African descent in America, that does not explain why they accepted White pastors, a move that native Blacks could neither understand nor sanction.

West Indians worshiped in the Roman Catholic and Episcopal (Anglican) churches, though a spattering of them could be found in the Baptist and Methodist churches, too. In 1928, St. Martin's Episcopal Church was established to meet their needs.[61] Regardless of where they worshiped, church for the West Indian was a place to meet and mingle with acquaintances from the old country. Yet the church performed another key role in the life of West Indian immigrants. It helped extend their culture and traditions. Harlem churches with overwhelmingly large West Indian populations celebrated some West Indian holidays and festivals, engendering a sense of connectedness and belonging to their native land. On these occasions congregants were encouraged not to forget from whence they originated and to give tangible evidence of their memory by donating generously to causes back home. When King George V was ill in 1928 and 1929, several of Harlem's churches with West Indians offered up prayers for his recovery.[62]

The West Indians who migrated to New York City at the beginning of the twentieth century were not primarily of the professional ilk. More likely to be laborers or servants, they did not differ markedly from the Blacks from the South in terms of occupational status. Still, they were decidedly more urbane than their American counterparts and more aggressive in pursuing opportunities to improve their lot economically, socially, and politically. Between 1900 and 1930, when they made up a mere 10 percent of the Manhattan population, they owned and operated 20 percent of the Black businesses in the borough, a fact that contributed in no small way to comparisons to Jews. Also during this time they had a lower crime and fertility rate than the indigenous African American population.[63]

While indigenous African Americans were involved in business ventures such as pool rooms and barber shops that catered primarily to the Black population, West Indians focused on mercantile operations in which there was competition from Whites, such as jewelry stores and food and vegetable shops. They did not shun even more risky business ventures and initiatives such as real estate and insurance and operated the only Black-owned casino and moving picture theater in Harlem during the 1920s.[64]

West Indians did not hide or deny that they had come to the United States with a view to bettering themselves economically. Consequently, they worked hard and saved their money. As an ethnic group they were the largest number of depositors at the Harlem branch of the Postal Savings Bank.[65] The word on the street was that as soon as a West Indian had "a dime more than a beggar," he or she would start a business that could range from a small fruit stand to a brokerage firm.[66] Classic among the tales told about the business acumen of the West Indian was the story of a Barbadian woman who owned and operated a rooming house.[67]

Three values shaped the West Indian experience in New York City during the first wave of their immigration to the United States: ambition, education, and pride. To the West Indian, ambition was setting realistic yet high goals and pursuing them with resolve and purpose. A necessary element of ambition was education, without which West Indians believed nothing worthwhile could ever be accomplished in life. West Indians pursued higher education with a determination that bordered on frenzy, seeing in educational attainments a source of both national and personal pride, and, more important, a way of moving up a few notches on the social ladder. Their desire to surge ahead educationally was evidenced by their presence at Harlem's libraries and the ubiquitous intellectual and social forums of the era. Dark-skinned West Indians believed that education inoculated them against racism and discrimination. Regrettably, West Indians sometimes indicted indigenous African Americans for having little or no ambition, desiring little education, and showing no racial or personal pride.[68]

With educational opportunities supposedly available to all, West Indians could not fathom why all Blacks could not avail themselves of these opportunities. Coming to America poor, the last thing they wanted was to return home poor. In fact, they considered poverty and America as being mutually exclusive. For this reason, they denied themselves some luxuries in which other racial and ethnic groups were known to indulge, opting to invest in property and savings. In addition, they sent shipments of American goods back home to prove how well they were doing and as convincing evidence that America was truly the land of opportunity.[69]

A number of scholars have studied the relative economic success of West Indians in the United States, and today the issue continues to pique the fancy of West Indian and American alike.[70] Some have concluded that the answer lies in the type of slavery that existed in the West Indies, arguing that it was not as brutal as that which existed on the North American continent.[71] In some cases, slavery in the West Indies was worse than in North America, particularly in regard to overwork and the devaluation of blackness. Unlike slaves in North America, those in the West Indies were allowed to grow and barter their own food and to use some of the proceeds from the sale of foodstuff to purchase an array of life's conveniences for themselves. As a result, West Indian Blacks could speak of a history of attending to their economic needs, their experience in a market economy supplying them with critical knowledge and, more important, motivation to negotiate and navigate in the world of business.[72]

Others, searching for reasons for the greater success of West Indians in the United States, have pointed out that West Indians never had to endure a Civil War to gain their freedom and that even in slavery there were never so many White lords around that their sanity and sense of self-worth were destroyed. In addition, they did not suffer through a long rehabilitation from slavery as Black Americans had endured during Reconstruction.[73]

Tending more toward pragmatism, some scholars have argued that the West Indians who came to America were the cream of the crop and that the long journey here sifted out the faint of heart and weak of character.[74] Inarguably, immigration often attracts the most resilient and resourceful people. West Indians were helped all the more because they settled in urban areas where they were able to command traditionally high urban wages.[75] West Indians did encounter one stark reality in America that immigrant groups from Europe and other parts of the world did not: discrimination based on color. Other groups blended into the White majority. West Indians could not and did not. Many of them returned home, and others formed and joined clubs and organizations in attempts to maintain the majority status they had experienced in their countries. West Indians themselves attributed their success in the United

States to their sense of "West Indianness," by which they remained focused on their primary reason for coming to this country.[76]

Whatever the basis or cause for the success of West Indians in the economic sphere, the fact remains that it was the burgeoning African American community that provided them with a favorable confluence of circumstances. Concomitant with the marked increased in the Black population was the development of a Black consumer market that beckoned for goods and services that Whites had previously supplied and monopolized. Enterprising West Indians saw and exploited this niche in the market, in time monopolizing some businesses and dominating the competition in others.[77] Given their penchant for pursuing higher education, not a few of them matriculated at universities in metropolitan New York and elsewhere, obtaining terminal degrees in the sciences and arts that they used to achieve economic success.

Perpetuation of West Indian Culture

In keeping with the scientific evidence that people socialized in one culture are never fully absorbed into another one even when they relocate, West Indians did not give up their folkways when they came to America.[78] The physical world they left behind had a different climate and geography. It was as different economically, socially, and politically as the one they encountered in the United States, where they ran head on into a diversity of unreconciled social mores. Cultural reorientation was made all the more challenging for them because of the issue of race.[79]

Some West Indians did not readily identify or resonate with the indigenous African American experience because they did not consider themselves Black. Distancing themselves from their American counterparts, they asserted that in the West Indies, where anyone 75 percent White was considered White, there were no distinctions of color.[80] They contended that they were free in the West Indies, anesthetizing themselves into believing that they were also free in the United States. They ignored the fact that freedom in the United States, as in the West Indies, was a function of, among other things, economic status. Some West Indians failed, or perhaps refused, to put themselves in the shoes of indigenous African Americans and were known to summarily and matter-of-factly wonder out loud why their American counterparts could not simply do what they were doing, which was buying and owning property. Knowing that they could abort their quest for economic advancement and return to their countries at any time in part accounted for this attitude, which distressed and angered American Blacks to no end.[81]

West Indians were conspicuous in Harlem because of the way they dressed, which was in tropical materials and bright, colorful prints. Their accents, which no amount of camouflaging could hide, only served to highlight their difference and distinctiveness from the American Black population. The West Indian accent was so thick that on first hearing West Indians talk some Whites thought that the West Indians were trying to entertain them.[82] Yet the accents of West Indians presented them with unique challenges in the area of education, making it difficult for them to excel and achieve in the classroom at least on the elementary and high school level.[83]

Between 1920 and 1930, West Indians could procure in Harlem's food stores items from the Caribbean, including pigeon peas, breadfruit, cassava, tannias, eddoes, guavas, and mangoes. They paid hefty prices for these fruits and vegetables, used to cook West Indian dishes they loved. In Harlem, they continued to cook cockoo, a Barbadian dish made with corn meal and okra and served with fish; pelau, a Trinidadian delicacy consisting of rice and meat flavored with spices; and callaloo, another Trinidadian dish made from okra and the leaves of a bush called dasheen and flavored with crab meat or pieces of ham. Sweet bread was a staple, as were ginger beer, sorrel, and mauby, a drink made from the bark of a tree which the taste buds of the local population found difficult to stomach because of its bitterness. Refusing to eat any leftovers, which they condemned as stale food to be discarded, West Indians believed in cooking everyday, a practice that contributed to their being labeled as haughty, proud, and arrogant.[84]

A rhythmic, musical people, West Indians brought their distinctive tempo and lyrics to New York City, too. The Trinidadian calypso was sung around Harlem, as were West Indian folk songs. The latter were used, as they had been for a generation earlier, to teach West Indian children the fundamentals of reading.[85]

CIVIC AND POLITICAL ORGANIZATIONS

Blacks from the West Indies arrived in Harlem unprepared for the social and political conditions they encountered. Their predecessors had failed to alert them to the oppression and racism in North America. In an attempt to adjust to their alien, hostile environment, they inaugurated social networks and organizations, much like the Jewish Landsmanschaft societies that integrated Jews into their new homes while perpetuating the traditions of the mother country. These organizations were more than just voluntary groupings that offered a sense of solidarity to the newly arrived immigrant groupings. Called benevolent and progressive associations, these bodies functioned in a number of ways, including surrogate family and integrating force in an otherwise disassociating society. To be sure, the associations appeared parochial and provincial on the surface, their names seeming to suggest that membership and involvement were restricted to their kind. Yet the associations, in addition to providing crucial connecting linkages between the newly arrived and the homeland and being a vital arena for social intercourse here, were all about economic survival, too. Thus, these organizations were attempts by West Indians to reconstruct their world.[86]

The Harlem West Indian organizations were not restricted to promoting the welfare of West Indians in the United States. At least one, the Hamitic League, was a Pan-Africanist organization. It was one of three Black world groups which in 1918 emerged as a rival to W. E. B. Du Bois and the NAACP. Among its members were G. McLean Ogle of British Guiana, Arthur Schomburg, and John E. Bruce, a journalist and later supporter of Marcus Garvey.[87]

Although West Indians were not known to have had many fraternal organizations in the islands from which they hailed, it is hardly surprising that, given the purpose and utility of these organizations, Harlem between 1900 and 1930 had a fair share of them. Fraternal organizations provided newcomers with critical information about employment and housing, served as a context for the perpetuation of old friendships and, by extension, the home culture. In addition, they offered a way for the expatriate to continue influencing the politics of his or her birthplace. More important, they represented a strain in the broader Black community for modalities of self-evaluation that did not emanate from the dominant White culture.[88]

WEST INDIANS AND POLITICS UP TO 1930

West Indians were actively involved in New York City politics from 1900 to 1930, their involvement the result of their drive and accurate read of the political scene in New York City. During the first three decades of the twentieth century Blacks in New York City remained loyal to the Republican party, doing so in spite of the fact that the Republicans had all but turned their backs on Black support. Mired in social, economic, and political isolation, Blacks still saw their best chances for rescue and inclusion in the Republican party. Yet during this time the Democrats made intentional overtures at capturing the Black vote, most noticeably through an organization they had created in 1898 called the United Colored Democracy. Rumored to be a "Tammany Club," the United Colored Democracy funneled Black votes into the Democratic party in exchange for token patronage jobs that represented neither political leverage nor economic empowerment.[89] W. T. R. Richardson, a West Indian who had migrated to the United States in 1884, was among the founders of the United Colored Democracy.

Initially, West Indians registered with and supported both the Republican and Democratic parties, though they campaigned hard for Theodore Roosevelt in 1912. They knocked on doors, speaking on Roosevelt's behalf and encouraging Blacks, West Indians included, to register and vote.[90] Yet by the 1920s they tended toward the Democrats, in part because they had no axe to grind with the Democrats. Putting pragmatism over ideology, West Indians concluded that since neither party was serious about addressing the concerns of the Black community they would at least get what they could from the Democrats, which was jobs. By 1930 they were moving away from the Republicans, especially at the state and local level, with a group of them, called the New Democrats, feeling no allegiance at all to the Republicans.[91]

Besides those West Indians who remained loyal to mainstream American politics in the Republican and Democratic parties were several who pioneered in the radical movement of protest and confrontation. As early as 1902, Hubert Harrison, from the Virgin Islands, was preaching radicalism on the streets of Harlem. Harrison founded the *Voice*, America's first militant Black newspaper, and authored two books, *The Negro and the Nation* (1917) and *When Africa Awakes* (1920), before his death in 1927.[92] A. Philip Randolph was mentored in socialism by Harrison. Yet it was W. A. Domingo, a Jamaican, who was considered the father of Harlem radicalism. Domingo served as associate editor of Garvey's *Negro World* before publishing his own newspaper, the *Emancipator*, in which he continued his radical writings. William Bridges's the *Challenge* and Cyril Briggs's the *Crusader* were two other Black socialist periodicals of the era. A former chief acting-editor of the *Amsterdam News*, Briggs launched the *Crusader* in 1918 in sympathy for Bolshevism. Eric Walrond, from British Guiana, served as associate editor of Garvey's *Negro World*, though he eventually joined *Opportunity* magazine. And Claude McKay for a time edited the *Liberator*, a white Marxist newspaper. The names of these periodicals tell the story of their objectives and activities. The United States government was so concerned with these publications that it took steps to suppress them, including the issuance of a report in 1919 entitled "Radicalism and Sedition among the Negroes as Reflected in their Publications."[93]

West Indian political radicalism was not limited to elective politics on the state, local, and national levels. It penetrated labor organizations as well. Ashley L. Totten and Frank R. Crosswaithe were standouts in this regard. Totten, from St. Croix, had migrated to the United States in 1915, immediately finding work with the Pullman Sleeping Car Company. Conditions in the company made him yearn for an organization that would speak to the issues of higher wages and less working hours as well as work toward eliminating the contumely heaped on Black workers. His efforts finally led to the creation of the Brotherhood of Sleeping Car Porters and Maids. By 1925 Totten was known around Harlem as a firebrand. Also from the Virgin Islands was Frank R. Crosswaithe, who in 1925 formed the Trade Union Committee to Organize Black Workers. This body urged African American workers to join trade unions and pursue equal pay and work conditions. Crosswaithe was so prominent in the labor union movement that during World War I former president Teddy Roosevelt made an appearance at the Palace Casino on 135th Street to denounce him and some fellow West Indian radicals.[94]

Because they had as little to lose as they had as much to gain, West Indians were at the helm of activities to better the economic, social, and political lives of the African American community. They did not much appreciate their loss of status in America, responding by aggressively fighting for their rights. West Indian women led the fight to integrate the garment industry in New York City, and Haitians played key roles in penetrating the fur industry toward the close of the 1920s. David E. Grange, a combative Jamaican, was the force behind one of the major strikes of the International Seaman's Union when he served as vice president. And it was Ashley Totten from the Virgin Islands who, as an officer of the Brotherhood of Sleeping Car Porters, mentored A. Philip Randolph. West Indians pioneered and provided leadership in the growth of left wing economic and political organizations in the country at large and

Harlem in particular not because they were innately leftist in orientation and outlook but in part because such forms of protest provided them with status.[95]

Detractors have attempted to discount the radicalism of West Indians, saying that in the Caribbean they were conservatives and that they only embraced radicalism when they came to the United States. The radicalism of the West Indian was thought to be insincere, the product of naïveté or ignorance, and the reckless abandonment of sanity and prudence by the temporary resident.[96] Yet political radicalism in Harlem did not occur in a vacuum but against a backdrop of overt and covert racism that West Indians found intolerable. Jim Crowism was rife, and Booker T. Washington's accommodationism did not sit well with West Indians. President Woodrow Wilson, his progressivism and campaign promises to African Americans notwithstanding, was responsible for an avalanche of segregationist legislation and practices in the federal government and nation that may have been the cause of the upswing in lynchings and was definitely a factor in the increase of Ku Klux Klan activity in the nation. Given that migrating itself is a radical act, representing a break with tradition, culture, and the past, it is far from surprising that West Indians did not cower in the face of American racism.[97]

Moore, Domingo, McKay, Briggs, Garvey, and others were part of a generation of educated, enlightened West Indians who, beginning in the 1880s, had emerged to protest the inherently oppressive nature of English colonialism. Products of the British educational system, they were proficient in the work of English literary giants such as Shakespeare, whom they quoted and recited lavishly. They were also adroit in the processes and procedures of politics, reveling in the bare knuckles world of political debates, sometimes for the sheer fun of displaying their competencies. Yet what troubled them most and provoked their strongest reactions was the disparity they saw in the society between the ruling minority and the majority. Although they lacked the financial and political wherewithal to effect change on a radical level, they nonetheless agitated for change, transcending their dismal socioeconomic levels in the process. In the end, these West Indian leaders in Harlem realized that in the political arena race more than ethnicity made for the amalgamation and contours of the African American community and that those who ventured into politics were seen and accepted not just as the spokespersons for West Indian interests but as the de facto representatives of the wider Black constituency.[98]

STEREOTYPES AND CONFLICT

Almost from the moment they first met, West Indian and American-born Blacks have viewed each other with a suspicion born in part by a misunder-standing and misreading of the motives of the other. By their very nature stereotypes are hardly ever based on objective, discernable, measurable cri-teria but on subjective, incomplete, and inaccurate information often viewed through myopic, jaundiced eyes. West Indians were stereotyped in many ways. They were thought to be stingy and thrifty and people who had to be moni-tored closely in matters of business. They were considered a haughty group who thought they were superior to American Blacks, clannish, all alike, brash and talkative, quick-tempered and overly sensitive, ambitious, aggressive, liti-gious, serious, hard working, and eager for education. West Indian men were said to rule their homes with a heavy hand, treating their wives as property. And West Indians were said to lack racial pride. They were not race conscious.[99] Conversely, West Indians stereotyped American Blacks as lazy, shiftless, loud, emotional in their religion to the neglect and detriment of rationality and sanity, and woefully mired in the past. American Black males were loafers who freeloaded off their women. American Blacks were not forward looking or long-term planners. They focused on the present, in which they hoped to find instant gratification. A widespread feeling at the time was that the ethos of the West Indian stressed frugality, industry, education, and investment, and that these qualities coalesced to make the West Indian dominant in professions such as medicine, dentistry, and the law. They were said to be better prepared for medical and dental schools, with deans of several medical schools profess-edly saying so.[100] Even James Weldon Johnson, whose parents hailed from the British West Indies, thought that West Indians were an outstanding people, mythologizing them as above average in intelligence and sane, sober people with a knack for business.[101] Around Harlem it was alleged that West Indians had come to Harlem to teach, start churches, or create trouble. Not used to discrimination based on color or ethnicity, they were generally unaccepting of the lot of African Americans and were perpetually agitating for change in their status. Because they dominated in the Black left-wing organizations that characterized Harlem during the 1920s, a Black West Indian radical thinker was once dismissed as an overeducated West Indian in search of a job.[102]

American Blacks, by no means immune from the anti-alien sentiments that permeated American society during the early twentieth century, were loathe to welcome West Indians with open arms, pejoratively dismissing them as out-siders bent on replacing them in the American mainstream. The misgivings that native Black Americans harbored toward West Indians were expressed in derogatory terms such as *monkey-chaser* and *tree-climber*. The West Indian's penchant for colorful clothes and unmistakable twang made him the target of crude jokes and comic misrepresentations in private and public. Street vendors particularly relished ridiculing West Indians, whom they sometimes physically assaulted. One ditty sung about West Indians had these words:

When I get on the other side
I'll buy myself a mango
Grab myself a monkey gal
And do the monkey tango

When you eat split peas and rice
You think you eatin' somethin'
But man you ain't taste nothin' yet
'Til you eat monkey hips and dumplin'.
When a monkey-chaser dies
Don't need no undertaker
Just throw him in de Harlem River
He'll float back to Jamaica.[103]

The cause for the strained relations between West Indians and Black Ameri-cans in Harlem lay equally with both groups. Indigenous Blacks had failed to differentiate among the West Indian groups, in time assessing the best by the worst. This failure caused the American Black to assume a posture of superior-ity, which was replaced later by jealousy when the attainments of West Indians forced their recognition. Yet West Indians helped fuel the fires of misunder-standing, if not discord, by their unyielding attachment to their homelands and all things British. They persisted in playing British sports such as cricket, the "game of gentlemen," and in recognizing British holidays and events. British subjects that they were, they naively believed that whenever they were discriminated against in this country they could appeal to the British govern-ment for redress. West Indians seemed to place a premium on their accents, stubbornly resisting to curb or change them for fear of being mistaken for an indigenous African American and being treated as such. Others refused to alter their style of dress, opting for the tropical attire that often solicited taunts and ridicule. Still others declined the invitation of native Blacks to join their churches, opting to remain Roman Catholic and Episcopalian. Yet what really irritated indigenous Blacks was the reticence, if not refusal, of West Indians to become naturalized American citizens, a move that kept them out of the polling booth. American Blacks rightly concluded that this diluted their clout in the electoral process. As African Americans saw it, the habit of West Indians in perpetuating their culture and folkways was intentional and a not-too-veiled attempt at distancing themselves from the native population.[104]

If, according to W. E. B. Du Bois, American-born Blacks at the start of the twentieth century were a cauldron of conflicting tensions brought about by their attempts to reconcile two identities—American and Black—West Indian immigrants found themselves in a similar predicament.[105] Like Black Americans who at once wanted to be Black and American, West Indians wanted to remain West Indian even as they cast their lots with African Americans. Lennox Raphael deftly captures this "two-ishness" in relating what happened when, years later, his aunt became an American citizen. Saying it did not mean anything to her, she still wished to be known as a West Indian. Raphael calls this the standard neurosis and color complex of the average West Indian, whom he claims does not want to be considered Black. He asserts that he never met a West Indian who did not feel superior to an American Black and that West Indians of his era seldom rented to American-born Blacks. Moreover, according to Raphael, West Indians believed that the British system of education was superior to the American and that America-born Black children not raised in a home with at least one West Indian parent were destined to be without ambition and develop behavior problems. Finally, West Indians could not understand why they could acquire property so quickly after coming to the United States while American-born Blacks continued to complain about the lack of equal opportunity. Raphael thoroughly rejects this "hysteria and false pride."[106]

West Indians resisted acceptance of the minority label because of this sense of two-ness. They resisted the label because they viewed doing so as giving tacit endorsement to the notion that people of African descent were inherently inferior to other races, which was one of the last things a West Indian was willing to admit. Thus, they opted to identify themselves by nationality more than by race.[107]

Their distrust of each other notwithstanding, West Indian and Black American cultures did affect each other in early twentieth century America. In the religious sphere, voodoo and obeah from the West Indies did intermingle with conjure, which had made its way to Harlem from the South. In time, West Indian fruits and vegetables decorated many Harlem food stores and tables. So great was the demand for these tropical products that a profitable business was spawned to make them available. Black Americans even took to West Indian music, finding in the rhythmic, pulsating tempo strains of Africa with which their souls connected and resonated. One song, "Sly Mongoose," could be heard being belted out on phonographs as early as 1915, and calypso music grew in popularity through the 1920s. So, too, did West Indian comedians and entertainers.[108]

West Indians contributed to Black life in the United States in other fundamentally significant ways. The persistent affirmation of the worth and dignity of their personhood in a society that systematically and structurally sought to discount people of African descent and to relegate them to positions of subservience is one such contribution and legacy. Generally, West Indians resisted the broader society's attempt to regularize them, to beat them into its idea of the standard. It was this attitude that in part explains the thought and activity of Marcus Garvey and Claude McKay, who immortalized this mindset when he wrote: "Like men we'll face the murderous, cowardly pack, Pressed to the wall, dying, but fighting back."[109] This West Indian attitude was most noticeable in Jamaicans, a proud people who refused to believe that they were in any way more deficient than other human beings. Unfortunately, this spirit was often mistaken for sassiness, and even African Americans bemoaned the West Indian penchant for standing up for his or her rights even if it meant going to court. Dismissed as troublemakers, West Indians were denied employment in some industries because of this attitude.[110]

For all of their accomplishments, West Indians were as circumscribed in their attempts at economic emancipation and empowerment as were American-born African Americans. Integral components of the Black community, they were destined to share in its triumphs and failures, its weal and its woes. When they aspired to leadership positions, they discovered that those that existed were restricted to the Black community. This was a rude awakening for the naive few who believed that educational and professional qualifications mattered more than the color of one's skin to the American society. More important, West Indians learned that ethnic identity and pride were detrimental to Black solidarity, the lesson being a primer for those who sought to serve the public sector as journalists or elected officials.[111]

Challenged by their leaders to see their coolness toward each other for what it was—an absurdity often exploited by the broader society to keep them perpetually locked in the throes of conflict—West Indians and indigenous Blacks forged and maintained genuine friendships and working relationships. Especially effective in this regard were the rebukes of those West Indians who pointed out to their fellow sojourners that it was patently foolish to excoriate the society to which they had come in search of economic progress. Taking aim at the ethnocentricity that seemed a hallmark of the West Indian community at the time, one West Indian leader reminded his fellow expatriates that they were still Black and looked down upon by an America that judged by the color of the skin more than anything else.[112] In addition, both groups were reminded that even though their forebears had been dropped off in the West Indies and North America, they had been carted to these points in the same boat.

In time, West Indians and indigenous African Americans realized that there was a commonality in the treatment meted out to them by the broader American society. This realization, coupled with the fact that segregation had physically placed West Indians and native Black Americans side by side, made for a coming together to combat the issues that dogged their paths, marred their lives, and threatened to permanently relegate them to a marginalized status in American society. As such, discrimination welded the two groups together into a formidable minority that could not be treated with benign neglect.

THE END OF THE 1920S

Harlem, like the rest of the country, was decimated by the Depression, which, according to Hughes, "brought everybody down a peg or two." Given that African Americans "had but a few pegs to fall," they did not fall far.[113] Ravaged by economic hardship, Harlemites staggered into the 1930s unsure of their future. Yet, few African Americans in Harlem would admit to the negative phenomena that were settling in and beginning to blight the area. A mood of euphoria, enlightenment, and emancipation permeated the atmosphere, and the few gains made by some African Americans were generally heralded and trumpeted far and wide as major success stories.[114]

The few who were willing to admit that beneath the veneer of good times were troubling signs of decay hastened to point out that Harlem was still in the process of becoming one of the most exciting communities in America and in a true sense transcended the accepted definition and understanding of community. Still deficient in many things, including economic development, which had not kept pace with its "development in politics, in the professions, and in the arts," Harlem was a "large-scale laboratory experiment in the race problem" where things were sure to get better.[115] Cast as a playground by writers, it needed to be recast as an important community in which "fundamental, relentless forces" were at work.[116]

SUMMARY

Harlem, New York, did not evolve as a distinctly African American community in a vacuum but in the context of unprecedented developments in patterns of race relations sweeping the United States in the early twentieth century. The changes in race relations that occurred in Harlem took place in the context of changes in the social and economic climate of the broader American society. The urbanization of African Americans, for example, was a product of the increased discrimination that Blacks experienced as they moved to the North, and Harlem's night life was not so much a symptom of the economic health and vitality of the African American population as it was stark witness to the exploitation of the area's residents.

By the 1920s, Harlem was the quintessential African American community, professedly a symbol of self-actualization and opportunity for Blacks. Those who streamed into Harlem sent word back that it boasted its own educational institutions, churches, stores, newspapers and other publications, and a host of lodges and organizations that catered to and were operated exclusively by people of color. To the newcomer and the uninformed, the community appeared self-contained and self-sufficient, an oasis of Black control in the midst of oppression, alienation and powerlessness. Yet, in the 1920s Harlem was anything but self-contained and self-sufficient, and no one was more aware that it was that way than the thousands of African Americans who lived there.

When West Indians and indigenous African Americans encountered each other for the first time, each reacted with a mixture of uncertainty and distrust born of ignorance. Their interactions were characterized by a complex web of likes and dislikes, attraction and repulsion. Both groups sensed differences and were disturbed, at times even offended, by them. The stereotypes they harbored about each other marred their relationship, fueling conflicts between them and engendering division in the West Indian community.

West Indians in New York City experienced several warring impulses. One was toward a larger Anglo-American culture exemplified by high church and cricket. Another was toward a unique West Indian identity, replete with West Indian cultural retentions not shared by either Whites or American Blacks. Last was toward Pan-Africanism. Of necessity, American-born Blacks and West Indians developed social relationships of reciprocity and mutuality to unitedly address the social and political phenomena that confronted people of color in the United States. Both groups aimed for rapport, the West Indian sense of an alternative nationality proving quite important in this regard.

That West Indians tended more toward radicalism is incontrovertible. It is explainable given the radicalism of the act of immigration itself. Immigration is a radical act of protest against an unacceptable status in the home country. Immigrants flee to new lands in search of self-enhancement not just as a means of escape. Hence the desire of West Indians to acquire an advanced education. With the West Indian there was an inflated preoccupation with higher education, Howard University facilitating more than a thousand West Indian students in the first three decades of the twentieth century. This heightened awareness and pursuit of an education in turn gave rise to the stereotype of the West Indian being smarter than American-born Blacks. The truth is that West Indian students may have been better educated to begin with and therefore more highly motivated whether or not they acquired a college degree.[117]

In spite of their indictment as anti-Black, West Indians reversed a trend of the early twentieth century, which was for Blacks to patronize White lawyers. They displayed greater confidence in Black lawyers by utilizing them, and the appointment of two Black municipal court judges in Harlem toward the end of the 1920s served as a catalyst in this regard.[118]

West Indian hard work and achievement are two elements that gave rise to the myth of West Indian superiority. That the West Indians who migrated to America tended to be the cream of the crop contributed to the perpetuation of the myth. The radicalness of migration was a significant factor in the West Indian penchant for protest during the first three decades of the twentieth century. Yet during this period Harlem had a significant number of indigenous African Americans who had also migrated there from the South.

In the end, the West Indian population in Harlem had more positive than negative effects on New York City in general and the native Black population in particular. West Indians contributed to the nation's economic life and to the perpetuation of American optimism. They provided evidence that in this country one can succeed if one is willing to work hard and make sacrifices. Both West Indians and native Blacks saw their social vision expand and their cultural sensibilities educated and enhanced as they were forced to deal with each other. More important, their shared experience of struggle caused them to refocus their vision. West Indians and indigenous African Americans wisely cast aside their differences to unitedly focus their energies on issues that benefited all people of color. The result of their collaboration on common issues may be characterized as unity and intraracial progress.

James K. Humphrey, therefore, ministered in Harlem in a time of volatility and change. The old Black community of New York City had undergone tremendous change, moving from the southern tip of Manhattan island to its northern tip. This community had been transformed from a colonial one to a community of people who, in spite of a shared racial heritage, was culturally diverse. The diversity of cultures in the African American community in which Humphrey lived and worked presented him with some unique challenges. Notwithstanding the cultural differences, African Americans and West Indians living in Harlem in the first three decades of the twentieth century had a shared experience of discrimination. Economic and political opportunities were extended to them only reluctantly, as were religious ones. Theirs was a common struggle for acceptance and respectability. African Americans, especially the few who were able to acquire an education beyond the high school level and those who experienced a measure of success as entrepreneurs and property owners, yearned to be recognized as legitimate members of the middle class. More often than not, their attempts were frustrated by a society bent on keeping them on its fringes. It is far from surprising that African Americans flocked to the standard of individuals such as Marcus Garvey, who held out hope of a better tomorrow and spoke unashamedly of racial pride, and James K. Humphrey, who agitated for self-determination for his congregants.

Chapter 4

The Black Experience in Adventism, 1840–1930

From the start of the Millerite Movement around 1840 to the time James K. Humphrey left the Seventh-day Adventist church in 1930, the African American experience in Seventh-day Adventism was a saga of paradox, ambiguity, and ambivalence. Born in the midst of the Second Awakening, the Adventist movement and later the Seventh-day Adventist denomination both demonstrated uncertainty, if not confusion, in dealing with the Blacks who filtered into their ranks in myriad ways. Adventists lacked a coherent, strategic plan to evangelize Blacks, hedged on declaring their position on the race issue shortly after their official organization at the height of the American Civil War, and only moved to intentionally minister to people of African descent in America after they were reprimanded by Adventist pioneer, Ellen Gould White, in the last decade of the nineteenth century. Their noble pronouncements to the contrary notwithstanding, Adventist resonance with the color issue during this period was one of pragmatism over principle and expediency over legality.

Adventist treatment of Blacks has led supporters and detractors among members and nonmembers alike to question the organization's sincerity, sensitivity, and commitment to inaugurating an age of racial healing and reconciliation. At the start of the new millennium, race, as in the broader society, was one of the most important challenges confronting the denomination, defining and contextualizing not a few of its policies, practices, and priorities. In the United States, the Seventh-day Adventist church is structured unambiguously along racial lines, a reality that eloquently tells that in the Seventh-day Adventist church race matters.

Historically, Seventh-day Adventists have viewed human history and the events of the world from a distinct perspective, ascribing meaning to world events in keeping with principles that rise above the earthly sphere and viewing the earth as the theater in which human history is played out. Adventists conceive of history as being purposeful, with events and personalities proceeding inexorably toward a meaningful, climactic end. As such, human beings should order their lives with an eye on the end, fully aware that their actions do have an impact on their future destiny.[1]

The distinctiveness of the denomination's cosmology began to emerge during the time the group existed as part of the Millerite Movement, evolving more between the Great Disappointment of 1844 and the formal organization of the denomination in 1863. Yet Seventh-day Adventism did not evolve in a cultural and historical vacuum, uninfluenced by larger political and economic forces and factors. Consequently, while Adventists conceived of historical forces in ways that caused them to be branded a cult, they tended to view people of African descent in very much the same ways that the broader American society did. Moreover, the evidence suggests that the denomination did so unquestioningly, accepting the theological and sociological framework and underpinnings for society's diminution and depreciation of the African American's nature, culture, and ability.[2]

James K. Humphrey joined the Seventh-day Adventist church shortly after the start of the twentieth century, when Africans from the South and the West Indies were beginning to stream into the urban centers of the North. Rising quickly through the denomination's leadership ranks, Humphrey, a proud Jamaican who was troubled by the racism he encountered in American society, early experienced severe pangs of conscience over the ways the Adventist church handled matters of race. Ultimately, Humphrey, unable to accept the marginalized status of African Americans in the Adventist church anymore, broke with the group.

THE MILLERITE MOVEMENT

Between 1800 and 1850, the land mass of the United States increased by approximately 50 percent and the population jumped 400 percent from approximately five to more than twenty million people. The young nation became home to millions of immigrants, many of whom were from Ireland and Germany. This influx of people to America was the first genuine mass immigration the nation experienced. Even though America welcomed new peoples to its shores, immigration created tension and antagonism among its population. This was particularly true with respect to religious orientation and allegiances, and, more important, the nascent spirit of nativism in the nation at the time. Americans viewed the growing Roman Catholic population with suspicion, labeling Catholics as anti-American for the premium they placed on promoting their own educational system. Early to mid-nineteenth century America saw religious uniformity come to an end and, concomitantly, a rise in the number of sects and religious groups that operated outside the margins of American society. So pervasive was the increase and spread of religious groups and activity during the period that it has been referred to as the time of religious ferment.[3] Yet, the rise of activity in the religious sector of the nation did not occur without other influences but mirrored tendencies that were occurring in the political and social spheres of the nation as well.

The two individuals who represented the strains and changes that took place in the social and political lives of the nation were Charles Finney and Andrew Jackson. To be sure, Finney was not Jacksonian in his political ideology. Yet Finney was vintage Jackson in his presuppositions and world view, siding with the little and marginalized peoples of the American society whose discontent he exploited. The activity of both men resulted in the elevation of ambition and initiative over wealth and ancestry, and for the first time the American dream was considered within the reach of all. Optimism and egalitarianism were the watchwords in both the popular religion and popular democracy of the day.[4]

It was in this context of hospitality to unconventionality in both politics and religion that Adventism was born and fostered. Its parent was millennialism, a Christian theology that includes the ultimate victory of Christ over the forces of evil and the deliverance and exoneration of his followers. Millennialism is best taught and understood in the context of the Second Coming of Jesus Christ, an event some Christians believe is synonymous with the end of human history. Millennialism in general, and apocalyptic millennialism in particular, invaded America from England in the first half of the nineteenth century, although William Miller, their chief American proponent, was not extensively versed in their British version.[5]

The Seventh-day Adventist church had its origins in the Millerite Movement that swept the American northeast from the early 1800s to the mid-nineteenth century. Millerism was inaugurated by William Miller, a farmer from Low

Hampton, New York, who began to seriously study the prophetic portions of Scripture around 1818.[6] A self-taught, self-styled Bible expositor and theologian, Miller concluded, based on his personal exegesis of Daniel 8:14, that Jesus Christ would return in 1844 to purify the earth. Miller initially was loathe to divulge his findings to the public, opting instead to talk and preach with small groups of people wherever and whenever the opportunity arose. He would have continued to do so but for the involvement in the movement of Joshua V. Himes, a Boston publisher who on hearing Miller's views embraced them and decided to publicize them.

From 1840 onward, Joshua V. Himes functioned as the chief organizer and promoter of Miller's beliefs, giving the Advent Movement shape and focus.[7] Were it not for Himes, Miller may never have had a place in American history. Later, Himes's skills were augmented by those of Charles Fitch, whose unique interpretation of Revelation 18:4 provided the movement with one of its defining moments. Together, these two men promulgated Miller's beliefs through the printed page and by organizing several general conferences in the northeastern United States to study the issue of the Second Coming.[8] Their efforts were not without success. As many as fifty thousand Adventists were spread across the northeastern United States by the mid-1840s, all eagerly expecting something of cataclysmic dimensions to occur. Nor were these people oddballs or fanatics woefully out of touch with mainstream America.[9]

Miller was modest in his ambitions and goals. For starters, he did not want to launch a new denomination or organization, believing that his convictions transcended sectarianism and division and that Christian unity was both a prerequisite and prelude to the second coming of Christ. Miller, at least up to 1844, was not a separatist and was so against separatism that he even rejected the second angel's message of Rev. 14 as preached by Charles Fitch and others, viewing the message as disruptive to the goals and mandate of the Second Advent movement.[10] Moreover, Miller believed that because his message was Bible-based, it had the special blessing of God. Miller remained a Baptist until late 1844 when the Low Hampton congregation in which he had held membership expelled him. Thereafter, his teaching on church membership oscillated between espousing separation and remaining loyal to one's congregation. One factor that contributed to Miller's calls for separation was the persecution that Adventists, as those who embraced Miller's teaching that Christ would return to the earth in 1844 were then being called, were receiving in their respective churches.

People of African descent were involved in the Millerite Movement. Among the first Blacks to embrace Miller's beliefs were John W. Lewis of Providence, Rhode Island, and Charles (Father) Bowles of Boston.[11] Before becoming a Millerite, Bowles was a Freewill Baptist who had organized many White congregations. Yet among the Blacks of the Millerite Movement no one stands out as much as William Foy, a light-skinned Black from Maine who received visions earlier than Ellen Gould White did. Until recently left out of or miscast in Adventist history books, Foy lived and preached at the peak of the Advent Awakening. He received a total of four visions, at least one of which occurred in a mixed congregation. It was originally believed that fearing prejudice and perhaps physical danger, Foy refused to publicize what had been revealed to him in vision. Yet his biographer has shown that after a three-month hiatus Foy resumed preaching, continuing to do so until close to his death on November 9, 1893. Although it is unclear how Foy felt about the Sabbath or whether he ever kept it, Foy was a genuine spokesperson for the Millerite cause, serving as a pre-Disappointment prophet who in no way competed or contradicted the post-Disappointment prophecies and ministry of Ellen Gould White.[12]

Lewis, Bowles, and Foy were but three of the Blacks who figured prominently in the Millerite cause. To be sure, only a sprinkling of Blacks ever encountered the phenomenon, and there are no figures indicating how many ever joined the movement. Still, these three individuals show that Blacks were involved in the cause. According to Seventh-day Adventist historian George Knight, Millerite leadership was strategic and intentional, if not aggressive, in their efforts to work among Blacks, demonstrating their commitment by investing not just time but money in their efforts.[13]

Were Millerites abolitionists? Did they aggressively work to eliminate slavery? Did they stand in solidarity with the slaves? Ron Graybill believes that the foremost abolitionist leader of the day, William Lloyd Garrison, was ambivalent toward Miller and his cohorts, viewing them as deranged individuals victimized by outlandish theories concerning the second coming of Jesus Christ that made them of no use to the abolitionist cause. Graybill says there is no record that Miller himself was actively involved in the antislavery cause and that Millerite publications are almost completely bereft of any articles designed to promote the elimination of slavery. Millerism, to be sure, had something in common with the abolitionist cause, including a similar concern with biblical predictions about the millennium, a mutual opposition to organized religion, and a shared quest for personal piety, perfection, and purity. Yet Millerism was a movement with a single focus that adherents refused to allow to be blurred by other tangential concerns. Concluding that Millerism did little to foster reform causes, Graybill alleges that it actually pulled many people away from active participation in the movement.[14]

Graybill seems to have an ally in George Knight, who says that by 1843 Miller "was at loggerheads with the reform movements, as well as with the church, in terms of a strategy for bringing in the kingdom." For Miller, "the second coming would be the reform of all reforms. It was the ultimate cause."[15]

George Knight contends that even though Garrison was "a bit discouraged" with Joshua V. Himes's "apostasy to Millerism" and "frustrated beyond measure when talented leaders converted to Millerism," Garrison's abolitionism was focused and intense, with the eradication of slavery "the central element in bringing about the millennium" in Garrison's thinking. For Garrison, talk of a millennial reign of peace that was not linked to the end of slavery was an absurdity. Knight also disagrees that Miller was not involved in the abolitionist cause, citing evidence that in 1840 Miller was touted as being an abolitionist in the *Liberator,* a Garrison periodical, and Knight asserts that Miller's involvement in the abolitionist movement must have been sustained, because two weeks after the October 1844, disappointment, Miller was identified as a "trusted participant" in the Underground Railroad.[16]

Some of the significant figures in the Millerite Movement did display signs of a social conscience. For example, Joshua V. Himes sponsored several reform causes before becoming Miller's chief promoter, and Charles Fitch wrote at least one article questioning slavery. In addition, Joseph Bates organized an antislavery group during the 1830s and a temperance society in the 1820s. Himes's involvement in the abolitionist movement was anything but peripheral. "A perpetual activist" who "did not sit on the sidelines in the struggles of the day," Himes plunged into the abolitionist cause when to do so was to endanger one's career, if not life, even in the North. His fervor and intensity so unnerved the members of the First Christian Church that Himes was forced to resign his leadership role in that congregation. He moved on to become the pastor of the Second Christian Church, which was formed by a core of those who left First Christian in the wake of Himes's departure. Charles Fitch was a "zealous abolitionist" whose discourses condemning slavery were thought to supercede Garrison's in terms of eloquence and vigor, and even though Fitch ultimately broke with Garrison, it was not because Fitch's antislavery sentiments had waned.[17]

Joseph Bates was among the foremost in terms of Sabbatarian Adventists who stood in solidarity with the slaves. Bates's passion for the Temperance and Abolitionist causes did not wane with his involvement in the Sabbatarian Adventist movement, even though he was reprimanded by some detractors for such. Bates refused to drive a wedge between social reform and expectations of the Second Coming of Jesus, arguing that, in a sense, they stood together or would fall if bifurcated. Indeed, Bates believed that anybody who did not believe in the second coming of Jesus would and could not serve the moral reform movement well.[18]

Malcolm Bull and Keith Lockhart argue that Adventist pioneers were involved in abolitionist activities before they became Adventist or before the group became an organized entity but that once they joined the group Adventist pioneers generally reflected the broader society's attitudes and practices with regard to the issue of race. The authors contend that Adventists early perceived the issues of slavery and racism in America less as matters that required social reform than as issues that underscored American hypocrisy and identified and situated the nation in the scheme of Bible prophecy. Not only did attitudes of prejudice inform and dictate early Adventist approaches to race, with church leaders adopting the policy that good race relations between Blacks and Whites are best fostered and facilitated by the separate-but-equal doctrine, but the authors believe that Jim Crow segregation found a prototype in Adventism.[19]

Not surprising, after the Great Disappointment of 1844, Adventists experienced a decline in their numbers. In 1846, a remnant of the disappointed merged with a group who believed in the sanctity of the Bible Sabbath, which they held was the seventh day of the week, becoming known as Sabbatarian Adventists. By the end of that year Ellen White, who had started receiving visions in December 1844, was generally viewed by the new group as heaven's special messenger to the remnant.[20] From that time on to the organization of the denomination in 1863, Sabbatarian Adventists worked at concretizing and systematizing their doctrinal tenets and beliefs, ultimately hammering out a theology that included an attempt to address the race issue.[21]

Sabbatarian Adventists held that slavery was antithetical to the biblical ideal of love and brotherhood and was a stain on the nation's moral fabric. They were particularly troubled by the Fugitive Act of 1850, viewing it as an intrusion by the federal government into the lives of citizens, whose freedom of choice Sabbatarian Adventists held was a biblical principle. Sabbatarian Adventists prized the notion of freedom of choice, rightly arguing that its denial or compromise in one sphere would spread to others, including themselves, a small, fledgling group operating outside the parameters of mainstream American religion. Yet, for all their lip service to the tenets of abolitionism, Sabbatarian Adventists stopped short of radical involvement in the abolitionist cause. Confronting the principalities and powers were not what they were about.

Douglas Morgan, while admitting that Sabbatarian Adventists "thundered against governmental actions favorable to slavery" and "sought to keep their own community free from the sin of slavery," claims that they did not aggressively or intentionally work to alter the American system. Their poignant, penetrating words in support of abolitionism notwithstanding, Sabbatarian Adventists "would not fight their war with bullets or . . . with ballots." As far as they were concerned, conditions in American society would only be remedied at the Second Coming of Jesus Christ, and even though it was incumbent on those preparing for the event to point out injustices in society, it was more critical that people ready themselves for the event.[22]

At best, then, Sabbatarian Adventists were moderate abolitionists whose preferred course of action was quiet diplomacy, not physical confrontation or even collective agitation. They believed that their target should be the moral and spiritual health of the American nation, not its political life. Sabbatarian Adventists were convinced that were the moral and spiritual fibers of the nation righted, an inevitable corollary would be an upswing in America's political life and institutions for the oppressed and marginalized. Among those who embraced and sought to advance the causes of both Sabbatarian Adventism and Abolitionism was Sojourner Truth, though she is more known and celebrated for her espousal of the feminist movement.[23]

Early Seventh-day Adventist Contact with Blacks

Organized during a time when the United States was locked in a conflict centering around the destiny of Black people, the Seventh-day Adventist church was sluggish in mounting an intentional, aggressive campaign to proselytize Blacks, who heard the Adventist brand of the gospel in as early as 1875 from a lay preacher named Silas Osborne.[24] A native of Kentucky who had migrated to Iowa in 1851, Osborne had accepted Adventist teachings there before moving back to Kentucky in 1871. His brother pressed him to share his newfound beliefs publicly, and after much cajoling, Osborne obliged.[25] Among Osborne's first Black converts to Adventism in Kentucky was a preacher named Edmund Killen, who went on to preach to African American audiences, although not much is known about the degree of success he experienced in winning Blacks to his new denomination.[26]

When Adventist pioneers began preaching to Whites in some parts of the South, they found a sprinkling of Blacks worshiping with the Whites. For example, C. O. Taylor, the first Seventh-day Adventist minister to preach the Third Angel's[27] message in Georgia, reported that he saw some Blacks present with the Whites in the Baptist church he used to attend, and D. M. Canright asserted that there were three African American Sabbath keepers among the White congregation to which he preached in Kentucky.[28] It is far from surprising that Blacks were found worshiping with Whites at this time, since before the Civil War slaves had generally worshiped in the churches of their masters.

Adventist pioneers to the South were not oblivious to the challenges inherent in witnessing to African Americans. For example, D. M. Canright, from Little Rock, Arkansas, related that they encountered no problems trying to preach to Blacks as long as they restricted their efforts to the Black community.[29] Years later, J. M. Rees stated that in Tennessee Black and White membership in Adventist churches presented no problem but that a minister who tried to preach to an integrated public audience would invariably see the Whites leave.[30] Two Adventist preachers in Georgia saw both Blacks and Whites leave their meetings when the two groups realized they would have to sit together for the meetings. Yet some time afterward African American evangelists reported successful attempts at preaching to White and Black congregations in the South.[31]

At the conclusion of a Tennessee camp meeting in 1889, a group of ministers and delegates spent time pondering "important issues," the race issue being the "most serious and perplexing." Reporting on the deliberations from back home in Louisville, Kentucky, R. M. Kilgore stated that for northern Whites to attempt to dismantle "the distinction between the races" would be "simply fanatical and unwise" and that those who had never worked in the South could not resonate with the situation there. He argued that Whites who labored "indiscriminately" among both races would "have no influence whatever among the Whites in any part of the South" and that only those Whites who restricted their efforts to Blacks could expect success to attend their work. Kilgore stated that Whites would have to accept that to labor exclusively for Blacks would make them of "no reputation among the Whites."[32]

The first Black Seventh-day Adventist church was established at Edgefield Junction, Tennessee, in 1886 by Harry Lowe, a former Baptist minister. It had been organized as a company in 1883.[33] In that year, J. O. Corliss reported that there were 267 White and 20 Black Adventists in the South. In 1890, R. M. Kilgore, the northerner heading up the Adventist work in the South, who would later urge the separation of Black and White churches, organized the second Black Adventist congregation in Louisville, Kentucky. Kilgore built upon the labors of A. Barry, who had started having meetings in Louisville after accepting Adventism as the result of reading an issue of the denomination's official paper, the *Advent Review and Sabbath Herald*. The following year, another Black congregation was organized in Kentucky, this time in Bowling Green, by Charles Kinney, a former slave from Richmond, Virginia, who had moved west after the Civil War.[34]

Known as the "Father of Black Adventism," Charles Kinney joined the Adventist church in 1878 through the preaching of two distinguished Adventist pioneers—John N. Loughborough and Ellen G. White. On July 30, 1878, Kinney heard Ellen White preach to a crowd of four hundred in Reno, Nevada. He was moved by the sermon, which was based on 1 John 3:1, "Behold, what manner of love the father hath bestowed upon us, that we should be called the sons of God." By the end of September, Kinney was keeping the Sabbath and experiencing belonging and fellowship among the individuals who would become the nucleus of the Reno church. Recognizing Kinney's competencies, church members elected him church clerk, and conference officials appointed him secretary of the Nevada Tract and Missionary Society. Kinney was ordained to the gospel ministry in 1889, in a ceremony that he never forgot and that changed the course of his service to the Adventist church. On the day of his ordination, church officials tried to segregate Kinney and his members at the camp meeting where the solemn service was to be held, only backing down when Kinney and his congregation threatened to bolt.[35]

Admitting that his ideas were radical and that his suggestions were ones he wished he neither had to make nor would ever be implemented, Kinney in 1889 began to call for separate services for Whites and Blacks in the Adventist church. He believed that inherent in the gospel was the power to break down all walls of prejudice resident in believers. Yet prejudice existed in society, creating barriers to the promulgation of the gospel. Kinney stated that the color question was an embarrassment to all Blacks, whose presence in meetings hindered Whites from joining the church. In an effort to ameliorate the situation, he offered twelve propositions, among them a call for a "frank understanding" between Blacks and Whites on all issues having to do with race. Kinney also advised that separation be pursued as a viable strategy wherever integration limited or negated church growth and that Christian community be fostered so that separation may be viewed for what it is—a strategic way to reach all people and not a monument to prejudice and alienation.[36]

A couple of years before Kinney began counseling General Conference leaders on the race issue, Adventist leaders had started wrestling with it. Vigorous debate about the race question had dominated the 1887 General Conference session, with the issue dividing the delegates. On the one hand were those who, citing the moral underpinnings and biblical principles attending the issue, found segregation offensive and unacceptable. They argued that Whites who refused to worship with Blacks were better left alone, their Christianity suspect anyway. On the other hand were the pragmatists who did not want to disturb the status quo or create controversy. They wanted the gospel to be preached without discrimination to anyone who wanted to hear but reasoned that elimination of prejudice in the hearts of Whites was a matter better left to the Spirit of God.[37] Still, a resolution recognizing no color line was introduced, with E. J. Waggoner amending it to say that Blacks who accepted the Third Angel's Message should be received into the Adventist church on an equality with White members and that no distinctions whatsoever be made between the two races in church relations.[38]

Between 1889 and 1895, Kinney, who had been ordained and commissioned with the expressed mandate to evangelize African Americans in the South, offered to the General Conference of Seventh-day Adventists strategies for the successful promulgation of his assignment. Stressing the egalitarianism inherent in Scripture, he appealed for White missionaries to penetrate the South with the gospel even as he admitted that structural racism would continue to frustrate those efforts. Kinney addressed the delegates at the General Conference session of 1891, speaking of the necessity of establishing a distinctly separate work for Blacks, especially in the South. Citing racial issues, he said that such a structure would lead to more effective soul winning efforts among Blacks. More than anything else, Kinney did not want to see the dignity and worth of his people trampled upon. At the same time, he did not want to see Whites refuse to accept the gospel because of the presence of Blacks in their churches.[39]

Seventh-day Adventist work among Blacks in North Carolina started in Greensboro in 1891 and in Texas at Catchings in 1893. Black congregations continued to be spawned in the South throughout the 1890s—in Memphis, Tennessee, in 1894; Birmingham, Alabama, in 1895; Chattanooga, Tennessee, and Charleston, South Carolina, in 1898; and in Orlando, Florida, Montgomery, Alabama, and Winston-Salem, North Carolina, in 1899. The proliferation continued in the first decade of the twentieth century, with Black congregations beginning in Atlanta, Georgia, in 1900; St. Louis, Missouri, in 1901; Kansas City, Missouri, in 1903; and in Jacksonville, Florida, in 1906.[40]

African Americans were not a drain or a financial burden on the Seventh-day Adventist church during this time. When Blacks first assembled for worship at Edgefield Junction in 1883, they contributed ten cents in offering. Ten years later they returned fifty dollars in tithe,[41] and five thousand dollars at the turn of the century. In Mississippi, where in 1903 Black Seventh-day Adventists numbered nearly as many as White ones, financial records reveal that Blacks returned approximately half of all tithe the previous year.[42] At the end of the first decade of the twentieth century, African Americans were returning $25,000 annually in tithe.[43]

Adventist efforts to educate Blacks during Reconstruction were as slow as those to expose them to the gospel. More than ten years after the end of the Civil War, a school for African Americans ranging in age from six to twenty-four, who were "more obedient than the White pupils in the surrounding schools," was finally operating in Ray County, Missouri. Not much is heard about the school after 1877.[44] From March through May of that year, however, reports were received at General Conference headquarters about a school for Blacks in Texas that had been started by a lay couple in a tent. Joseph Clarke and his wife were pleased when Blacks replaced the tent with a building they built themselves.[45] Yet Adventists launched their most ambitious project to educate Africans Americans in the mid-1890s when the Oakwood Industrial School was established in Huntsville, Alabama. Named Oakwood because of the preponderance of oak trees in the vicinity, the school aimed to develop the moral, mental, and physical faculties of Blacks so as to prepare them for the "practical duties of life." Students were expected to work as well as to study and to conform to the religious and ethical ideals of the denomination and institution, with expulsion from school the penalty for the infraction of any of its rules. In 1904 Ellen White, whose counsel was key in the establishment of the institution, visited the campus, later dispatching an inspirational letter informing students that they were acquiring an education to better prepare themselves for service to God and reminding them that God, as their great teacher, was ever willing to bestow wisdom upon them.[46]

In 1903, General Conference president George I. Butler called for "greater and better facilities" to be provided at the Oakwood Industrial School. Noting that Oakwood was the only institution in the world established for training people to work among Blacks in the context of the Third Angel's message, he admitted that the undertaking called for more resources than the Southern Union Conference of Seventh-day Adventists could supply. Butler believed that only a collaboration between southern and northern forces could help Oakwood meet its objectives. Yet what stands out in his address to the delegates assembled for the Thirty-Fifth Session of the General Conference was his admonition that the Session not adjourn without voting policies that would place the educational institution at a level that would match its needs and the demands of God at that time.[47]

In 1901, with Oakwood's enrollment hovering around fifty, Black Adventist church membership approximating three hundred, and church leaders still caught up in the throes of debating the race issue, the Seventh-day Adventist Mission Board dispatched Anna Knight to India, where she labored as a missionary for six years. A Mississippi Black whose love of reading had exposed her to Seventh-day Adventist literature, Knight became convinced of the Bible Sabbath after an intense study of the issue and was baptized in Graysville, Tennessee. She later attended the Adventist College in Battle Creek, Michigan, graduating from the school's nursing program. In 1896, as the Oakwood Industrial School was opening its doors for the first time, Knight returned to Mississippi, where she launched a mission school for impoverished Whites in her hometown of Gitano. When Blacks heard of her school, they requested that she start a Sunday School among them. Knight obliged, operating two Sunday Schools concurrently, one for Blacks and the other for Whites.[48]

In New York City and Los Angeles, Seventh-day Adventist contact with African Americans followed divergent paths, with an ordained Adventist pastor and church leader establishing the Adventist presence in New York City and a layperson doing the same in Los Angeles.[49] Stephen N. Haskell pioneered the Adventist work among Blacks in New York City in 1902. Working out of a room on West 59th Street in the Borough of Manhattan, Haskell began canvassing Blacks in the neighborhood. Toward the end of that year the fledgling group he had started rented a hall for twenty-five dollars. When the year ended, a church with a charter membership of eleven had been organized. H. W. Cottrell and

E. E. Franke, who organized the congregation, left J. H. Carroll, a layperson, in charge. Carroll plunged into his work with such enthusiasm that by early 1903 the membership of the church had increased by 300 percent and a night school providing instruction in reading, writing, Bible, history, grammar, and other subjects was in operation. Among Carroll's first converts was James K. Humphrey. Yet no action was taken at the first annual session of the Greater New York Conference of Seventh-day Adventists, held October 7 to 12, 1902, in New York City, to target the African American population.[50]

Four years after Adventist work among Blacks started in New York City, an African American then holding membership in the White Seventh-day Adventist congregation in Los Angeles started giving Bible studies to interested Blacks in the burgeoning population. As a result, two years later the first Black church in the West was established.[51]

What attracted African Americans to the Seventh-day Adventist church during this era? To be sure, Blacks did not flock to the church in significant numbers. Still, more than a handful saw in the unorthodoxy of the church's teaching a body of truth uniquely suited to bring them the mental, spiritual, and physical uplift they needed. Victimized by slavery and segregation, they found in the teaching of the imminent return of Christ the hope of rescue from oppression and injustice. The doctrine of the Sabbath offered a much-needed respite from the daily, unrelenting grind of labor in the fields of the South and urban centers of the North. And the denomination's still-evolving health emphasis held out an antidote for their physical needs. In sum, Adventism offered a system of Bible teaching and truth that powerfully appealed to the desire of African Americans for a better life in this world, not to mention in the one to come.[52]

ELLEN G. WHITE AND THE RACE ISSUE

A survey of the African American experience in Adventism would be incomplete, if not problematic, without an investigation of the thought and writings of Ellen G. White, whose work continues to be a formative and guiding influence in the Seventh-day Adventist church. Ellen White had much to say about slavery, people of African descent, and how Christians should have related to the newly emancipated slaves.

Slavery was a volatile, divisive issue that fractured many denominations and polarized the membership of others. The Methodist church split over the issue in 1844, the year of the Great Disappointment for Millerites and Adventists, and the Baptists followed suit the following year. As the Civil War raged in 1861, three denominations with huge memberships split over the issue—the Episcopalians, Lutherans, and Old Side Presbyterians. Because Sabbatarian Adventists during the period from 1844 to 1861 drew heavily from the Baptists and Methodists, it is not surprising that Adventist theology and practice reflected the struggle of these two denominations to reconcile the issue.[53] Of course, Adventism's unique interpretation of prophecy made for a radical connection between slavery and prophecy.[54]

Among the myriad of thorny issues with which the infant Seventh-day Adventist church wrestled was church race relations. Still experiencing the pangs of birth, the denomination could not rationalize, on biblical grounds, the nonacceptance of the essential humanity and equality of people of African descent, though it relegated them to the fringes socially. One year after the church nearly splintered over the theological issue of righteousness by faith,[55] it was forced to confront the race issue in 1889 at its annual Fall Council meeting of world church leaders.[56] Ellen White, conciliatory and pragmatic, would then begin to issue a series of thoughts and admonitions on the race issue that speaks to its complexity, ubiquity, and irrepressibility. The first of White's messages, entitled "Our Duty to the Colored People," was delivered to world church leaders on March 21, 1891.[57]

Ellen White asserted the intrinsic equality of Blacks, saying that in heaven's recordings the names of Whites are juxtaposed with those of Blacks, an axiomatic truth she believed shows that in God's reckoning no difference is found between Whites and Blacks. Arguing that God's love for his creation knows no division and shows no preference based on race, nationality, or gender, she said that the soul of the African is as precious in God's sight as that of any of his covenant people of ancient biblical Israel and that those who speak ill or harshly of Blacks are guilty of misappropriating the blood of Jesus Christ, which makes of all people one nation. White reminded Seventh-day Adventists that, contrary to popular belief, there would be no segregated neighborhoods in heaven.[58]

White bemoaned the 1889 General Conference resolutions on the color issue, claiming that they were not only unwarranted but precluded the miraculous intervention of God, and she cautioned church leaders against cementing prejudices that should have expired with Christ on the cross. She believed that sin was marring the church because it had made only lackluster efforts at winning Blacks to Christ and warned that the church had received no permission from

God to bar Blacks from their assemblies. Encouraging White church members to exploit every means possible to make amends for the injustices meted out to Blacks, Ellen White asserted that Blacks, like Whites, had souls to be saved and were the property of Christ, too. Yet White's most telling admonition at this time was that Blacks hold membership in White churches.[59]

Ellen White was all for the development of American-born Black leadership, holding that many Blacks were intelligent, competent individuals whose abilities could be honed and sharpened should Blacks only be given the same opportunities as Whites. She believed that even though slavery had degraded and corrupted the Black race, many African Americans possessed "decided ability" and "more intelligence than do many of their more favored brethren among the White people."[60] She perceived Blacks as an "ignorant and downtrodden class" with emotions and customs so hardened by years of degradation that arresting and reversing them posed no small problem. Yet she claimed that a corresponding situation existed among Whites and that success could still be realized if efforts were made to salvage African Americans. Even so, White did not condone the penchant among some Blacks of aspiring to preach to White audiences. Believing that such a move was a mistake, she encouraged Black preachers to focus on their own race, saying that such an emphasis would have as a corollary contact with White gatherings.[61]

White continued admonishing the Adventist church on the race issue throughout the 1890s, her appeals being pointed and passionate. For example, she indicated that the church needed to "repent before God" because it had failed to perform missionary work in the "most abandoned part of God's moral vineyard" and stated that a concern for people of African descent should be central and foundational to the church's missionary endeavors. Indeed, to continue to neglect African Americans in favor of others overseas betrayed a tragic misunderstanding of the priorities and purposes of God. Yet White's most poignant statement during this period was that the darkness of the skin of African Americans was not a measure of their sinfulness or wretchedness and that much of what African Americans were then experiencing was the direct result of how they had been treated by Whites.[62] The church's neglect of the African American had left it unprepared for the coming of the Lord, Ellen White stated.[63]

The United States did not escape the indictment of White, who claimed that the entire system of slavery had been originated by Satan, a tyrant who fiendishly delights in pitting people against each other.[64] She informed the nation that it owed a "debt of love" to the African American, telling it that God had ordained that the nation make restitution for past wrongs and that accountability rested as squarely upon the shoulders of those who had not enforced slavery as upon those who had.[65] To Ellen White, the Emancipation Proclamation freeing the slaves ranked in significance with the deliverance of the children of Israel from Egyptian bondage. In both cases God had miraculously intervened to bring deliverance to an enslaved people. Yet God did not leave freed slaves to fend for themselves but placed on the American people the responsibility of empowering African Americans. To the detractors who claimed that Blacks were hopelessly mired in a downward spiral of wickedness and depravity, Ellen White said that Whites were to be blamed for spoiling the morals of Black people.[66]

Ellen White criticized her church for not moving quicker to bring relief to the plight of the freedman, saying that conditions in the South would have been markedly different if strategies had been initiated immediately after the proclamation of freedom. Alleging that only about 1 percent of what could have been done there had been done, she said that angels in heaven were then stifling their music in displeasure. She argued that God had bestowed upon many people of African descent "rare and precious talents" that were only waiting to be tapped and unleashed, a reality aggravated by years of resistance to educating Blacks. Calling the South a "sin-darkened" field, she claimed the church had no excuse for not working it.[67]

Ellen White's counsels on the race issue during the 1890s were consistent with her earlier expressed views. She had opposed the Fugitive Slave Law of 1850 that demanded the return of runaway slaves, encouraging church members to disobey it and suffer the consequences. As the nation was becoming embroiled in its Civil War, White received what may only be termed a watershed vision about slavery. She called slavery a horrible curse and "high crime," asserting that through the Civil War God would punish the South for perpetuating slavery and the North for allowing it.[68]

Delbert Baker deftly summarizes Ellen G. White's comments on the race issue by saying that they revolve around seven principles: (1) the biblical, which calls for Christians to preach Christ worldwide; (2) the moral, which requires that Christians do what is right; (3) the humanitarian, which calls on people to be compassionate; (4) the empathetic, which challenges Christians to try to understand what others are experiencing; (5) the restitutionary, which calls for a restitution of things to the exploited; (6) the societal, which argues that reciprocity is what has made society strong and vibrant; and (7) the eschatological, which asserts that judgment will be meted out to the oppressors of society, especially to those who have done nothing to correct wrongs done to the poor.[69]

Notwithstanding her pointed statements condemning slavery and racism, Ellen White was a product of her times, whose social theories and practices conspired to produce in her a pragmatism that continues to confuse Blacks to this day, and that begs for explanation and understanding. To the uninformed Ellen White comes across as contradictory and confusing, and detractors have not relented in questioning and castigating her for comments she made that seem to compromise the biblical principles she espoused. For example, while encouraging Whites to work for the rights of Blacks, Ellen White still cautioned against "fanaticism," specifically saying that interracial marriage should neither be taught nor practiced.[70] More specifically, White seemed to give tacit sanction to "separate but equal" facilities and operations for Blacks, her reasons ostensibly driven by both social realities and private concerns for the growth of the "Black work."[71]

Saying that efforts put forth on behalf of Blacks in the South should be done in such a way as not to trigger the prejudice of Whites, Ellen White cautioned workers there to pay close attention to what they said about Black-White relations. Workers were especially admonished not to criticize Whites about their treatment of Blacks. Still, White appealed for manpower and resources to be poured into the region, taking the time at one General Conference session to point out to the delegates that when previously she had talked about the "Southern work," some had mistakenly assumed she meant the White work when in reality she had been using the terms "South" and "Black" synonymously.[72] Her appeals for workers notwithstanding, White admitted that she had once counseled her son Edson, who pioneered Adventist work among Blacks in the South, to move on to another field of labor, though admittedly for health reasons.[73]

In 1908, Ellen White stated that separate churches were one way of effectively promulgating the evangelization of Whites. Integrated churches, she believed, presented serious obstacles. Specifically, White stated that "in regard to white and colored people worshiping in the same building, this cannot be followed as a general custom with profit to either party." She argued that "the best thing will be to provide the colored people who accept the truth, with places of worship of their own, in which they can carry on their services by themselves." These places of worship were to be "neat, tasteful houses of worship." Separation of the races was particularly necessary in the South, "in order that the work for the white people may be carried on without serious hindrance," and the practice was to be continued "until the Lord shows us a better way."[74]

Even though a careful reading of her statements shows that they were conditional—that is, that Ellen White did not consider segregation to be the ideal but a pragmatic way for the church to deal with a nettlesome issue—many believe that they are a reflection of the church's true position on the issue and that White's statements helped determine Adventist policy throughout the twentieth century. Bull and Lockhart, for example, believe that the Adventist church is a White body with a mission to White America, and that, its liberal statements to the contrary notwithstanding, the church did not want this fundamental objective imperiled by forays into the African American community.[75]

Yet Roy Branson vigorously defends Ellen White, arguing that, in an era when "many fine Christians" defended slavery as an economic or political issue, Ellen White viewed it as a moral matter. Pointing out that Ellen White felt so strongly about the issue she even recommended that public defenders of slavery be removed from the fellowship of the church, he states that White anchored her beliefs of race on not only eschatological grounds but on the doctrines of creation and redemption as well.[76] Bronson admits that the doctrine of redemption, with its emphasis on Christ's atoning work, which links all people together into one community of faith, appeals more to Christian believers but says that even nonbelievers should see in the doctrine of creation more than hints of the commonality and equality of human nature.[77]

Addressing Ellen White's statements that seem to promote segregation, Branson explains that it was not her theology that prompted them but the "crisis of the nineties," which Jim Crow legislations and severe economic conditions in the South had conspired to produce. He argues that White's remarks were a concession to what she hoped to be a temporary situation and that when White cautioned Blacks not to seek equality with Whites she was referring to some particular social arrangements and not to the fundamental nature of human beings. Moreover, her counsels reflected a concern for those Whites working in the South who throughout the 1890s had borne the brunt of aggression provoked by their humanitarian work. Branson concludes that Ellen White was no "gradualist, no moderate" but a "zealous reformer, vivid and full-blown."[78]

Branson finds an ally in Ron Graybill, the Seventh-day Adventist denomination's first and foremost expert on Ellen White and church race relations. Stressing that Ellen White "held no latent doctrine of inherent inferiority for the Negro,"[79] Graybill says that she never supported the popular notion of a contented slave or the southern White man as the best friend of Blacks, two widespread beliefs of her time. Furthermore, White firmly believed Blacks and Whites were inherently fully and totally equal people headed to and preparing for the same heaven. He concludes that Ellen White's counsels regarding separate religious services and facilities were a "temporary expedient" based on "conditions in a country mired in the depths of its deepest pit of racism."[80] Furthermore, the expedience "was necessitated by the force of law and the threat of violence, loss of life among Negroes, and the abrogation of the opportunity to work among all classes of mankind."[81]

EDSON WHITE AND THE MISSION TO BLACK AMERICA

The individual credited with spearheading Seventh-day Adventist work among African Americans in the South is Edson White, the second son of Adventist pioneers and leaders James and Ellen White. Inspired to do so at the conclusion of a Bible training conference held at the denomination's headquarters in Battle Creek, Michigan, in 1893, Edson White immediately began to strategize as to how he could bring spiritual and social enlightenment to rural poor Blacks in the South. His plans gained momentum when he stumbled upon the counsel his mother had given to the church's leadership in 1891 that the organization should evangelize Southern Blacks. At a loss to explain church leaders' neglect of his mother's plain counsel, Edson forged ahead, preparing himself for his mission by attending a three-week seminar in Atlanta, Georgia, in January 1894.

Returning home from the Atlanta Conference, Edson settled upon an educational and vocational program as the best way to address the social, spiritual, and educational problems of Blacks in the South. This program would be modeled after that of famous Tuskegee Institute educator Booker T. Washington. Yet the denomination preempted White when it established Oakwood College in Huntsville, Alabama, in 1896. Edson did finally see his dream of evangelizing Blacks come true; he helped finance the project by printing and marketing a small instructional manual he called *The Gospel Primer* and procured and outfitted a boat he called *The Morning Star*[82] for his expedition into the South.[83]

Six months after launching, Edson White and his crew arrived in Vicksburg, Mississippi, in early January 1895, receiving hospitality from the Mount

Zion Baptist church, a Black Baptist congregation in Vicksburg. A year before their arrival, a Black minister from Arkansas had come to town preaching a combination of fire and brimstone that provoked the ire of civic leaders. The preacher, Alonzo Parker, was martyred by an incensed mob, though not before predicting that the city would receive another opportunity to mend its wicked ways before receiving the judgments of God. When *The Morning Star* steamed into port, many of Vicksburg's Black population were convinced that the boat represented the fulfillment of Parker's prophecy.[84]

White and his company promptly started to instruct interested Blacks in the rudiments of the three R's—Reading, 'Riting, and 'Rithmetic. Their progress was slow and difficult and was made more so when White learned that the denominational publishing house had decided to suspend publication of *The Gospel Primer,* a move that threatened to bankrupt the project and bring it to a halt. Yet White encountered his stiffest challenge from local authorities, who twice threatened to run him out of town. Once, White was denied permission to erect a church in Vicksburg. On another occasion he was asked to cease teaching Blacks. Permission was ultimately given for the erection of the church, which was dedicated on August 10, 1895, with General Conference president O. A. Olsen preaching the dedicatory sermon.[85]

Not only did Edson encounter passive and active resistance to his efforts from Southern Whites, but he did so from the Blacks as well. Southern Whites, still seething from their defeat and humiliation in the Civil War, viewed Northern Whites as outsiders intruding on their sovereignty and economic well-being. The Blacks, experiencing a measure of freedom and self-determination for the first time in their existence in America, tended to look askance at White and his strange religion, which, among other oddities, proclaimed that Saturday was the Bible Sabbath and the day God wanted Christians to keep holy. In addition, Edson encountered Blacks who seemed bent on preserving whatever vestiges of their ancestral past still remained among them.[86]

The Morning Star tooled up and down the Mississippi River from late 1894 into the twentieth century, docking along its banks to bring enlightenment and empowerment to interested African Americans. Yet White was stung by charges that his project was being financed by the poor—the very people it was designed to liberate and empower. Meeting those charges head on, Edson informed a session of the General Conference that *The Morning Star* was his own property and had been financed with his own money and that all operating expenses had been met by him. He asserted that at the start his personal income had been used to pay the salaries of the ten to eighteen individuals who had been deployed in various capacities upon the steamer and that only when the operation had expanded had donations been used to help meet payroll. Yet Edson did not want *The Morning Star* to be looked upon as his personal endeavor but as God's plan and work. In responding to a query about where he had gotten the money to sustain his operation, Edson stated that the Lord had given it to him.[87]

One year after docking in Vicksburg, Mississippi, *The Morning Star* began serving as the headquarters of the Southern Missionary Society, a semi-independent arm of the organization that Edson White had established to bring focus, contour, and direction to the work among Blacks in the South. The Southern Missionary Society would later become an arm of the Southern Union Conference, which was organized in 1901. Relocated to Nashville, Tennessee, shortly before the establishment of the Southern Union Conference, the Southern Missionary Society functioned as the vehicle for the promulgation of the evangelistic, educational, and health programs of the church for Blacks. Its functions were assumed by the Negro Department of the General Conference, which was established in 1909.

The Morning Star thus represents the first sustained attempt by the Seventh-day Adventist denomination to evangelize Blacks. Yet it was the brainchild of a creative maverick whose ideas and plans created friction along the way. White's program was successful only because of his dogged determination and the encouragement of his mother.

Six years after arriving in the South, Edson rejoiced to see a permanent church building erected in Vicksburg, Mississippi. The speaker for the dedicatory service was his mother, whose sermon was "Trust in God." Ellen White, whose visit to the South was made while she was very ill, was impressed with the building, in the basement of which was a school and to which was annexed a two-story mission house and another four-room house. Yet what struck Ellen White was the congregation, which was made up almost entirely of Black people whom she characterized as "bright and sharp of intellect." Ellen White "never felt more pleased to break the bread of life" than at that moment.[88]

It was no accident that the Vicksburg congregation was almost all Black. Edson White disagreed with Adventists who believed that Blacks and Whites in the South should worship together no matter what dangers attended such an arrangement. For him segregated services was a matter of expedience, with experience showing that mixed congregations had adverse effects on both

Black and White church attendance. Edson had scoured his mother's writings for instruction that even remotely suggested it was "obligatory upon us to force the two elements together." Coming up with nothing, he sought direct counsel from her, intoning, "If I am wrong in this, I want to be right." As far as he was concerned, "no masterly effort" to dismantle Southern prejudice was required of him. Furthermore, any compulsion to bring Whites and Blacks together in the South would leave him without a viable strategy of motivation to work there. As far as Edson was concerned, only a miracle of God could change the situation in the South.[89]

Painfully aware that working among Blacks posed barriers to working among Whites, Edson proposed a separate camp meeting for Blacks in Tennessee in 1900. He counseled that Black ministers should be brought in to run the meeting but that control of it should rest in the hands of Whites. Edson was particularly distressed by the forwardness of Chicago Blacks, whom he claimed were "absolutely and aggressively persistent in pushing what they claim to be their rights in spite of all reason." He could not fathom why Chicago Blacks failed to see the damage they were doing to the advancement of Adventism by their presence and behavior in the church there. According to White, their behavior had been so "outrageously offensive" that many interested Whites had left vowing never to return.[90]

Edson White's position was in keeping with the denomination's history of subordinating sensitive issues to the greater good of the church and of prizing expediency more than disturbing the status quo. To church leaders, maintaining popularity was more critical than being pushed to the margins, or worse, being viewed as irrelevant. Ample evidence of this may be seen in the way one of White's associates responded to an editorial in a Yazoo City, Mississippi, newspaper criticizing the mission activities of the White group. F. R. Rogers, the associate, responded to the editorial by saying that Seventh-day Adventists did not believe in, teach, or practice social equality. Accused of adopting two Black girls who dined at his table with the rest of his family, Rogers denied the charges, informing readers that he had had servants who had been treated as such and that his group had exercised every care to follow the customs of the city and state because they were peaceful, law-abiding citizens. Yet Rogers left Yazoo City for Vicksburg soon after denying the charges, prompting the rapturous applause of both Yazoo City newspapers.[91]

Edson and his associates did not view their duty in the South as that of contending with insolvable problems or irremediable difficulties. Instead, they were to preach "Present Truth," leaving all social and political conundrums to God, who in his own time and way would resolve all wrongs and bring deliverance to the oppressed and exploited.[92] White decried attempts by northern Blacks and southern Blacks who had received educational training in the North to bring about social changes in the South. It was impossible to reform the social customs of the South, Edson believed, saying that an individual might as well try to alter the course of the Mississippi River. He asked potential workers who did not have the simple objective of working for the salvation of souls in mind and who were unable to accept conditions in the South as they found them to stay away, intoning that his operation did not want "reformers" on social equality to enter the field.[93] Edson's thoughts and comments resonated with those of his mother, who cautioned Blacks not to press for social equality with Whites, ostensibly because of unregenerate Whites who were the real cause of the race problem.[94]

As pioneering and as groundbreaking as was Edson White's southern project, it may not be classified or viewed as a strategic, focused plan of the Adventist denomination to evangelize African Americans. The fact is that initially White met with fierce resistance from Adventist leaders, who even diverted funds for its upkeep, and the denomination did not craft any coherent plan to evangelize Blacks in the South until White had experienced a measure of success doing so. Edson White's experience with Adventist church leaders amply illustrates the ambiguity, if not confusion, that permeated and characterized the denomination's attitudes toward reaching Blacks in the South toward the end of the nineteenth century. To be sure, it may be that control was the issue at stake. Edson White was somewhat of a maverick whose vision and resolve may have disquieted church leaders.

The seeming contradictions and ambivalence that Ellen G. White, Edson White, and other Seventh-day Adventists displayed on the issue of race were not unlike the feelings harbored by other nineteenth-century Christians. This was especially true of Christians in the South, where slavery had been the backbone of the economy. Even some abolitionists who vigorously fought for the termination of slavery were not free of racial prejudice, and many were conspicuously contemptuous in their treatment of Blacks, even refusing to associate with them. Some Whites in the abolitionist movement held that people of African descent should be represented and their causes championed while at the same time they believed that Blacks were intellectually, socially, and morally inherently inferior to Whites.[95]

THE NORTH AMERICAN DIVISION NEGRO DEPARTMENT

In 1890, Black membership in the Seventh-day Adventist church was approximately fifty, with not more than twenty Black Seventh-day Adventists living below the Mason-Dixon. As the twentieth century dawned, there were more than three hundred Black Seventh-day Adventists in seven organized churches in the South, and Oakwood's enrollment hovered around fifty. By 1908, Black church membership was more than a thousand, and there were thirteen canvassers[96] spread out over the South promoting church literature uniquely geared to the African American community. Coordination to reach African Americans was provided by the Southern Missionary Society, and church leader Ellen G. White continued to agitate on behalf of the Black work. In 1909, Seventh-day Adventist church leaders recognized the need to create a centralized entity to direct the Black work with intentionality and purpose.[97]

The creation in 1909 of the Negro Department of the General Conference of Seventh-day Adventists illustrates the move in America at that time to address issues of self-determination among Blacks in substantive, meaningful ways. In 1905 the Niagara Movement had committed itself to the abolition of all distinctions centered around race. A few years earlier a Black Adventist minister named Louis C. Sheafe had issued a call for Black representation in the leadership of the church, claiming that as he traveled around the country he was inundated with questions and concerns about the treatment of Blacks in the church. Sheafe believed the work among Blacks would be accelerated if spearheaded by Blacks themselves.[98]

In spite of the call for Black leadership, a White person was appointed the first director of the Negro Department, with three more White individuals succeeding him until 1918, when the first African American was appointed director. William H. Green, a brilliant attorney who had argued cases before the highest courts of the land, led the department from 1918 until his death on October 31, 1928. Throughout the 1920s the General Conference continued to tinker with the structure it had set up to facilitate work among Blacks, finally voting at its Fall Council meeting in 1929 an action that even today is considered a watershed—in Union Conferences with at least five hundred members, a Black would be elected as union secretary.[99]

The General Conference was on record as saying that the office of the director of the Negro Department would be at its headquarters. It was that way until 1918 when Green was elected head of the department. Prejudice precluded the continuation of that policy so that Green's was a roving office away from the world headquarters of the denomination. In 1930, the year Humphrey and his congregation were officially severed from the Seventh-day Adventist church, the General Conference again reaffirmed its wish that the head of the Negro Department be situated at its world headquarters building in Washington, D.C. Even so, prejudice again derailed the implementation of the action.[100]

The evidence shows that the Negro Department did realize its major objectives of facilitating and fostering work among African Americans and of helping to develop indigenous Black leadership. Among the Black Adventist ministers nurtured and developed during the early twentieth century was Sydney Scott, who in 1913 baptized more than one hundred people in Wilmington, North Carolina. Known and remembered for his masterly use of graphics that visibly illustrated the prophecies of the Bible books of Daniel and Revelation, Scott conducted several evangelistic campaigns during this period in North and South Carolina. Another successful Black Adventist minister was Matthew C. Strachan, who, before assuming in 1924 the pastorate of Harlem Number Two in New York City, was a notable minister in Florida. J. S. Green, Floyd Stevens, and John Manns were three other successful ministers. Manns, who baptized about 150 in Savannah, Georgia, ultimately left the organized Seventh-day Adventist church over the race issue, taking much of the membership and church property with him. The remnant of the Savannah, Georgia, congregation was organized under the leadership of W. S. Willis, who in 1916 went to Washington, D.C., to stabilize the remainder of the Sheafe apostasy there.[101] Yet the standout among Black Seventh-day Adventist ministers in the early twentieth century was James K. Humphrey.

AFRICAN AMERICANS AND THE SDA CHURCH

African Americans have struggled for full participation and self-determination within the Adventist church from at least the early twentieth century. Calvin Rock submits that their protest movements fall under three broad categories: (1) the struggle for participation, 1909–1929; (2) the push for structural accommodation, 1929–1944; and (3) the battle for modified autonomy, 1969–present.[102] The goals of Black protest during the first period were "job opportunities, equal pay within the system, and adequate representation on committees and boards," showing that what Black Seventh-day Adventists wanted was essentially "complete acceptance within the church as a whole." The goal of Black protest during the second period was the development of Black churches and institutions along the lines of White ones.[103]

For Rock, it is far from surprising that Seventh-day Adventist church leadership opposed Humphrey's drive for self-determination. Rock, a retired denominational Black leader, asserts that the Seventh-day Adventist church has a tradition of resisting every type of integrationist model that Blacks have ever proposed. Rock argues that both when Blacks sought access to power under the "separate but equal" policies of the first half of the twentieth century and when they later pursued the power of self-determination, White Seventh-day Adventist church leadership opposed them.[104] Yet, the fact that Seventh-day Adventists have, at least theoretically, embraced the notion of egalitarianism is beyond dispute. Adventists accept that it is the goal for which all Christians should strive. Still, Adventists have historically struggled to translate their mental assent to equality into credible policies and practices, and when it comes to their practices, the value of expediency has often trumped the principle of equality.[105]

Rock takes this assertion further, contending that the Seventh-day Adventist Church has experienced little, if any, dissonance or trauma complying with laws antagonistic to racial equality but has demonstrated a stubborn reticence in endorsing and complying with laws seeking to bring about racial tolerance and acceptance. He allows that this is not how it was at least up to the early 1890s. Before that decade, Ellen White generally espoused a position of race relations that challenged the status quo, and early Adventists did have somewhat of a social conscience.[106]

In seeking the reasons that Blacks have had the experience of second-class citizenship in the Seventh-day Adventist church, Calvin B. Rock submits five: (1) Adventists tend to be conservative politically and socially; (2) Adventists, theologically, are fundamentalists; (3) Adventists have given up any hope of effecting any substantive, meaningful change in the world, in part because of the complexity and difficulty of the issues involved; (4) the denomination's mission and church growth initiatives have been aimed at "upper-lower and lower-middle class" Whites, groups that are especially unnerved by the upward social movement of Blacks; and (5) "political expediency."[107]

Rock later refined and nuanced his reasons that African Americans have had to struggle for full acceptance in the Seventh-day Adventist church, submitting that there are theological as well as socioreligious and sociopolitical constraints. The theological constraints are: (1) an apocalyptic eschatology,

(2) a sectarian ecclesiology, (3) a radically deterministic doctrine of God, and (4) the free-will image of man. Adventism's apocalyptic eschatology sees the end of the world as imminent and as an event that will be catastrophic and cataclysmic. More important, according to Rock, is the impact of the denomination's apocalyptic eschatology on its social understandings and ministry, which has been conservative. As such, attention to societal ills is not given the priority it deserves, not with the end of the world and the Second Coming of Jesus so imminent.[108]

Adventism's sectarian ecclesiology has led to the denomination isolating itself from the rest of Christianity, which Adventism views as nominal. Initially, Seventh-day Adventists resolutely resisted the idea of concretizing themselves into an organized religious body, their reasoning against such a move driven by, among other things, their experience of persecution in their former churches and the imminence of Christ's return to earth. Yet most significant in this regard was their view that church organization smacked of Babylon, in Adventist theology signified to mean confusion about religious and spiritual things as well as a system opposed to truth and aligned with error.[109] In time, Adventists did formally organize themselves, quickly adopting a stance of isolation from the rest of Christianity and calling on all people who are opposed to doctrinal error to leave apostate religion and embrace fully God's truth.[110]

Calling the Seventh-day Adventist denomination's attitude and practices toward Blacks "the dirty linen of discrimination within Adventism," Rock in 1970 called on both White and Black Adventists to alter their thoughts, attitudes, and actions based on race, reminding all that Blacks never elected to pursue an independent route to the kingdom of God. Rock claimed that Blacks were forced to pursue such a course because of the "long, discouragingly weak record of race relations" within the SDA denomination, which "clearly negates any optimism" that things will be much better anytime soon. Yet Rock understood that the "Better Way" was at once possible and probable, in part because of the power of God to impact and transform lives "by whatever circumstance necessary."[111]

As compelling and as desirable a goal as full integration is, it is not enough for Frank W. Hale Jr., like Rock a former president of Oakwood College, who suggests that integration without a full sharing of power, resources, and opportunities is vacuous and palpably unfulfilling. Hale believes that it was to register their discontent with just such an integration that Richard Allen left the Methodist church and James K. Humphrey could remain no longer in the Seventh-day Adventist denomination. For Hale, when Whites retain all power in their hands, integration is of a "false kind," especially when African Americans are made to experience its "indignities."[112]

That more Black Seventh-day Adventists did not splinter from the Seventh-day Adventist denomination because of its history on race relations is "remarkable" to Calvin B. Rock, who cites as reasons the following: "a) an apocalyptic emphasis which minimizes hope or need for social change; b) a system of 'belief transmission' or socialization through church schools and youth societies which incorporates succeeding generations and maximizes loyalties to the larger religious body; c) a combination of 'plausibility structures' both *theoretical and structural*, which legitimates one's religious world in ways that provide binding intellectual and psychic security; d) the stellar efforts of a long line of eminent black preachers, . . . who, with pen and voice, have proclaimed a gospel filled with exhortations of fidelity to the church which they hold to be God's chosen people."[113]

African American Adventists conceive of the Adventist church as a unique group of Christians called into being by God to proclaim and embody a heretofore unheralded, perhaps even neglected, gospel. The embodiment and proclamation of this gospel message is embedded in the prophecies of the books of Daniel and Revelation and will result in people, who will not number many, leaving apostate churches and joining the Adventist church. Yet Black Adventists have not been oblivious to the conditions and practices of the Adventist church that have militated against their inherent right to equal treatment and have a history of pointing out the dissonance in what the denomination says and what it does in the area of race relations.

Can African Americans in predominantly White denominations be both committed to their church and true to their racial heritage simultaneously? Although a quick look at the history of independent Black religious movements would seem to suggest that Blacks are more at home in their own churches, at least as far as worship is concerned, Rock contends that Blacks in predominantly White denominations "can be at once racially formidable and denominationally loyal."[114]

SUMMARY

The Black experience in the Seventh-day Adventist Church began when a few Blacks joined Millerites in expecting the advent of Christ in 1844. Blacks who embraced Millerism, associated with Sabbatarian Adventists, and joined the Seventh-day Adventist church did so on their own, in part because the three groups lacked a coherent, intentional plan of attracting African Americans, whose status as slaves and then as freedmen posed problems for them. Seventh-day Adventist pioneers were involved in some antislavery causes, to be sure, though the reasons for their involvement are debatable. One reason that issue continues to be made over whether Adventists endorsed segregation in the nineteenth century is the absence of any official record of the denomination's position on the issue.

Not until 1887 does the issue of segregation appear in official church records. At an official meeting of Seventh-day Adventist church leaders that year, delegates passionately exchanged views on a resolution calling on the church to erase all lines of distinction between Whites and Blacks. A three-member committee was empaneled and empowered to study how the resolution may be implemented, reporting one week later that it did not sense a need for the church to enact laws or guidelines on so delicate an issue. As with other sensitive issues, the denomination left the matter up to the dictates of individual consciences.[115]

Seventh-day Adventists began their attempts at attracting Blacks in the South after the Civil War, when the region was undergoing reconstruction. Not all Southern Blacks resonated with the politics of Reconstruction, tainted as it was with Jim Crow legislation and de jure segregation that made a mockery of the Thirteenth Amendment. Neither did all Southern Blacks flock wholesale to the Northern Whites then canvassing the South, the altruistic pronouncements of these Whites notwithstanding. Southern Blacks viewed Northern Whites with deep-seated feelings of suspicion, and in their attempts to redefine themselves spiritually and socially, most Southern Blacks opted to remain with their churches, "The Invisible Institution" that had functioned as a balm for them during the Antebellum period.[116] Yet some Blacks did exploit the educational and vocational opportunities offered to them by Northern Whites.

Adventist ministry to and among Blacks in the South received a boost when Ellen G. White's son chanced upon counsel she had given to church leaders years earlier. Pointed and passionate, Ellen White had called upon the church to not neglect the freedmen in the South, claiming that Whites and Blacks were equal in the sight of God. Edson sailed into Mississippi in January 1885, plying the Mississippi River for almost a decade thereafter evangelizing the African American community. Yet both Edson's and his mother's writings on matters of segregation call for sober, in-depth, and reasoned analysis because of their seeming contradictions.

As the twentieth century dawned, James K. Humphrey, passing through New York City on his way to Africa, accepted the teachings of Adventism from a layman. A former Baptist minister, Humphrey embarked upon a career of service to the Seventh-day Adventist church that was marked with distinction. In time, he pastored the largest Black Seventh-day Adventist church in North America, ending his service only when his congregation and he were expelled.

Delbert Baker sees five themes running through the Black experience in Adventism. First, he believes that the development of the Black work was in keeping with, and an integral part of, God's plan for Seventh-day Adventists to evangelize the entire world. Second, he posits that God designed that the Seventh-day Adventist church be multicultural and all-inclusive. Third, he identifies Ellen G. White as the single most important Adventist leader for championing Adventist ministry to Blacks. Fourth, he submits that the relationship between the Seventh-day Adventist church and Blacks was a mutually beneficial one, in that African Americans helped the church to "mature in its outlook on multiculturalism." In this regard, he cites Ellen White, who pointed out the incongruity of the church sending missionaries overseas when a mission field in the South lay right before it. Finally, Baker calls for a celebration of the strides made in winning Blacks as a result of the collaborative efforts of the entire church.[117]

Chapter 5

THE CHURCH HISTORY OF THE
SABBATH-DAY ADVENTISTS

If the decade of the 1920s was a period of vigor and optimism in Harlem, New York, that of the 1930s was full of uncertainty and tension. With the stock market crash of 1929, not only Harlem but the entire United States was shoved into an economic crisis that tested the American people. On that fateful October day in 1929 the "Roaring Twenties" gave way to "Hard Times." Truly, the 1930s were turbulent years for America, with the Great Depression at home contributing to the economic and political instability around the world.[1] It was in this crucible of economic and political uncertainty that the Sabbath-Day Adventist organization was born. Coincidentally, the historic meeting between Seventh-day Adventist world church leaders and the members of First Harlem that led to their parting took place at the end of the week of the stock market crash.

The church history of the Sabbath-Day Adventists, not unlike that of other small, independent, urban movements of the twentieth century, is one of struggle and challenge, and the organization's early history does not markedly differ from its recent history. Sabbath-Day Adventist doctrine and church polity, when compared to Seventh-day Adventist doctrine and polity, shows significant similarity, and there is ongoing debate as to whether the Sabbath-Day Adventist denomination reflected the crucial political and social events of the twentieth century. For example, how did it respond to World War II, the Korean War, the Vietnam War, and the Civil Rights struggle? What kind of approach did Sabbath-Day Adventists have to twentieth-century social problems, and do Humphrey's writings and sermons provide clues to his theology?

How did Sabbath-Day Adventists relate to Humphrey, how was he remembered at the turn of the millennium, and what functions were served by membership in the organization?

An Oral History Retrospective
of James K. Humphrey

What was Humphrey like as a pastor and leader? Was he autocratic or democratic, and how was his preaching affected by the split with the Seventh-day Adventists? What were the worship services and ministries of the Sabbath-Day Adventists like under his leadership? How did members feel about him and about being a part of the religious organization he founded? Were their emotional responses primarily centered around Black pride? And what functions were served by their being Sabbath-Day Adventists?[2]

Shortly after his break with the organized Seventh-day Adventist Church and the launching of his independent organization, James K. Humphrey assumed the title of bishop.[3] Why did Humphrey opt for this designation? According to Ucilla Shillingord La Condre, Humphrey assumed the title because he felt he had labored long enough and had started enough congregations to be elevated to the position. La Condre, who was born in New York City and raised in Harlem by a father from Dominica and a mother from the South, was married in 1943 by the bishop, who blessed both her children. A Bronx, New York, resident who subsequently returned to the Ephesus Seventh-day Adventist Church during the 1960s, La Condre says that since nobody would lift him up, Humphrey did so himself, his action receiving ratification from his congregation. In her view, Humphrey's appropriation and use of the title had less to do with biblical or theological assumptions than with issues of power and utility.[4]

Irene Jarvis remembers that when Humphrey assumed the title of bishop, the youth of the church began calling him "The Great I Am." Unsure of whether they did so because they thought Humphrey believed he was Moses or God himself,[5] the youth did think that he was succumbing to a type of megalomania. This theory of the youth was not based on the number of people who swelled the small sanctuary to hear Humphrey preach or because he lived in palatial quarters or tooled around Harlem in expensive cars but on his bearing. Like most of the other youth, Irene, the last of six children whose mother had been a member of First Harlem Seventh-day Adventist Church from 1918, was struck by Humphrey's "dignified bearing." Born in 1924, Jarvis was baptized by Humphrey in 1939, and the Brooklyn resident was a member of the United New York congregation in 2000.[6]

In establishing the United Sabbath-Day Adventist organization and in assuming the title of bishop, Humphrey followed in the tradition of a long line of Black religious leaders who challenged the status quo.[7] Almost without exception, Black religious leaders who founded their own organizations assumed the title of bishop. Not all these groups were unambiguously religious. Some, like Garvey's UNIA, were quasi- or para-religious. Neither did all these leaders conceive of themselves as messiahs or Moses-type deliverers of their people. Finally, not all of them called upon their followers to reject the White Christ for a Black one, as did George Alexander McGuire, the former Episcopalian priest from Antigua who worked for Garvey's UNIA before establishing the African Orthodox Church.[8]

Humphrey was not perceived as one who utilized an autocratic or dictatorial style of leadership. Shunning heavy-handed rule, he was a democratic leader who encouraged discussion, moderated debate, drew ideas from members, and respected differences. When a group of members left to form a splinter group, Humphrey was unhappy and disappointed but not bitter. Yet the bishop was not loathe to maximize his power on occasions, often informing members that a course of action or a policy he sought to implement had been revealed to him directly by the Holy Spirit. Such a revelation almost always quelled discussion and eliminated opposing viewpoints. Still, in claiming divine revelation and inspiration, Humphrey was operating less in the tradition of cult leaders than reaffirming his divine call and commission.

While he did not rule with an iron hand, Humphrey did manage his church closely. The bishop authored all the materials used for study in the Sabbath School, and beginning in 1934 served as editor of the *United Sabbath-Day Adventist Messenger*. A gifted musician, he was a key player in both church choirs, as well as director of New York United's orchestra. Bernice Simmons Samuel says that New York United was known for its outstanding music and boasted a senior and youth choir that both performed to rave reviews. In addition, the choirs recruited and drew people to the young congregation. Samuel states that Humphrey, who married her sister in 1939, was often present for rehearsals and occasionally directed the senior choir. Samuel, who was born in New York City in 1920 to an Antiguan mother and a Barbadian father, was a member of New York United until 1963, when she left over disparaging remarks that William Samuels, the pastor then, made about the youth. Residing in the St. Albans section of the borough of Queens in 2000, she was a member of the Linden Seventh-day Adventist church in Laurelton, New York.[9]

The role Humphrey played in the church's treasury department amply demonstrates his management style. Ucilla La Condre states that Humphrey taught the staff how to "keep the books," even showing them how to wrap coins.[10] That Humphrey was a demanding manager and workaholic who seldom took vacations is a reasonable inference. Most of his traveling was to visit branches or to establish congregations. Return trips to his native Jamaica were rare, and it was during one of those rare trips to the land of his birth that an opposing faction broke away, taking "the cream of the crop" along.

Unlike the majority of African American pastors in Harlem at the time, Humphrey never donned a pastoral or preaching robe when he mounted the pulpit. He preferred to preach in a plain black suit, believing that robes, even black-on-black ones, called attention away from the message to the messenger. Yet in opting for the plain suit Humphrey may have been exposing West Indian cultural tendencies. More important, he may have been showing vestiges of Seventh-day Adventist culture.[11] Olga La Beet, a member of New York United until her death in March, 2001, remembered that as a public speaker Humphrey seemed a combination of Martin Luther King Jr., and the Reverend Jesse Jackson. A former teacher, guidance counselor, and high school principal, La Beet said that Humphrey exhibited the cadence and rhythm of Jesse Jackson and the deep thought and insights of Dr. King, adding that members were unable to detect an accent in him by the 1930s. She concluded that his lack of accent and his preaching style may have accounted for Humphrey's broad appeal in the African American community.[12]

Humphrey was an ardent student of the Holy Bible, which he would often wave in the air as he preached, and he particularly enjoyed studying and preaching its prophecies. Both as a credentialed Seventh-day Adventist and as an independent minister, he used the Sunday evening service to pound home Bible prophecy, especially those found in the books of Daniel and Revelation. The Sunday night service was evangelistic in nature and almost always drew a standing-room-only crowd. Both Ucilla La Condre and Dorothy Simmonds remember Humphrey encouraging members at New York United to stay home on Sunday nights so visitors could get a seat. They say that to make the prophecies as clear as possible, Humphrey used charts, graphs, and other visual aids, and a rule to point out items and to maintain the interest and attention of his ever eager listeners. His members remember him as erudite and scholarly, adding that Humphrey relished the role of teacher more than that of preacher and that he had the gift of making the complex and difficult simple and understandable.[13]

Dorothy Simmonds had an association with James K. Humphrey that predates the founding of the United Sabbath-Day Adventists. Born at Harlem Hospital on December 19, 1914, she was taken at six months of age to Barbados by her parents and returned to the United States in 1926. The family became members of First Harlem, and young Dorothy remembers sitting in the balcony as a teenager and hearing Humphrey calling for volunteers to help out at Second Harlem. Her recollection of the stormy meeting of November 2, 1929, is faint, though she states that the Seventh-day Adventist church leaders present that night were run out by members loyal to Humphrey. Baptized as a United Sabbath-Day Adventist by Humphrey in 1933, she was married in 1942 by the bishop, who also blessed her children. A year earlier he had eulogized her mother. A loyal member of New York United in 2000, Dorothy, whose husband was secretary of the church until his death, is fierce though objective in her defense of Humphrey, saying that the bishop was a great minister but not a good business person. She claims that Utopia Park failed and caused the bishop to lose money because he lacked business acumen not because he was not well meaning.[14]

Two other individuals, Ermie Chandler and Mirian Flatts, remember Humphrey as an outstanding evangelist. Flatts, who was born in 1894 on the island of Barbados and had been baptized into the Seventh-day Adventist Church there, arrived in New York City in 1922. She became a member of First Harlem, serving the congregation as a kindergarten Sabbath School teacher. Flatts says Humphrey was a good leader, "a vibrant evangelist," and "a fiery preacher."[15]

What Ermie Chandler remembers most about Humphrey was his ability to answer any question posed to him. Expressing her admiration, Chandler, who was baptized by Humphrey in the Hudson River, adds that Humphrey once offered a thousand dollar check to anyone able to disprove that Saturday was the Bible Sabbath. On another occasion when the bishop was stumped by a question, he paused, bowed his head in prayer, and opened the Bible exactly at the spot where the answer to the question was. Chandler says that action really impressed her and convinced her that Humphrey was anointed by God. Born in 1907 in Barbados, Chandler was married in 1925 by Humphrey, who also blessed her children. Chandler and her family returned to the Ephesus Seventh-day Adventist Church in 1939 because they wanted to be a part of the larger, "more stable" organization, and although she stops short of speaking ill of Humphrey, she does says that Humphrey did not have enough patience "to wait on the Lord."[16]

Throughout the 1930s James K. Humphrey maintained the evangelistic flavor of his preaching, believing that preaching that was not evangelistic was inherently unbiblical. Almost always, he ended his sermons by lifting up Jesus and with an appeal for those who had not yet accepted Christ as their personal Savior to do so. Passionate and persuasive, these appeals struck a responsive chord in not a few of his listeners. The result was that regular baptisms were conducted in Pelham Bay and the Harlem River, as well as in the baptistry at the church. Jarvis and Simmonds recall that before being baptized, people interested in joining the church were required to spend at least six months in a baptismal class, where they received thorough instruction in the fundamental tenets of Christianity. Only after individuals showed convincing proof that they understood the teachings of the church were they baptized. Sabbath-Day Adventist baptismal services were not the spectacularly staged events that drew a horde of curiosity seekers like the baptismal services of some of the other religious groups of the era. On the contrary, they were low-key events that powerfully impacted the lives of the faithful.[17]

Humphrey did not restrict his teaching and preaching to the prophecies and doctrines found in the Bible. Asserting that the bishop was knowledgeable almost to a fault, La Beet says that he went on a search for the Black presence in the Bible and that the quest resulted in him preaching frequently on the subject. She opines that the bishop saw as a critical aspect of his ministry the raising of the consciousness level of his congregants with respect to their history both within and without the Christian church. Race consciousness was a readily identifiable element in his persona and world view, though he was not consumed by it. Dubbed "The Man of the Hour," Humphrey particularly liked to zero in on current events, especially those taking place in Harlem. He believed that his finger was on the pulse of world events, and, consequently, he was in a position to alert his hearers as to what they could expect to see transpire in their lifetime.[18]

According to La Condre, Humphrey was a community-minded leader who believed in tearing down the walls of separation between religious groups and building bridges to other groups and people instead. Humphrey kept abreast of issues and developments within the World Council of Churches. In this regard, the bishop demonstrated a marked contrast to Seventh-day Adventists, who, at least up to the time, distanced themselves from the World Council of Churches, holding that involvement in the organization smacked of ecumenism. Humphrey reached across denominational lines to collaborate with other Black religious leaders on initiatives to improve the conditions of Black people and was not averse to inviting Black pastors of other religious persuasions to preach at his church or to lecture on social and political issues. Like other African American pastors, Humphrey wanted his group to be a seven-day-a-week provider of ministries and programs that benefited the community spiritually, economically, politically, and socially. He encouraged members to vote and admonished his youth to stay in school and to pursue careers in medicine, law, and other professions historically off limits to Blacks.[19]

Irene Jarvis states that each week Humphrey visited the Children's Division of the Sabbath School, where he reveled in listening to the children recite Bible verses. Often, he would assign Bible verses to the children, returning the following week to hear them recite the verses. He affirmed the children, and they in turn loved him. Humphrey would gather the youth in the front of the sanctuary, where he spoke to them about issues with which they were wrestling. He counseled them about courtship and dating, encouraging them to marry within the church family, and of the importance of personal grooming, the value of an education, and the need to set goals in life. The bishop frowned upon mediocrity, dismissing it as a curse to the Black race. More than anything, he wanted his youth to know that their potential was limitless, and that in their hands were the keys to success.[20]

United Sabbath-Day Adventists in general and Humphrey in particular gave more than lip service to their youth, providing them with opportunities to participate in all the services of the church and to function in various officer personnel capacities. These opportunities went beyond those in youth groups, such as the youth choir and the weekly youth meeting. La Condre says that at New York United, youth served as ushers, as choristers for the Sunday night evangelistic meeting, and as counters in the treasury department. The message Humphrey and his leadership team wanted to convey was that their church did not view youth as irrelevant members to be banished to the fringes of the church but as leaders in training.[21]

On Saturday nights the youth of New York United went roller skating and bowling and to the beach and Coney Island on some Sunday afternoons and holidays. Humphrey often packed his car with young people for the trip to Jones Beach on Long Island. One such youth was Aileen Samuels Hunter, whose father succeeded Humphrey as bishop of the United Sabbath-Day Adventists and who was a close friend of Ruth Humphrey, the bishop's only child. Fondly does Hunter remember being taken as a child to the beach by the pastor and of being knocked down by a wave. Hunter, whose parents were from Antigua, was born in New York City in 1924, baptized by Humphrey in 1936, and married by him in 1946, the year before her father assumed leadership of the organization. She is a retired high school assistant principal who also tutored at Mercy College in Dobbs Ferry, New York. Living in Nanuet, New York, in 2000, she commutes to New York United faithfully every Sabbath.[22]

Bernice Samuel opines that boat rides up the Hudson offered a respite from the pell-mell pace of life in Harlem. So too did the lyceums and other cultural programs that were conducted for the youth on some Sunday afternoons and the occasional trip to Carnegie Hall for a special presentation. According to her, these social and cultural activities engendered a sense of belonging among not just the youth but all church members and caused several youth to marry within the church family.[23]

In spite of the premium early Sabbath-Day Adventists placed on mentoring youth, few things about the membership of the New York congregation at the start of the twenty-first century stood out as starkly as the absence of youth. In 2000, New York United was composed of approximately sixty members, almost all of whom were adults. Indeed, members who date their association with the congregation from the Humphrey era constitute an appreciable percentage of the current membership, making New York United a veritable coterie of senior citizens. Feisty and resilient, the group cherishes the church's history and guards Humphrey's legacy with uncommon loyalty.

Agatha Phillips, who was ordained as a female elder on January 6, 2001, states that notwithstanding his sensitivity to social and community issues, Humphrey nonetheless counseled his members that above all else they should stand in the Christian faith and never forget their Lord Jesus Christ and what he had done for them.[24] This stance of Humphrey's shows he was not a radical doctrinally. In many ways Humphrey was a conservative in doctrine and church polity. For example, Humphrey denounced life insurance as an evil to be shunned by his members. He exhorted members not to spend their hard-earned dollars to procure a commodity that only fattened the coffers and pockets of grafters and extortioners, and he believed that life insurance betrayed a lack of faith in God and a preoccupation with life on earth, both of which were at variance with the principles of God's everlasting kingdom. Bernice Samuel remembers that when two members who did not have life insurance died, the New York United Sabbath-Day Adventist congregation was thrown into a disarray that resulted in a split between those who embraced life insurance as a necessary and intelligent way of planning for the inevitable contingencies of life and those who resolutely maintained that it was an evil.[25]

For La Condre, La Beet, Jarvis, Samuel, Hunter, Simmonds, and others, New York United was, as La Condre aptly puts it, "a place of refuge."[26] More a family than even a community of faith, members shared what they had with each other and knew that temporal as well as spiritual help could be procured at the church. Simmonds says they were a "happy group of Sabbath keepers" and that she was proud to be a member of the group.[27] In a similar vein, Jarvis, who remembers that as a youth it was not an option if you were going to church, states that it was "fun being in church." One reason it was fun being in church was because the friends she had there were different from those she had at home and school.[28] The joy and satisfaction that these individuals derived from being associated with New York United is noteworthy, given that as Sabbath keepers they could not participate in activities other youth did.

E. Forrest Harris Jr. contends that the independent Black church movement and the Black cults and sects of the North were "unique expressions of Black people's quest for collective self-consciousness through religious commitments." These religious bodies functioned as a "source of power and self-definition alternative to the dehumanizing anti-self images" in the broader society, providing members with "hope, assurance, and a sense of group identification."[29] Thus, for United Sabbath-Day Adventists, church was a place where relationships were formed and nurtured, life partners were procured, children were socialized, youth were trained to assume positions of responsibility in society, and, most important, a religious organization was built through which they expressed their dreams and aspirations.[30] Humphrey is remembered positively by these individuals. He was the religious leader who studied the Bible with them as a prerequisite to their baptism. He married most of them, blessed their children, and presided over the burials of their parents, spouses and, in some instances, children. Willing to admit he was a human being with flaws, they nonetheless still held him in high esteem.

Establishment of United Sabbath-Day Congregations

Sabbath-Day Adventists came into existence, they claim, as a result of the treatment people of African descent had received in the Seventh-day Adventist denomination almost from the time Blacks started attending the meetings of this unique religious group. From the start, Black Seventh-day Adventists had attempted to "secure adequate returns and proper recognition" from the organization. Yet their efforts had met with frustration, if not failure. Attempts by African Americans to matriculate at the denomination's educational institutions had met with sparse success, and the racism the few who were admitted encountered often caused them to withdraw prematurely. The situation was not much different from that of those who tried to enter Seventh-day Adventist medical facilities, either for treatment or training. Opportunities in the organization were restricted to teaching, preaching, and selling church literature, with little consideration given to the educational achievements or vocational competencies of African Americans. Frustrated that the denomination had failed over the years to give them "due consideration" in spite of their faithfulness and loyalty and, more important, had failed to "show a better example of Christ-likeness in Righteousness, Justice and Equity," James Kemuel Humphrey and his loyalists believed they had ample reason to disassociate themselves from the Seventh-day Adventist denomination and form their own.[31]

The group adopted the name United Sabbath-Day Adventists in January 1930 after a committee of twenty-three individuals had given extended study to the matter. The committee, which voted twenty-one to two in favor of the name, believed that it could not continue using the name Seventh-day Adventist because that name stood for "unfair treatment of colored people through discrimination and 'Jim-Crowism.'" United was chosen because of the premium the Bible placed on unity and because unity is a hallmark of true Christianity. In addition, the new religious body would try to effect unity between individuals and groups, including racial and ethnic groups. This unity would authenticate and motivate the group's endeavors to preach the gospel worldwide. Still believing in the sanctity of the Sabbath, the group used the term Sabbath-Day in its name, going a step further to assert that people who keep the Sabbath day holy must of necessity be holy themselves. Finally, because members were convinced that Jesus would be returning to the earth soon to end the reign of sin and usher in an age of peace and holiness, they kept the word Adventists.[32]

United Sabbath-Day Adventists were buoyant and optimistic at the start of their organization. They believed that American society, especially in the South, was ripe for proselytizing. The group decried the sluggishness with which Seventh-day Adventists had tried to reach African Americans and was particularly chagrined that after almost sixty years of contact Black Seventh-day Adventist church membership was only approximately nine thousand. Sabbath-Day Adventist outlook was going to be global, and the new religious body would give specialized focus and attention to their marginalized brothers and sisters in the United States, whom they characterized as "susceptible to the religion of Jesus Christ, and are so willing to hear any one speak of the Savior who died for them."[33]

A year and a half after their inauguration, United Sabbath-Day Adventists were being ridiculed and vilified by Seventh-day Adventists as a scattered, inefficient, and ineffective organization. Reminding its detractors that at eighteen months it was still an infant and should not be compared to organizations sixty and more years its senior, the group pointed out that it had been born of love—as Christ had been—and was in need of love, affirmation, and empathy. It requested that instead of the disparaging barbs it be offered substantive and substantial gifts in the form of financial contributions to its domestic and foreign initiatives, and offerings of time and labor. United Sabbath-Day Adventists dismissed the criticisms as untrue, claiming that their strides in evangelism and church growth outdistanced those of the denomination from which they had extricated themselves. In addition, they claimed that their progress mirrored that of African Americans in the general population, who, shaking loose from the shackles of slavery, also had faced seemingly insurmountable barriers in their drive for self determination.[34]

The evidence appears to substantiate the claims of the Sabbath-Day Adventists. In quick succession, they spawned branches in the United States and overseas. Not surprising, the largest United Sabbath-Day Adventist congregation was in New York City, where Humphrey lived and was well known. Mother of every other Sabbath-Day Adventist church, this congregation, which by mid-1931 numbered 530, was committed to fostering evangelistic efforts worldwide. Its Sabbath School was touted to be the best organized among Adventists in the world, and the church boasted a youth membership well in excess of two hundred. By late 1931 other United Sabbath-Day Adventist congregations had been spawned in Chicago, Boston, St. Louis, Omaha, Milwaukee, Newark, and Kingston, Jamaica. How United Sabbath-Day Adventists established these churches is unclear, though it appears that people sympathetic to Humphrey and his cause contacted him with a request that he organize them as a church.[35]

These small congregations were saddled with pressing needs, which, given their Depression-era context, is understandable. Forty-four individuals constituted the church in Omaha, which had M. M. Boodle as its pastor. This group worshiped in a large two-story frame house it was attempting to purchase as 1931 drew to a close. Still, members were encouraged by the prospects for growth, evidenced by three persons who had recently "taken their stand for baptism." The Milwaukee congregation, led by Moses M. Payne, a local elder, was a vibrant group that had forty-five people attending Sabbath School. In addition, its young people's meetings were "very interesting and enjoy a good attendance," with a "number of visitors attending and participating in the services and meetings of the congregation."[36]

The first United Sabbath-Day Adventist Church in New Jersey was established in July 1930 in Newark with a charter membership of twenty-four, almost all of whom had been former members of the Seventh-day Adventist denomination. By the end of 1931 the group had grown by 25 percent and was functioning as a full-fledged church. Its Sabbath School was "wide awake," and its Missionary Department was "working for the conversion of souls." The Newark congregation did not have a building of its own, yet that did not stop the group from trying to meet the material needs of its constituents and community, an objective that was anchored in its belief that the mission of a church is more than that of ministering to the spiritual needs of people. Sabbath-Day Adventists held that feeding the hungry, clothing the naked, and sheltering the homeless constituted the mission of the church, too. Church leaders informed readers of the *Messenger* that the pastor of the Newark congregation, who during 1931 was a guest columnist for the *Newark Herald,* had seized the opportunity to explain in a series of articles the reasons behind Humphrey's split with the Seventh-day Adventist denomination. "Convinced that under the circumstances Elder J. K. Humphrey was right in the stand he took," readers were "grateful for the information."[37]

In the fall of 1930, a small congregation was organized in Ashbury Park, New Jersey. Committing itself to justice and equity between the sexes and among races, the group, constituted mostly of former Seventh-day Adventists, found it difficult to achieve its goals and objectives because of financial constraints. Like other Sabbath-Day Adventists congregations, this group also appealed for funds to carry on its work.[38]

On May 30, 1931, James K. Humphrey, acting in his capacity as founder and president of the United Sabbath-Day Adventist General Conference, organized a branch in Boston with a charter membership of thirty-three. Like other congregations, this one operated without a local minister for a time. Yet that did not derail its outreach activity, and five months after its organization its membership had grown to forty. Attendance at Sabbath School was double the church membership, and all departments of the church were functioning optimally.[39]

By the end of 1931 United Sabbath-Day Adventists had established a presence on the island of Jamaica with churches in Kingston; Higgins Town, St. Anns; and Waltham Park and Ewarton, St. Andrews. The Kingston congregation, which supported the group at Waltham Park, was permeated by a "good spirit" and a "strong determination to stand together for the furtherance and establishment of the despised cause," and a baptismal class of seven proffered evidence of the group's evangelistic zeal. Established amid severe conflict, the Higgins Town congregation had quickly secured a lot of land on which, with the help of the Kingston congregation, it had constructed a church building. Though still unfinished, a condition which was an inaudible but eloquent appeal for financial assistance, the facility doubled as a school building, providing space for at least forty children. Ewarton was a relatively recent church plant that had come about as the result of the visionary labor of a focused local leader but was suffering because of the lack of a permanent, stable place of worship.[40]

Humphrey alleged that a torrent of calls for the organization of Sabbath-Day Adventist congregations had been received from Jamaica and from Central and Latin America. The calls had prompted Humphrey to appeal for human and financial resources, and only the lack of help had thwarted a more aggressive response from the new religious body. A dearth of financial resources had prevented Humphrey from visiting Panama, although it did not stop two Sabbath-Day Adventist congregations from organizing themselves there during 1931.[41]

By August 1932, United Sabbath-Day Adventists were lauding their rise and progress, accomplished "under the courageous and energetic leadership of Elder James K. Humphrey." In spite of severe opposition from detractors, the organization had moved "forward steadily," disproving predictions of an early demise and standing tall as a "challenge to the bigotry and selfishness of those who once exploited them."[42] The organization claimed a worldwide membership of twelve hundred people worshiping in fifteen congregations and missions in places as far away as Jamaica, West Indies. Humphrey, saying that a "good report maketh the bones fat," informed members that the New

York congregation, the flagship church of the denomination and home to the General Conference of Sabbath-Day Adventists, had a membership of approximately six hundred. Once more, he alleged that Seventh-day Adventists were only interested in the financial contributions of Blacks, specifically of "getting the most out of them that is possible, rather than doing the most for them that is possible." He told his followers that the New York Supreme Court, ruling in their favor, had directed the Greater New York Conference to return the deed of the group's property to it, saying that this was an answer to prayer for which the church was happy and grateful. Humphrey believed that in "every respect" the new body was much better off than "when she was connected with the Seventh-day Adventists." [43]

The Brooklyn and Newark congregations, both pastored by R. Leo Soaries, vice-president of the General Conference, were raising funds to procure adequate worship facilities. Organized in May 1930 with a charter membership of fifteen, the Brooklyn membership in August 1932 stood at twenty-nine. Soaries asserted that members were "conscientious Christians" who were standing "squarely for the Bible and the Bible only, and Jesus Christ as their Savior." Rejoicing in a "present salvation and a deep knowledge of Christ," the group was "praising God for the organization of a Negro Sabbath-keeping body where promising young people can hold positions of trust and responsibility in service for God and humanity." A gifted writer, Soaries had recently produced a play entitled "Deliverance," which the youth of the church, whom he characterized as "refined, cultured, and energetic," had dramatized to rave reviews. The pastor said that everybody who had seen the play commended "these talented young people for the able manner in which they played their parts." Soaries was convinced that Blacks were at a point in their existence that called for them to find their niche, and, not unlike his leader, was sure that Blacks more than any other racial group were suited to "conscientiously preach the gospel of Christ to the world." This was the case because a requirement for preaching the gospel effectively was a life devoid of hypocrisy and untarnished by feelings of superiority. With their "superiority complex and racial antagonisms," Whites, Soaries thought, were incapable of convincing people "that they are the representatives of an impartial God." [44]

In the Midwest, the Chicago church, which had survived the onslaughts of an "unfaithful few" who had been associated with the church, was moving forward in 1932 under the competent and loyal leadership of a lay couple, Joseph Lumley and his wife. The Milwaukee congregation, "one of the strongest and most faithful companies" in the conference, was also operating under lay leadership. The Depression was having an adverse impact on the ability of members to support the church financially in Milwaukee. Still, the church was well organized, according to Alice E. Nogest, missionary leader, and because it believed that civilization was in its eleventh hour, it was "trying to improve the time." As such, the congregation had targeted its youth for service, organizing a "Girl's Douglas Club to help in the way of providing wholesome recreation" and a "Surprise Package Club." Remembering that the "Son of Man came not to be ministered unto, but to minister," the youth had been busy "cleaning rooms for sick people, going on errands, and doing things in general to bring bliss to others." The St. Louis church, which had survived "great tribulation because of unfaithful ministers," had recently received the services of some lay preachers, and in Omaha, where Morrell Boodle and his wife had not been "without troubles and trials," the church was repairing and decorating its auditorium.[45]

Back East, there were United Sabbath-Day Adventist Sabbath Schools operating in Baltimore and in Jamaica, New York, and the membership of the Boston congregation, thirty-three when the group started in 1931, stood at forty-three in 1932. Attendance at the Sunday evening evangelistic meeting in Boston was high, as was the case with Sabbath School, where sixty-seven people were usually in attendance. A branch Sabbath School had been started in Newburyport, Massachusetts, and the Boston congregation boasted a baptismal class of several. Over the previous thirteen months the church had collected $565.98 in offerings. Boston was aspiring to lead the Conference in activities and was purchasing more *Messengers* per capita than any other Sabbath-Day Adventist congregation. The success of this congregation was all the more significant because its pastor had recently been transferred to the Southwestern region.[46]

In Humphrey's country of birth, the work of the Sabbath-Day Adventists was also moving forward. On August 3, 1932, the cornerstone of a new church building in Kingston was laid. The Reverend G. Hargis of the Seventh-day Baptists was the keynote speaker for the occasion, returning a favor Humphrey had performed for him when the United Sabbath-Day Adventist leader preached the dedicatory sermon for a Seventh-day Baptist building in 1930. Calling Hargis a "brother minister," Humphrey thanked him for his services.[47] At Higgins Town enrollment at the Sabbath-Day Adventist Church school topped thirty, and plans called for it to increase to fifty by the opening of school the following month. Sickness and lack of a worship center had conspired against members at Ewarton.[48] Humphrey ended his 1932 report of the church plant-ing and church growth activities of his still infant organization by claiming that calls for organization of Sabbath-Day Adventist congregations were pour-ing in from "all parts of the world and especially from the United States." He stated that as soon as funds allowed, the calls were going to be answered.[49]

The establishment of Sabbath-Day Adventist congregations in the United States and the West Indies continued throughout the 1930s. For example, in the summer of 1938, a group was organized in Indianapolis by Humphrey, who placed at its helm a former Baptist minister who had joined the Seventh-day Adventist church a year and a half before. J. J. Freeman quickly became disen-chanted over the experience of African Americans in the Seventh-day Adven-tist church. On learning about the United Sabbath-Day Adventists through one of their publications, Freeman requested to meet with Humphrey, who gladly facilitated his wishes to become a part of the United Sabbath-Day Adventists. By then, Humphrey had also traveled to Bermuda and established a "splendid group of believers there." As the Ninth Annual Session of the Gen-eral Conference of the United Sabbath-Day Adventists convened in New York City in 1939, calls requesting organization were coming in from Detroit, Cleve-land, and Cincinnati in the United States and from Antigua, Barbados, British Guiana (now Guyana), and Trinidad in the West Indies.[50]

The establishment of United Sabbath-Day Adventist congregations in the West Indies is noteworthy. Like some West Indians of his era, Humphrey believed that race relations in the West Indies were starkly different to those that existed in the United States. To be sure, slavery had been as oppressive in the West Indies as it had been in the United States, and the situation was the same with racism. Yet some West Indians, including Humphrey, held to the ungrounded belief that conditions in the West Indies had changed. For example, when in 1913 a move had been made to drop the words North Ameri-can from the North American Negro Department of the General Conference of Seventh-day Adventists, Humphrey spoke out against the recommendation, arguing that he did not want conditions in the United States to spread to the West Indies, where they were not in existence.[51]

Who were the people that joined the Sabbath-Day Adventists? Did the group attract only urban slum dwellers, immigrants from the South and the West Indies searching for stability and meaning in an unfriendly, alien environment? Based on the photos and articles in the denomination's official organ, the *United Sabbath-Day Adventist Messenger*, a reasonable conclusion is that the group attracted educated, middle-class, well-to-do individuals, as well as those mired in poverty. Almost without exception, pictures of church leaders and members show well-dressed, immaculately coiffured people. Children are adequately and tastefully clothed. Even snapshots of the Kingston and Higgins Town, Jamaica, congregations tell a story of Blacks being able to clothe themselves well in the midst of a worldwide depression. In addition, one is able to detect a sense of pride in the people, a feeling that in spite of the odds they were going to triumph and that they had nothing for which they should be ashamed.

The artwork on the cover of the November 1931 and August 1932 issues of the *Messenger* was the creative expression of a United Sabbath-Day Adventist young adult. In the picture, Claudius Frederick attempted to capture "the universality of the gospel commission" by depicting an angel flying in the sky while blowing a trumpet to make people aware of "the commandments of God and the faith of Jesus Christ." The airplane, ship, train, and automobile convey the thought that "by land, sea, and air the message of Jesus' soon coming must be disseminated." Tasteful and attractive, the cover of the periodical tells that at New York United youth were provided with avenues to develop and display their talents and competencies. Indeed, the November 31, 1931, issue of the magazine, in calling attention to its cover, stated: "We are glad that this young artist, as well as other young people of our group, can now be given an opportunity to use their talents in the service of Christ who died for them."[52]

True to its claim, the *Messenger* was a medium for the growth and expansion of the skills of Sabbath-Day Adventists, especially the young. J. R. Williams, a medical doctor with a degree from McGill University, contributed health articles monthly, and S. H. Craig, a dentist and World War I veteran who had graduated from Harvard University with "the highest ranking in the class of 1929," wrote a regular column on oral health.[53] Poetry and other expressions of creative genius dotted the pages of the periodical, which always carried an assortment of portraits of members and pictures of congregations. In the early 1930s the assistant editor of the periodical was C. J. Lewis, a "promising" young man, and the editor, P. J. Bailey, was not much older. In addition to editing the journal, Bailey ran the departments of the Conference, suggesting he had organizational, managerial, and administrative skills. A serious, scholarly-looking gentleman, Bailey gives evidence of an appreciable grasp of theological themes. Whether he was trained in theology is unclear, but his articles, especially one entitled "The Scope of the Gospel," demonstrates that he was steeped in Scripture and resonated with theological nuances. In this article, Bailey provides a

panoramic sweep of the plan of salvation, his soteriology consonant with traditional Adventist and evangelical Christianity's understanding of the issue.[54]

In the August 1932 issue of the *Messenger*, three pictures speak to the sense
of pride that Sabbath-Day Adventist leaders had in the accomplishments of
their youth. On page four was a picture of C. J. Lewis, the handsome assistant
editor of the paper, who had just received a Bachelor of Arts degree in Education from New York University. On page fifteen was the picture and story
of Dr. Kathleen H. Jones–King, "an unassuming young woman of refinement
and ambition," who had recently finished a medical internship at Freedman's
Hospital in the nation's capital. A member of Howard University School of
Medicine's class of 1931, Jones–King, who was practicing in Philadelphia, was
one of the first women doctors of Howard University to pass the National
Board Examination, and she had been licensed to practice in forty-six states.
Jones-King had been baptized by Humphrey in 1926 and credited her aca-
demic and vocational success to prayer, hard work, and the financial help of a
younger sister, who, together with the rest of the family, was a member of the
Brooklyn Sabbath-Day Adventist congregation.[55]

Yet it was a picture on page twelve of that issue that tells eloquently of the
premium Sabbath-Day Adventists placed on ambition and success, especially
as it related to their youth. Ten-year-old Elaine Moore is shown clad in a plaid
coat. Her hair pulled back to show her beautiful face, her penetrating eyes
reveal, according to the periodical, a "forceful personality" and tell a tale "of
innate intelligence and ability." The journal claimed that when the qualities
young Elaine exhibited are harnessed and used for and by God, "great good is
accomplished." Endowed with a good mind, Elaine had been able to commit to
memory and repeat without help several passages of Scripture and was lifted
up as a prototype of the kind of children being nurtured in the church.[56]

Human-interest stories accompanied by pictures were not restricted to
the young. Occasionally, the autobiographies of seniors were run, especially
those who had experienced slavery firsthand. For example, in 1932 readers were
treated to the story of the odyssey of Mrs. Bell Crowder, a member of the
St. Louis church. Born in Louisville in 1852, she and her three siblings were
taken to Tennessee when her mother was sold to a slave trader. There her two
brothers were separated from the rest of the family. Taken to church where she
heard White preachers speak every Sunday on the theme "Servants, obey your
masters," Crowden believed for a while that that was the only verse in the Bible.
After the Civil War her family moved a couple of times, finally locating her two

long-lost brothers. Eleven months shy of her eightieth birthday, Bell Crowder looks many years younger in the picture, taken on the front steps of her home, clutching what appears to be a well-used Bible.[57]

Notwithstanding what seems like the proliferation of United Sabbath-Day Adventist congregations during the 1930s, the fact is the organization never experienced great success attracting the unchurched and nonbelievers to itself and only limited success in proselytizing former Seventh-day Adventists. Humphrey may have been one of Adventism's premier evangelists before he was defrocked by the denomination, but once he became the titular head of the Sabbath-Day Adventists he ceased to engage in evangelism on the scale he had done previously. More important, from their inception United Sabbath-Day Adventists had one major goal—survival. Struggles with the Seventh-day Adventist denomination and internal conflicts only made their major goal more acute. Yet United Sabbath-Day Adventists during this time may not be characterized as an insular, self-conscious bunch preoccupied with self-preservation and self-perpetuation. The group did articulate a theology of mission that transcended its precincts and did reach out to its community in tangible ways.

TENETS AND CONSTITUTION OF THE SABBATH-DAY ADVENTISTS

In his seminal work, *The Social Teaching of the Black Churches*, Peter J. Paris argues that the major objective of the independent Black church movement was "the institutionalization of the Christian faith in a nonracist form" and that the founders of independent Black churches never intended that their churches differ from those of their White counterparts in policy and doctrine.[58] Attempting to remain loyal to the principles of the nation and their race, these Black churches differed from White ones in purposes more than in doctrine and polity. According to Paris, two factors accounted for this reality. The first is that Black churches were dependent on the cooperation of Whites for both their emergence and development, often needing their help to procure loans to acquire property. In addition, because Blacks resolutely believed in the ideal society they saw Black churches as a necessary, and perhaps temporary, phenomenon prompted by the contingencies of race.[59]

Were the United Sabbath-Day Adventists a Black duplication of the Seventh-day Adventist Church? Were their tenents or fundamental beliefs reflective of those of the Seventh-day Adventists?[60] The closest thing to a fundamental set of doctrines that Sabbath-Day Adventists adopted was authored by R. Leo Soaries, vice-president of the organization. Published in 1935, it shows that, in the main, United Sabbath-Day Adventist tenents mirrored those of mainstream Christianity in general and the Seventh-day Adventists in particular (see Appendix A).

Fundamental Beliefs of Sabbath-Day Adventists

Sabbath-Day Adventists believed:

1. In the infallibility of Scripture, which they affirmed is the word of God and amply supplies the "wisdom, knowledge and understanding" needed for salvation. The holy corpus was the product of neither the initiative nor intelligence of people but of a sovereign God, who, through the ministry of the Holy Spirit, inspired holy men and women to write Scripture. 2 Tim. 3:15, 16; 2 Pet. 1:20, 21.

2. That Jesus Christ, who was used by God to create all things, was both human and divine while on earth and had to be the God-man in order to accomplish the work of redeeming humanity. John 1:1–5; Col. 1:13–16; Heb. 1:1, 2; Phil. 2:8; Matt. 1:21, 23; Heb. 2:14–18.

3. That Jesus Christ is able to save the most wretched from eternal death, which is the consequence of a life of sin. Christ offers eternal life as a gift. Matt. 1:21; Acts 16:31; Rom. 5:1; John 3:16; Matt. 9:13; Rom. 6:23; Rom. 5:12–19.

4. That people are mortal beings, having been created into a situation where death was a distinct possibility. Human beings are unified creatures of body, soul, and spirit who expire at death and remain unconscious until Jesus returns. Gen. 2:7, 16–17; Gen. 3:22; Eze. 18:4; Rom. 16:3; Job 14:7–15; Job 17:13.

5. That those who have accepted Jesus Christ as their savior will be rewarded at his second coming and that those who have rejected him will reap the consequences of their actions, "complete annihilation," after the millennium. Isa. 40:10; Isa. 62:11; Rev. 22:12; Rev. 20:7–9; Mal. 4:1; Psalms 37:10, 20, 38; Psalms 34:21; Prov. 2:22.

6. That the judgment takes place after the second advent of Jesus Christ. Psalms 96:13; Psalms 50:3; 2 Tim. 4:1; Matt. 25:31–40.

7. That the testimony of Jesus Christ is the spirit of prophecy, Christ having been the one who prompted and actuated the prophets. Christ was "the directing intelligence behind every statement made." Indeed, "it was Christ who testified through the prophets." As such, "the testimony of Christ is the spirit of prophecy, and not the gift of prophecy." Throughout the Dark Ages, Christians suffered and were martyred for the testimony of Jesus Christ. 1 Peter 1:10, 11; Rev. 1:9; Rev. 19:10; Rev. 20:4.

8. That the Holy Spirit, who sealed Christ at his baptism, seals the believer. Given to lead and guide the believer into truth and to glorify Christ, the Holy Spirit is the divine Comforter who abides with Christians forever. Eph. 4:30; Eph. 1:13–14; 2 Cor. 1:22; John 16:13–14; John 14:16–17.

9. That conversion is a requirement for entrance into the kingdom of God through baptism and that the "born again" person lives a temperate, holy life. John 3:5; Matt. 18:3; Titus 2:12, 14; 2 Pet. 3:11–14; 2 Thess. 4:14–18.

10. That God's Ten Commandments law, as a "transcript of His character," is eternal and immutable. Psalms 111:7–8; Psalms 89:34.

11. That Saturday, the seventh day of the week, and not Sunday, the first day of the week, is the Bible Sabbath and should be "observed as the day of worship by all Christians." Gen. 2:1–3; Exod. 16:23, 28; Exod. 20:8–11.

12. That the "proper means for the support of the church" is the "Bible plan of tithing and the giving of offerings." Mal. 3:8–11; Matt. 23:23.

13. That civilization had reached its penultimate hour and that Blacks had been conscripted to proclaim the gospel to the world since both Jews and Gentiles had missed their opportunity to do so. Matt. 20; 6; Matt. 16:21–24.

14. That Gentiles were the Japethites, or "the white race," and that the terms *Ethiopian, Egyptian, Hamite,* and *Cushite* all applied to people of African descent. Gen. 10:5; Mark 10:33; Rom. 11:11, 25; Isa. 19:23–25; Isa. 11:11.[61]

It is uncertain if this list represents the complete set of cardinal doctrines of the Sabbath-Day Adventists. Some pivotal Christian beliefs and teachings are missing. For example, nothing is said about the resurrection of Christ or about his co-eternity with God, the Father. To be sure, that Christ possesses all the attributes of deity is implied in their document, and perhaps no mention of

Christ's resurrection is simply that and nothing more. Items 13 and 14 show that Sabbath-Day Adventists were no mere duplication of their White counterparts, the Seventh-day Adventists, but a group acutely conscious of its Black heritage. Whether this slate of beliefs was ever officially voted or adopted by Sabbath-Day Adventists is unsure. It is also uncertain if members or those interested in joining the group had to vow allegiance to the doctrines before they could be accepted into membership, either by baptism or some other method.

Constitution and By-Laws of the Sabbath-Day Adventists

The Constitution and By-Laws of the United Sabbath-Day Adventists identify the New York congregation as the body to which the document applies, leaving one to speculate as to whether the Constitution and By-Laws also applied to all branches. A reasonable inference is that other than for Article One, which identifies the church by name, it did. The Constitution is specific yet comprehensive, painting in broad strokes yet supplying detail, too.

Acknowledging Jesus Christ as the head of the United Sabbath-Day Adventists and recognizing the Bible as the enduring guide of rightful living for all Christians, the document states that the fundamental mission of the group was to facilitate Christianity in keeping with "Sabbath-Day Adventist doctrine." Church membership was open to all who believed in the second coming of Jesus Christ, the seventh day of the week as the Bible Sabbath, baptism by complete immersion, the unconscious state of the dead, dress and health reform, and those who committed themselves to paying a tenth of all their income as a tithe to the church. It was the responsibility of the Board of Trustees to levy and assess tithes and other financial contributions.

Precise as to the officer personnel of the church, their responsibilities and the formula for their election to and removal from office, the document does not state their terms of office.[62] The exception was the elder, whose tenure was indefinite. The president had broad powers, including authorization to sign all contracts and agreements and "all checks for the withdrawal of funds." Yet the treasurer was expected to pay all the bills of the church and the financial secretary to keep accurate records of all receipts and expenditures, showing that the organization sought to decentralize its financial operation, undoubtedly with a view to minimizing the probability of wrongdoing. Showing that it prized good music, the group placed matters relating to the choir in the document, going so far as to state that rehearsals were to open and close with prayer "so that God might be well pleased." Only sickness and uncontrollable contingencies, in which case a written excuse was called for, were recognized as legitimate excuses for nonattendance at rehearsals.

United Sabbath-Day Adventists considered church membership a sacred matter and the dismissal of a member an action to be taken only after all attempts at restoring the individual had failed. Citing Matthew 18:15–19, which outlines a procedure for dealing with the errant in the community of faith and differences among Christians, the Constitution and By-Laws state that dismissal of members could take place only after the detailed procedure had been exhausted. Still, members were expected to deport themselves in ways that would be "a credit to the church and to God" and were expected to "bear their share of the responsibility for the upkeep of the church."[63]

General Conference Sessions

Almost from the start, United Sabbath-Day Adventists convened General Conference Sessions annually. The objectives of these sessions included the receiving of reports from the satellite groups around the country and in the West Indies, and the dissemination of information from headquarters to the constituent churches. Committees on Nominations, Constitution and By-Laws, Entertainment, Plans and Recommendations, and Credentials and Licenses were impaneled, and the committees usually completed their tasks before the sessions adjourned. Humphrey was never averse to injecting devotional elements into these business sessions of the organization. As such, each session started with much singing, and whenever there was not much business to attend to or there were lapses in the agenda, delegates took to the floor to testify of God's blessings and the joys of being associated with the organization. Seldom were doctrinal or theological issues taken up at these sessions, although ministerial credentials, ministerial licenses, and missionary licenses were granted and withdrawn. A General Conference session more often addressed housekeeping matters and served as a rallying point for the faithful and a motivational device for the feeble of faith.[64]

At the Ninth Annual Session of the General Conference of United Sabbath-Day Adventists, convened in New York City May 19–26, 1939, in the denomination's newly purchased property located at 36–38 West 135th, delegates were seated from Bermuda (2); Boston (1); Indianapolis (1); Milwaukee (1); Newburyport, Massachusetts (1); Omaha, (1); Philadelphia, (1); and New York City (thirty-two regular delegates and eleven alternates). In addition, there were eight delegates-at-large, led by James K. Humphrey and including his wife, Viola R. Humphrey, and his brother, Benjamin Humphrey. No mention is made as to the criteria utilized for the selection of delegates. At this session, as was the case with all others, James K. Humphrey presided.[65]

The General Conference of Sabbath-Day Adventists had officer personnel and directors for the Sabbath School and Youth departments. It is certain that all these positions, with the exception of the presidency, were up for reelection at a General Conference session. For example, at the Ninth Session the Nominating Committee recommended individuals for the positions of secretary-treasurer, Alvin Simmons; secretary of the Sabbath School department, Viola R. Humphrey; and secretary of the Young People Department, Elsie Stulz. The Committee also recommended a five-member Executive Committee consisting of five men to assist the president in the execution of his duties and responsibilities. Conspicuously absent from the Nominating Committee's report was a recommendation for the position of president of the organization. Obviously, that Humphrey would continue on as leader of the group was a matter not up for discussion, debate, or a vote. The United Sabbath-Day Adventist denomination was his brainchild, and he would be at its helm, at least for the foreseeable future. Indeed, that Humphrey was the indisputable leader of the organization is evidenced by the way he conducted the business of these sessions. It was Humphrey who opened and closed each session—always with a prayer.[66]

Unarguably, men dominated the leadership roles of the United Sabbath-Day Adventists. Humphrey was not threatened by male leadership. On the contrary, he prized having men of uncommon ability around him and took the matter of legacy seriously. Humphrey believed that one of his primary responsibilities as a leader was the cultivation and development of men to carry on the work of the organization. He continuously assembled about him a group of competent men whom he groomed to become deacons, elders, and trustees. To them he also offered instruction regarding the management of a secular business and about being a leader in one's household. Most of the men he drew to him remained loyal, although two did level charges against him that led to the establishment of two splinter groups.[67]

Yet the two departmental directors voted at the Ninth Session were women. In fact, women delegates at that Session outnumbered men, and of the eighty-four people named as financial contributors to the Session seventy-one were women. Still, all six persons receiving ministerial credentials then were men, as were those who received ministerial licenses. Only three men out of a total of thirty obtained missionary licenses in New York.[68] These facts demonstrate that in spite of the fact that women provided much of the financial support for the Sabbath-Day Adventists, the organization's leadership was almost exclusively male.

Humphrey's report to the delegates at the Ninth Session shows that the organization was experiencing acute growing pains at the time. He bemoaned the lack of attendance at, and an interest in, the Sabbath School of the church. Pleading for at least 95 percent of members to attend, he cited numerical and financial growth of the church as the by-products of an increase in Sabbath School attendance. He called upon parents to encourage their children to attend, reminding parents that their children's attendance would "protect and preserve" them from the vices characteristic of large metropolitan areas and out of the nation's jails and prisons. Referring to his experience as a Seventh-day Adventist minister, Humphrey stated that Sabbath School attendees made the strongest church members. His slogan was "Every member of the church, a member of the Sabbath School; and every member of the Sabbath School, a member of the church." [69]

Not surprising, the lack of support for the Sabbath School had a negative impact on overall church attendance, a matter that was also dealt with at the Session. Believing that when they relocated interested members should inform the church of their whereabouts, delegates unanimously voted to conduct a membership inventory of all churches with a view to removing from membership lists anyone who had not been heard from in six months. Sabbath School attendance was also affirmed, with the delegates again voting unanimously to encourage members to support the Sabbath School with their attendance and involvement. Yet it was in the matter of financial responsibility that the Session spoke out most sternly, recommending that a special offering be donated for Humphrey to travel the country and West Indies to organize interested groups and that a sacrificial offering be collected quarterly to help promulgate the organization's outreach efforts.[70]

Financial challenges had an adverse effect on the group in more ways than one. They led to a reduction in the number of times the denomination's only paper, the *Messenger*, was to be published. Initially published every month, the *Messenger* began to be published quarterly in the late 1930s. Even so, continued lack of support for the paper from members caused the General Conference to go into debt with each publication, a situation Humphrey found totally unacceptable. Humphrey called on members to commit themselves to $1 a year to keep the periodical afloat. Yet financial challenges did not have a negative impact on the publication of the *Sabbath School Tutor*, the teaching journal of the organization that was published quarterly. A series of lessons centering around one theme that was intended to lead members to a deeper understanding of Scripture, the *Sabbath School Tutor* was must reading for all members. Recognizing the importance of studying the word, members rallied to Humphrey's cry to save the *Sabbath School Tutor*, with only one congregation refusing to pay its fair share of the cost of publishing the journal.

A major factor in Humphrey's break with the Seventh-day Adventist denomination had been the denomination's policy regarding church property. Humphrey could not accept that the title of properties owned by a local congregation had to be held by the local conference, the immediate governing entity of the organization. Yet at the Ninth Session of Sabbath-Day Adventists, the Constitution and By-Laws were amended to reflect the policy of the Seventh-day Adventists. Humphrey asked for and received a vote that the endorsement of the General Conference be procured before an organized United Sabbath-Day Adventist congregation could acquire or dispose of property. Moreover, such property would be part of the property of the General Conference. Much discussion attended these suggestions before they were voted, and the recommendation that the property of a defecting congregation be retained by the General Conference engendered even more discussion, no doubt because delegates viewed the recommendation in the context of their own experience within the Seventh-day Adventist organization. Still, delegates ultimately adopted the resolution by majority vote.[71]

EARLY CHALLENGES

Humphrey's problems with the Seventh-day Adventist church did not end in January 1930. One of the struggles United Sabbath-Day Adventists had with the Seventh-day Adventist denomination during the 1930s was for the property United Sabbath-Day Adventists believed was rightfully theirs. Quite understandably, Humphrey wanted the deed to the church building located at 141 West 131st Street turned over to his group. Sabbath-Day Adventists sued to recover the building, and a lower court sided with them. Yet the New York State Supreme Court reversed the lower court's decision, stating in its judgment that for the group to retrieve its property it would have to rejoin the Greater New York Conference of Seventh-day Adventists. Sabbath-Day Adventists refused, electing to stand in solidarity with Humphrey. In a move replete with irony, Humphrey's new congregation was forced to rent the building from the Baptist congregation that had purchased it.[72] An avalanche of negative emotions inundated Sabbath-Day Adventists as a result. Exacerbating the unhappiness, disgust, and resentment of the Sabbath-Day Adventists was the fact that promptly at 6 P.M. every Saturday janitors moved in to begin readying the facility for the Sunday morning services of the landlord. Often interrupted, if not aborted, by this practice was the Youth Meeting. Yet one of the practice's enduring legacies is the support it gave to the erroneous notions that the Sabbath begins at 6 P.M. on Friday and ends at the same time on Saturday.[73]

Sabbath-Day Adventists had a difficult time procuring adequate, affordable facilities in which to worship in New York City during the 1930s, and the Great Depression conspired with other factors to make their quest more difficult. Their General Conference session of 1938 met in rented quarters for which they paid twenty dollars per Sabbath, the "heavy financial burden" causing them to groan. The following year they were able to convene the session in their own facility, a fifty-thousand-dollar structure that they had purchased for twenty-seven thousand dollars with a down payment of three thousand and a twenty-four-thousand-dollar mortgage at 4 percent interest. The building, located at 36–38 135th Street, became home to the New York congregation and the headquarters of the General Conference.[74]

Today the New York United Sabbath-Day Adventist congregation worships in a structure they funded themselves. Completed three years after their founding pastor died, the one-story stone and brick structure is located on 110th Street in Manhattan, just across the street from Central Park North. As such, it is a prized piece of real estate that is well kept. The sanctuary on the first floor seats approximately four hundred, and in the basement is a spacious fellowship hall and several offices, including the pastor's study. Huge pictures of some of the first General Conference sessions of the United Sabbath-Day Adventists adorn the walls of the fellowship hall. The pictures tell a poignant tale of the origins of the group and serve as a stark reminder of the birth pangs it experienced. United Sabbath-Day Adventists are proud of their facility, which has the distinction of being the only Adventist church building in New York City that was not purchased from another organization.

Conspicuously displayed on the walls in the narthex of the building are plaques bearing images of Humphrey. Identified as the pastor of the organization from 1929 to 1952, Humphrey is eulogized as a great leader who was "faithful unto death." Another plaque places the date of the organization of the church as 1936 but does not cite Humphrey as its founder. To be sure, Humphrey's name and image are also on that plaque, leaving one to imply that he was the founder. Yet that Humphrey was pastor and not founder of the group underscores an important point in Adventist ecclesiology. That point is that God and not a human being is the foundation of his church.

Sabbath-Day Adventists did not only face challenges from without but from within as well. Almost from their inception, United Sabbath-Day Adventists experienced internal conflict. To be sure, the squabbles never imperiled their existence or dampened their determination to press on. Still, they consumed time and resources and detracted from the primary objective of the group. It appears that as early as 1934 the Sabbath-Day Adventists organization became caught up in the throes of a power struggle. At the Fourth Annual Convention of the General Conference, held May 18–27, 1934, R. Leo Soaries, vice-president; Hubert Gauntlett, secretary; and P. J. Bailey and C. J. Lewis, editor and assistant editor of the *Messenger* respectively, were all removed from office and church membership. No reasons for the actions were ever divulged, although notice of them was given in the January 1935 edition of the *Messenger*.[75] Also at the Fourth Annual Convention, Humphrey's title was changed from president to moderator of the Session. Saying it regretted that some members were not present at the Session and thereby were unable to hear the discussion that resulted in the action, William Samuels, the newly elected secretary of the General Conference, informed readers that "it was decided that the word 'President' is more political than religious." Samuels, who succeeded Humphrey as leader of the organization in 1947, claimed that the only religious body that used the term for its chief officer was the Seventh-day Adventists and that since moderator denotes a chairman, "it seems to us more fitting than the word 'President.'"[76] That the change in Humphrey's designation, at least for General Conference sessions, may have been the result of a power struggle is a reasonable inference given the fact that years later Samuels, when he became the leader of the denomination, assumed the title of "President."[77]

The immediate impact of the departure of Soaries, Gauntlett, Bailey, and Lewis could be seen in the appearance and content of the *Messenger*. The January 1935 issue of the paper carried only one picture, that of James K. Humphrey on the front page. Humphrey's caption identified him as moderator of the United Sabbath-Day Adventists. Noticeably absent were the reports from around the field and articles challenging readers to a higher level of living. The issue was half the length of previous editions and listed Humphrey and Samuels as its new editor and the assistant editor respectively. A lengthy, detailed article painstakenly detailing the activities of a recent "Man's Day Program" at New York United and naming the twenty-eight individuals who planned and executed the event suggests that the new editor may have been desperate for material. An "Aunt Lou" appealed for stories for children, and even the article on the edition's front page, a "New Year Greeting" penned by Humphrey, seemed lackluster.

Sometime between their 1938 and 1939 General Conference sessions, the Chicago congregation withdrew from the organization's sisterhood of churches, the reasons for the group's action never being tendered or divulged to the delegates at the 1939 Session. Humphrey did inform the delegates to this Session that the organization had not heard from congregations in Jacksonville, Fresno, and Boston.[78] One year later, a major split of the New York congregation occurred. Centering around allegations of financial and marital improprieties by Humphrey, the split was a major blow to the organization. Yet to this day the few individuals who were a part of New York United at the time resolutely defend Humphrey. To them he was a leader of unassailable character, though, admittedly, a human being subject to temptations, as all people are. Early in the tenure of Humphrey's successor another group left to form their own church because members disagreed with the new leader's recommendation that tithe funds be used with the proceeds from the sale of the building on West 135th Street to procure property on which to build a church.[79]

To this day, speculation abounds about Humphrey's marriage, with detractors claiming that Humphrey was an incurable womanizer who maintained a formal relationship with his wife only to preserve his position as founding minister of the Sabbath-Day Adventists. Humphrey's wife, Viola R. Humphrey, remained with her husband until her death. Fully aware of the rumors about her husband's philandering, she responded with stoic dignity and grace, telling those close to her that it was difficult being married to a minister. Yet the difficulty was due to the long hours and unpredictability of the ministry and not to her relationship with her husband. Violet Humphrey did not work outside the home but was an untiring worker for the church. She founded the Women's Week and superintended the Sabbath School on numerous occasions.[80]

The *United Sabbath-Day Messenger* kept the face of Mrs. Humphrey before readers, once captioning her as the "Wife of the President, who has stood faithfully by him for over 30 years."[81] The picture of the "First Lady" was of a serene, confident woman devoid of the trappings of worldly success. Like her husband, Mrs. Humphrey shunned fanfare and ostentation, weaving her hair simply yet stylishly in the bun fashion of the day. At the Ninth Session of the General Conference of United Sabbath-Day Adventists, Ada Daley, a New York delegate, singled out Humphrey's wife for her "courageous spirit." Mrs. Humphrey had been among the first to address the delegates, declaring that she was thankful for her role in the organization. She introduced several motions at the Session and was elected to direct the Sabbath School department.[82]

Humphrey had one child with Violet Humphrey, a daughter they named Ruth. Always referred to as "My Ruthie" by Humphrey, she was quick-witted, intelligent, and outspoken. Ruth graduated from college and pursued a career in nursing, later working for the United States Army. She was a registered Democrat and community activist who marched and picketed, claiming that she derived her activist proclivities from the father she adored. Ruth married twice and lost several babies at delivery. Humphrey's progeny ended with Ruth, yet Ruth claimed that her father had other children, and she traveled to Jamaica on numerous occasions to search for a brother she had heard lived there. It is unclear whether she ever met this person, although she often shipped foodstuff and other commodities to Jamaica addressed to him.[83]

Humphrey's detractors have been prone to cite his challenges from both within and without the religious organization he founded as proof that his judgment was rash and unsanctified, and that his move to splinter from the Seventh-day Adventist denomination was ill-advised. Yet in facing these challenges Humphrey was following in the tradition of other Black religious leaders who founded independent churches. Richard Allen, the first Black religious leader to splinter from a predominantly White church and establish an independent body, certainly faced his share of challenges. According to Albert Raboteau, "interdenominational squabbles and church politics harassed Allen's entire ministry." Raboteau asserts that Allen "aroused his share of jealousy and animosity," even being accused on one occasion of mishandling church funds while serving as a church treasurer. Not all Blacks in the Methodist Church left to join Allen's new group; some viewed Allen as "ambitious and opportunistic," and on at least one occasion Allen was spat upon by a Black rival while he was preaching.[84]

THE THEOLOGY OF JAMES K. HUMPHREY

Born in Jamaica, James K. Humphrey came to America in search of a better life. Here he heard stories of what the American brand of slavery had been like, and here he experienced firsthand Jim Crow practices that provoked his racial consciousness. He lived through World War I, the Harlem Renaissance, the stock market crash, the Great Depression, World War II, and the start of the cold war. The first half of the twentieth century was a period of upheaval and "Hard Times" interspersed with stints of glamour and vigor. When Humphrey died, America was entering the "Fabulous Fifties."

A product of his times, James K. Humphrey was not trained in theology and may never have attended a seminary for ministerial instruction. Yet as a minister he performed with distinction and exhibited an appreciable knowledge of the Bible. His theological understanding was grounded in the Bible, which was his standard and rule. Humphrey believed that "the Bible and the Bible only is the indisputable word of God." "There is no other book upon which the world may depend for the gospel but the Bible," he said. He appealed to his members to live up to "the truths of the gospel brought forth in God's holy book."[85]

Humphrey held that history was purposeful, with events moving inexorably toward a definite goal. He based his belief on the "biblical" passage: "There is a time and place for everything under the sun."[86] For Humphrey, time was about to run out. His was earth's last generation, making the preaching of the gospel of the kingdom an urgent matter. "Jesus Christ is very near at hand," Humphrey affirmed, calling upon followers to "prepare the people to meet this solemn event." Yet to do so meant paying heed to and proclaiming God's Ten Commandments Law, especially the fourth, which "calls upon every man, woman and child to remember the Sabbath Day which is the seventh day of the week (Saturday) to keep it holy." Humphrey contended that Scripture contained no warrant or backing for the observance of Sunday as the Bible Sabbath.[87]

For Humphrey, the time was right for "members of the Ethiopian race" to take "a pure and true gospel" to the world. To be sure, the gospel was not the exclusive property of any race or group of people. Yet it had been bequeathed to the "dark-skinned peoples of the world who have been slighted and segregated and discriminated against by both Jews and Gentiles." God, in his providence and wisdom, had elevated "downtrodden and despised" Blacks by giving them an opportunity "to help themselves in the knowledge of the Gospel of the kingdom of the Lord Jesus Christ." It was now the "duty and obligation" of the people of African descent to promulgate the gospel.[88]

Referencing Genesis 10:1–5, the bishop posited that Jews had descended from Japheth and were once the chosen people of God but that they had been replaced when, believing themselves better than the rest of humankind, they had failed to share their knowledge of God. Subsequently, God conscripted the Gentiles for service. Yet the Gentiles had failed "just as lamentably as the Jews," discriminating against both Jews and Blacks and becoming in the process "unfit to proclaim the gospel." It had become the lot of Blacks to preach the gospel, and Humphrey, as an "Apostle to the Negro race," felt constrained to "point out the prophecies that relate to the dark-skinned peoples of the world in the call to give the closing message to mankind." This call to service humbled the bishop, who believed that all people were to be addressed with the gospel, even though some would reject it.[89]

Humphrey believed that the worldwide economic depression was the direct result of humanity's selfishness. One reason he believed this was because he understood God to be omnipotent and, as such, able to supply all the temporal needs of the human family. The Depression was viewed as an embarrassment to individuals and entire nations alike, with England and the United States the two main culprits. As a consequence, these two nations were primarily responsible for implementing the drastic measures needed to deal with the crippling effects of the Depression. The selfishness of humanity was at variance with the love and benevolence of God, which, coupled with his power and mercy, were reason for thanksgiving. Yet the Thanksgiving season of 1931 would be marred because of the crippling effects of the Depression.[90]

Humphrey thought World War II was a fulfillment of Bible prophecy and a sure sign that the end of human history was imminent. To be sure, war had always been a fact of human existence, with nations and empires rising and falling by war. Yet World War II was a unique conflagration in which new artillery was being used for the first time, causing the bishop to cast and view the war in apocalyptic images. His fundamentalism showing, Humphrey saw no safety or deliverance for the faithful in human ingenuity but in God, who was an ever-present recourse and refuge. Moreover, in spite of the breathtaking inventions of humanity, the victory of God's people was guaranteed. The bishop did not advise congregants if they should enlist in the armed forces or seek employment in any industry directly tied to the war.[91] Yet Humphrey supported the New Testament teaching that Christians ought to support their governments and leaders, leaving members with the impression that the church would not look with disfavor upon those who enlisted in the armed forces or worked in the defense industry.

According to Ucilla La Condre, Humphrey claimed he had received information from the Spirit of God about World War II and some of the political, social, and economic developments that would occur during and as a result of the conflict.[92] She says that he urged members to pray, keeping them informed about the war as it progressed. In addition, he appraised members of other social issues, including the civil rights movement then emerging. The bishop may have been in agreement with the New Testament teaching that Christians should be supportive of their leaders and governments, but he approved of civil disobedience as a legitimate strategy to call attention to the inequities in society. La Condre avows that Humphrey believed that people who were angry as a result of being oppressed should register their anger in tangible, recognizable ways. Yet he condemned the looting that often accompanied civil disobedience, saying that looters were lawbreakers who should be arrested, prosecuted, and imprisoned.[93]

That Humphrey was not a crusader who espoused views that pushed the boundaries of the church is seen in elements other than his preaching style, which was anything but the animated, expressive type of many Black preachers in Harlem at the time. Evidence of the bishop's conservatism is seen in some of the policies he adopted. For example, Humphrey allowed no one who was not in full agreement with the doctrines and practices of the denomination to teach in the Sabbath School department. Freedom of thought did not apply in this regard, his teachers having to march to the drumbeat of conformity to the organization's policies. To be sure, for Humphrey this was a matter of setting the right example for the rest of the membership. The same principle applied to the support of the church through the tithes and offerings. Humphrey resolutely refused to allow anyone delinquent in remitting a faithful tithe and returning a freewill offering to hold a church office. The bishop also spoke out against the practice of some of his branch churches of using the tithe for reasons other than for that of remunerating clergy, asserting that such a practice was contrary to God's plan. In addition, he bewailed the fact that some United Sabbath-Day Adventist ministers had to work at other jobs to sustain themselves, a contingency he held was in opposition to the biblical Old Testament model.[94]

Like Seventh-day Adventists, Humphrey made a sharp distinction between the use that could be made of tithes and offerings. The tithe was to be used exclusively for the support of the credentialed and licensed clergy. Humphrey appealed to the Melchizedek model of the Old Testament Scriptures for warrant and backing for his position.[95] He said that Jesus was now the High Priest of the Christian, and, as such, desired to see "his ministers kept on the job by the faithfulness of His people bringing their tithes into the storehouse." Offerings were intended either for foreign or home missions. As the former, they were to be used beyond the precincts of the church that generated them; home mission offerings could be used to meet the operating expenses of the local congregation, including the salaries of church personnel other than the minister.[96] Founded around the stock market crash and weaned during the Great Depression, the Sabbath-Day Adventist organization struggled to meet its financial obligations throughout its history. Consequently, Humphrey and his leaders were forced to utilize fund-raising techniques that did not reflect biblical stewardship principles. For example, La Condre recalls that Sabbath School classes competed with each other for the honor of raising the most money. Members utilized financial rallies to solicit funds from relatives and friends, often taking to the streets to canvass well-wishers and sympathizers, too. Still, members were encouraged to commit sacrificially to the church and some went into debt to do so.[97]

Humphrey prized young people, whom he believed faced an inordinate amount of temptation to evil. He frowned upon the penchant of adults to condemn youth for the "frivolity and fickleness" that often come about because of their distaste for religion, reminding the adults that they were still in the process of becoming, too. At the same time, adults were not to give blanket endorsement to the activities of youth and were not to indulge their every whim and fancy. Youth needed to be taught, and it was incumbent on adults to mentor and model for them. Of special concern to Humphrey was the practice of parents of criticizing the church and its leadership in the presence of children. Such a practice almost always engendered profound feelings of apathy in youth, whose parents would then seek out the bishop to decry their children's attitude. Humphrey reminded parents that their most effective teaching was a life that exemplified the truths and principles they expected their posterity to emulate.[98]

Citing the economic crisis then gripping the world as proof that governments and nations were unable to provide meaningful relief for the critical challenges and issues of life and that past successes do not guarantee future triumphs, the bishop believed that the youth of society constituted the best hope for the future of the church and the world. He called upon churches to partner and collaborate with homes to "understand the thoughts, feelings, interests, and actions of the youths committed to their care." With a view to making Christianity "real, practical, and meaningful," Sabbath-Day Adventist youth systematically visited the sick and suffering, leaving behind cheer and goodwill. The New York congregation often partnered with other congregations in these humanitarian services, realizing that in unity there is strength.[99]

A COMPARATIVE ANALYSIS OF SEVENTH-DAY ADVENTISTS AND SABBATH-DAY ADVENTISTS

James K. Humphrey and the United Sabbath-Day Adventists may have splintered from the Seventh-day Adventist denomination in name, but not much in theology, ecclesiology, or church polity and organization. The bishop's troubles with the Seventh-day Adventist church did not center around these elements, a fact that made for much similarity between Sabbath-Day Adventists and Seventh-day Adventists.[100] Sabbath-Day Adventists did hammer out a set of "fundamental beliefs," frowning, like their Seventh-day Adventist counterparts, upon the notion of dogmas and creeds. They opted for the less problematic term, *fundamental beliefs*, to designate the set of biblical truths and doctrines they considered critical mass for membership in the organization, and a comparison of the fundamental beliefs of the two religious groups shows many similarities. Yet it is possible that Sabbath-Day Adventists do not believe that the prophetic gift was bestowed on Ellen G. White, something the group's Fundamental Beliefs do not address. Little editing or updating of their fundamental beliefs has been done by Sabbath-Day Adventists since their adoption. This is also true of their Constitution, which was ratified by 1936.[101]

The idea that Sabbath-Day Adventists do not believe that Ellen G. White was an authentic prophet may have been fueled by Humphrey himself. To be sure, Humphrey initially believed in the authority of Ellen G. White, who was a contemporary of his for almost two decades of his association with the Seventh-day Adventist denomination. It is uncertain whether the two ever met,[102] but it is true that Humphrey became increasingly disillusioned with White's counsel on the race issue. It is also true that there was one significant development in the bishop's teaching and preaching after his break with the Seventh-day Adventist organization. Noticeably absent was an emphasis on Ellen G. White as an authoritative prophet sent by God with an urgent message for earth's last generation. Humphrey never quoted Ellen G. White to augment the material in his church's Sabbath School booklet. This fact alone made the publication stand out in sharp contradistinction to the *Sabbath School Lesson Quarterly* published by the Seventh-day Adventists, which is always buttressed with quotations from Ellen White. More significant, Humphrey, unlike most Seventh-day Adventist preachers, never used Ellen White in any of his sermons. For him the Bible was the only source he needed, and it required no outside interpretation or elaboration. The bishop painstakingly stressed the difference between the writings of Ellen G. White and the Holy Scriptures and argued that White was to be used and understood as a reference only. For him, White's works could never approximate the canonicity of the Holy Bible. Humphrey did so good a job at explaining the difference between the writings of White and the Bible that some members concluded that their leader neither believed in nor accepted her works.[103] Others have asserted that the founding pastor's position on Ellen G. White is the main reason the Sabbath-Day Adventists have never been able to reconcile with Seventh-day Adventists.[104]

Sabbath-Day Adventists were comfortable with most of the doctrines and teachings of the Seventh-day Adventist church, their theological beliefs not just approximating those of their former associates but mirroring them. Sabbath-Day Adventists accepted the teaching of the Holy Spirit as the third member of the Trinity, emphasizing that a belief in, and, more important, a reception of the Holy Spirit did not entail glossolalia[105] or the emotional outbursts that others claimed it did. They believed in the imminency of the Second Coming of Jesus Christ, salvation through faith in Jesus Christ alone, the efficacy of Christian stewardship, and the power of the gospel to transform lives and characters through the indwelling of the Holy Spirit. Obedience to the Ten Commandments of God continued to receive special emphasis from them, as did faith in Jesus Christ. As Christians everywhere, they desired to see the gospel preached around the world, believing that transformed lives on earth offered a glimpse and foretaste of life in the world to come.[106]

Like Seventh-day Adventists, United Sabbath-Day Adventists believed that the gospel of the kingdom was to be preached to everyone as a prelude to the second advent of Jesus Christ. The objective of the gospel is to prepare people to live at peace with God in a society ruled by God. Given first to the Jews, the gospel was then directed to the Gentiles, who, after two millennia, had failed as miserably as the Jews to execute the mandate. Segregation and discrimination were two of the evidences of this failure, Sabbath-Day Adventists held. Yet Sabbath-Day Adventists took their theology of the gospel farther. They held that as had happened with the Jews, the gospel was retrieved from the Gentiles and given to the dark-skinned peoples of the world, who, fully aware that civilization was in its eleventh hour, were working feverishly to alert all people that "the coming king is at the door." [107]

Not surprising, the sanctity of the Sabbath was an item on which both groups agreed. While Humphrey contended that Sabbath keeping did not inherently contain any soteriological or salvific properties, he believed that it was the single most distinguishing feature of his group. He often reminded members of this fact, imploring them to exercise maximum care with the start and conclusion of the Sabbath, when people are prone to violate the Sabbath. In encouraging greater fidelity in Sabbath keeping, Humphrey cautioned against the temptation to lapse into spiritual pride or the "holier-than-thou" attitude of many Christians who fall victim to a "works theology." Yet he asserted that more faithfulness in Sabbath keeping would engender conversions among neighbors, whom the bishop believed were hungry for truth. Getting people to keep the Sabbath was Humphrey's focus, and the spiritual leader of the Sabbath-Day Adventists preferred that the heretofore unchurched joined his congregation rather than former Seventh-day Adventists disgruntled with their organization. [108]

An emphasis was placed on Bible study by United Sabbath-Day Adventists, who bemoaned the unacceptably high level of biblical illiteracy among the population in general and youth in particular. Members took special note of the results of a test that had been conducted some time earlier among the "best families" that revealed an ignorance of biblical knowledge thought to be elementary by Sabbath-Day Adventists. Believing that knowledge of the Holy Scriptures benefited people both spiritually and socially, United Sabbath-Day Adventists sought to engender a love for the Bible among its members by offering a plethora of opportunities for its study. More important, Humphrey anchored his preaching in the Bible, unapologetically pointing members to the Bible's primacy and potency and reminding them that the Bible supplied powerful antidotes for the vicissitudes and voids of life. [109]

One tool used to encourage Sabbath-Day Adventists to study the Bible was the *Sabbath School Tutor*. Authored by Humphrey and with the text "Thy Word is a Lamp unto my feet, and a light unto my Path—Psalm 119:105," the *Sabbath School Tutor* was a virtual spinoff of the *Sabbath School Lesson Quarterly* of the Seventh-day Adventists. Its lessons consisted of a main passage of Scripture to be memorized, and a series of questions followed by a verse of Scripture that supplied the answers. Little supplementary material was used, although, from the way the material was presented, one could detect the influence of outside sources. The lessons were well-written and attractively presented, each lesson ending with a thought provoking question on a practical element of faith, and a reminder that members not forget to support the Thirteenth Sabbath offering.[110] Each *Sabbath School Tutor* contained a review of the quarter's lessons and a series of lessons for the youth, too.[111]

Sabbath-Day Adventists also believed in the primacy and power of prayer. For them, God was capable of doing anything, including restoring health to the sick. God was an unchanging God, who, to the extent of the faith exercised in him, could repeat any of the miraculous feats recorded in sacred Scripture. An objective of United Sabbath-Day Adventists was relating to God in such a way that they would be in a position to receive from him spiritual help and physical healing. Believing that the human being is an integrated whole, the bishop sought to bring spiritual, social, and physical healing to his members. In keeping with the biblical injunction found in James 5:12, the bishop prayed for the sick, anointing them as he laid hands on them. Humphrey also believed in the power of God to bring deliverance to demon-possessed people. Yet the bishop's anointing and liberating services were not like the flamboyant ones practiced by some of the African American preachers of the era.[112]

According to members of the congregation, uncommon phenomena were known to occur at New York United. On one occasion while Humphrey was preaching about spiritualism, a strange figure assumed a position behind him and began to tap him on the shoulder. Humphrey tried brushing the hand away, finally spinning around to see who was trying to distract or interrupt him. As mysteriously as the figure had appeared, it disappeared. On another occasion an impeccably dressed man entered the church as the bishop was preaching and sat down on a chair behind him on the rostrum. Tall and handsome, the stranger, who vanished without a trace during the service, caused a commotion among the young women. Members interpreted both incidents as extraordinary phenomena orchestrated by the devil himself.[113]

In matters of lifestyle, Sabbath-Day Adventists did not always live what they preached and believed. For example, in the area of dress members early demonstrated a stubborn independence, opting to wear jewelry, even though the absence of such was a hallmark of Seventh-day Adventism at the time.[114]

United Sabbath-Day Adventists continued more than the doctrinal traditions of the Seventh-day Adventists, perpetuating also many of the programs, ministries, and organizational structure of their former associates. For example, the Sabbath-Day Adventists continued the annual Fall Week of Prayer, publishing the readings for the week in their official organ, the *United Sabbath-Day Adventist Messenger*, in much the same way as Seventh-day Adventists published their readings in the *Review and Herald*, their official organ. Yet it was in structuring their congregations like the Seventh-day Adventists that Humphrey showed a disinclination to veer away from his former church in discernible and distinguishable ways. The religious services and ministries of United Sabbath-Day Adventists were like those of Seventh-day Adventists. In addition, Humphrey grouped his congregations together in conferences, calling his flagship · group in New York City the General Conference. Like Seventh-day Adventists, he convened General Conference sessions, holding his sessions annually for the first decade of the organization's existence. To be sure, other Protestant organizations are structured along similar lines to this day. Still, given Humphrey's experience within the Seventh-day Adventist organization and the deep-seated feelings of disappointment and disillusionment engendered as a result, his decision to maintain so much of the Seventh-day Adventist church is noteworthy. Indeed, the similarities between the two religious bodies have created confusion among the uninformed, and not a few individuals have associated with the United Sabbath-Day Adventists thinking they had joined the Seventh-day Adventist church.[115]

In the end, Humphrey's troubles with the Seventh-day Adventist church did not center around the denomination's theology or with its ecclesiology; his preaching remained mainstream Adventist, and his orthodoxy did not veer much to the left or right of Seventh-day Adventism's fundamental beliefs. In spite of the negative experiences he had had in the Seventh-day Adventist denomination, James K. Humphrey never publicly condemned or spoke ill of the denomination. In the pulpit he was all dignity and decorum. The bishop never used the "sacred desk" as a vantage point from which to lob verbal assaults or denunciations. When the situation warranted it, Humphrey did use the pulpit to deny allegations of wrongdoing leveled at him. He also tried to clear up some of the controversy surrounding Ellen White's counsels regarding African Americans from the pulpit. Even then, he was not harsh or accusatory but civil, choosing to remain busy "preaching the word."[116]

A Comparison of J. K. Humphrey and Black Religious Leaders

How does James Kemuel Humphrey compare to some of the Black religious leaders in whose tradition he followed? The most celebrated of those leaders, of course, is Richard Allen, who left the Methodist Church and formed the African Methodist Episcopal denomination. Allen's break with the established church continues to this day to inspire and enthrall admirers and detractors alike. Allen was a practical theologian, for whom "theology, in its practical manifestations, should mean the liberation from oppression and injustice of people whose hopes had previously been directed to the City of God rather than the City of Man." When Allen perceived that "Methodist theology was not going to be applied to the solution of black problems," he concluded that "such theology was meaningless theology." Indeed, any "theology that failed to deal with earthly oppression was not a viable one." Though Allen is credited with starting the first independent Black religious organization, the truth is that other Blacks before him had tried. Allen succeeded where others had failed by a combination of sheer will, ambition, charisma, and leadership.[117]

Richard Allen, like J. K. Humphrey, believed in hard work, thrift, modesty, and simplicity. As Allen neared his death, he could attest to the fact that he had received no handouts from his new organization. Recognizing that providing for one's own family was not enough, Allen had established several charities to address some of the social pathologies and ills that then permeated the Philadelphian community. Allen was all for self-help organizations and, believing that there was a direct link between morality and prosperity, called African Americans up to a higher moral existence. Such a life, Allen believed, would give a lie to the negative stereotypical image Whites harbored about Blacks and would contribute to Black race pride. To the end, Allen's leadership, like that of Humphrey, was pastoral. Like Humphrey, Allen shunned show and ostentation, eschewing the life of flamboyance for that of sobriety and plainness, which is not to say that either man lived a dull life.[118]

Allen may have pioneered in the establishment of the African Methodist Episcopal (AME) Church, but it was Henry McNeal Turner, one of America's prominent Black leaders between the Civil War and World War I, who had a profound impact not only on the AME church but on African American religion as well. After Turner, the AME church was a national movement. Born free in 1834 in South Carolina, Turner joined the Methodist church in 1848, switching to the AME at the behest of William R. Revels years later because of what Turner perceived as the Methodist church's lack of fervor in working among African Americans. Turner went on to serve the AME denomination for fifty-seven years, rising to the rank of bishop and commanding the respect and admiration of all who came to know him.[119]

Turner was a Black nationalist who believed that "every colored man in this country who is not proud of himself, his color, his hair, and his general make up is a monstrosity." He regarded such a Black person as a curse to himself and his posterity, saying he was "no lower than a brute, and does not deserve the breath he breathes, much less the bread he eats." He continued: "Any man, though he be as black as midnight, who regards himself inferior to any other man that God ever made, is simply a walking ghoul and ought to join his invisible companions at the first opportunity."[120]

Turner was fiery and combative like Marcus Garvey after him, and though he may have come across as uncompromising, he knew when to be accommodating. Like Garvey and Humphrey, he rose from humble beginnings to become a leader of his people, and he never forgot that. Turner was fundamentalist in his understanding and interpretation of the Bible and was particularly drawn to the Exodus event, the story representing "both the culmination and cornerstone" of his theology. He was disturbed by the theological significance of Whiteness, refusing to sing hymns that equated whiteness with purification, and he saw no wrong in mixing politics and religion, serving briefly in the Georgia Legislature and associating with Black and White politicians all his life.[121]

Turner's Black nationalism morphed into a stubborn emigrationism that called for African Americans to return to Africa, something for which James K. Humphrey never called. Turner was uncompromising in his calls for Blacks to return to Africa, though he wanted only the best and the brightest among Blacks to do so, and he resolutely opposed other Black leaders such as Booker T. Washington, who embraced the ethic of accommodation. For Turner, no compromise was to be made as far as a person's dignity was concerned, and not until Marcus Garvey came along did any Black leader speak out as forcefully as Turner had, claiming that Blacks had as much right to self-definition and self-determination as any other race. Yet, in spite of his calls for Blacks to return to Africa, Turner never did so himself. Turner called for the repatriation of Blacks to Africa not because he was a separatist but rather because Turner concluded that, at least in America, Blacks and Whites could not peacefully live together.

Like Humphrey, Turner's was a practical theology that resisted neat, clear categories that could be codified or written down. Ever pragmatic and complex, both men believed in a God who acted on behalf of the oppressed and exploited and that God was just and benevolent. Long before James Cone declared that Jesus was Black, Turner believed that for Blacks God had to be Black. Paradoxically, Turner did not see Jesus as such, his view of Jesus reflective of that which most African Americans had at that time. Yet Turner was suspicious of the Bible as translated by Whites and believed that the Black community needed a translation of the Bible that spoke to the community's needs. Short of that, the Bible was ever to be read with a sniff of suspicion by Blacks.[122]

Tunde Adeleke views Bishop Turner as a standout among the Black nationalists that permeated the late nineteenth to early twentieth century, arguing that Turner's "disdain and hatred for White values" approximated those of Marcus Garvey and that they both "perceived American society as inherently and irredeemably racist." With his eyes fixed on the African continent, Turner held up emigration to Africa as the panacea for the African American's troubles, and he believed that extinction was the only viable alternative to emigration. For Turner, integration was untenable because it required that one sacrifice one's dignity, and he believed that self-determination was the truest and most telling evidence that one had been civilized.[123]

Another outstanding late–nineteenth century African American religious leader who had similarities with James K. Humphrey was Francis J. Grimke. Born on November 4, 1850, in South Carolina to a White slaveowner and Black slave woman, Francis Grimke went on to study law at Howard University after graduating from Lincoln University in Pennsylvania in 1870 as valedictorian of his class. He aborted law school for the ministry, studying at prestigious Princeton University before embarking on a distinguished career as a Presbyterian minister. Grimke's passion was pastoral ministry, so much so that he declined the presidency of Howard University to remain a pastor. Grimke was a moralist with firm, unbending standards for behavior. For him, character determined the value of people more than their heredity or earthly possessions. Like Bishop

Turner, Grimke did not harbor the accommodationist tendencies of Booker T. Washington, though all three believed that Blacks were morally bound to seek to improve themselves. And Grimke went further, asserting that Blacks who were educated had a greater responsibility to help those less educated.[124]

Grimke differed from Richard Allen and James K. Humphrey in one significant regard. As a Black minister in a predominantly White denomination, Grimke did not leave his church, and even though his voice remained prophetic to the end, challenging Whites to repent of their racist tendencies and practices, Grimke, of necessity, had to be on at least cordial terms with his White peers. Grimke also attempted to prove that Blacks were equal to Whites by relocating to an all-White neighborhood. The subsequent flight of his White neighbors proved to him that White racism, at least at that time, was based on the color of one's skin and not on the content of one's character or economic status. Grimke's educational accomplishments also got in the way of his attempts to motivate Blacks, though his experience in this regard did not cause him to stop thinking that everybody could achieve.[125]

Perhaps Grimke remained a Presbyterian to the end in spite of the undeniable wrongs committed against African Americans because of the premium he placed on loyalty, which he claimed had always been a hallmark of the Black experience in America. Grimke believed that the African American, who had been "oppressed, down trodden, discriminated against, denied even the common civilities of life," was "always ready to stretch forth his strong black arm in defense of the Nation." Though Grimke was hard pressed to explain what he thought was a seemingly axiomatic truth, he claimed that this fact was more true than for any other racial group in America. Grimke called upon African Americans to put the good of the national community before their personal interests, obviously seeing greater value in expediency than in principle.[126]

No mainstream African American religious leaders had as telling and enduring an impact on early twentieth century Harlem as Adam Clayton Powell Sr. and Adam Clayton Powell Jr. The senior Powell was a light-skinned Black who escaped abject poverty in Virginia and West Virginia to become pastor of the Abyssinian Baptist Church in New York City about the time Adam Clayton Powell Jr. was born. The senior Powell, to his enduring credit, relocated the Abyssinian congregation from mid-town Manhattan to Harlem at the start of the "Roaring Twenties" as both Marcus Garvey and the Harlem Renaissance were about to take root in Harlem. The move of the Abyssinian congregation to Harlem was not without controversy; the senior Powell threatened to resign if his congregants did not forsake "their penny-pinching" penchants, which imperiled their move to Harlem. The reticence of his parishioners, the pastor believed, indicated that they did not believe "in progressive and aggressive leadership." In 1937, when the senior Powell finally gave up the leadership of Abyssinian Baptist Church over the vehement objections of the church's Deacon Board, which wanted him to continue as pastor, he had achieved iconoclastic status among African American religious leaders.[127]

The senior Powell was critical of American Christianity, branding it unorthodox and hypocritical and contending that together with America's foreign polity, it wrecked havoc on the cause of God and democracy. He believed that only a person who has "purged himself of all hatred toward all fellow men" can be fully aware of God. Outward display does not engender a relationship with God. Yet Powell claimed to disbelieve that the Bible was the word of God because it was "too filled with contradictions." For him, truth does not contradict, and since God is a God of truth, the Bible should cohere. Powell asserted that the Bible was a work in progress to the extent that people continue to encounter God and hear God's truth on reading it. He refused to be caught up in theological debates concerning events surrounding the birth, life, and ministry of Jesus and was opposed to any discussion that sundered instead of united the family of God.[128]

The emergence of Adam Clayton Powell Jr. as a Harlem leader began in the spring of 1931, about the same time as the organization of the United Sabbath-Day Adventists. The junior Powell officially entered the ministry on April 24, 1931, his installation service bringing together a cadre of other ministers and well-wishers. That spring, five Black doctors were fired from Harlem Hospital, by then the African American community's leading, if not only, medical institution in the area. At city hall, the younger Powell led a demonstration protesting the firings as well as the deplorable conditions at the hospital, and the event catapulted him into the city's limelight as an activist minister determined to better the lot of his people. When he assumed leadership of Abyssinian in 1937, Powell was thought by some to be too radical for the leadership of the church, which, throughout the Depression, was heavily involved in humanitarian and relief work in Harlem. Seven years later, Powell was elected to Congress and became the undisputable spokesperson for the Harlem community and one of its most extraordinary leaders.

In Adam Clayton Powell Jr. was wrapped up pastor and politician, and he saw no cleavage between the two.[129] Flamboyant, debonair, urbane, and educated, the younger Powell was a gifted orator whose words wooed and won over even detractors. Marcus Garvey was jet black and claimed that there was not an ounce of White blood in him. Powell, who was unsure of his ancestry, could, and in his early life did, pass for White. As an elected Congressman, Powell became a credible, potent force to be reckoned with, and he had personal conferences with presidents and United States and world statesmen. James K. Humphrey spoke up for his people on the local stage, but Powell spoke authoritatively with others on the national and world stage. What all these Black religious leaders had in common was a sense of self and the magnitude of the moment. They knew that history was beckoning to them, issuing a call they could not resist.

For Adam Clayton Powell Jr., "America is not a Christian country. It is a country of pretensions, of 'churchianity,' where the institution of Christianity has been perverted into an instrument to perpetrate if not to propagate, directly and indirectly, anti-Christian doctrines of segregation and discrimination." He believed that "the only Christian church in the United States are those churches that, at all levels, welcome and encourage the participation of all the sons of God." [130] This view of America led Powell to conclude that African Americans would be the people to salvage America because Whites lacked the "moral capacity to take the initiative in guaranteeing racial justice." [131]

Powell never claimed that God or Jesus is Black, neither is he on record as saying that Black people are inherently or innately better or superior to White people. He did assert that the religion of African Americans is "more mature" than that of Whites. He refused to endorse the notion that the religion of the African American was an emotional roller coaster devoid of theological substance and integrity, arguing that because "religion is a joyful thing" there is a time and place for the emotional in religion, and he pointed out that the fervency of the religion of America's Pilgrim Fathers had atrophied into a dry ritualism that was patently unfulfilling. According to Powell, one reason African American religion was "more mature" than that of Whites was because of the discrimination and oppression Blacks have experienced, making the African American's "search for God an everyday, twenty-four hour job." [132] Powell was decidedly and unambiguously pro-Black. "Black self-determination, Black self-reliance, Black self-development, Black racial pride, Black responsibility, and Black self-respect" was the hallmark of his mission to the church, and for Powell Black power was "consistent with the will of God." [133]

A critical examination of these Black religious leaders shows that they had a deep appreciation for the Christian faith taught and bequeathed to them by slave masters. Their Christianity boasted a God who is strong, fair, and just, a God who is all-powerful and who utilizes His power on behalf of the oppressed. The Bible was the sacred record of God's acts in history and without question the inspired word of God. To be sure, Adam Clayton Powell Jr. had a theology of inspiration that was not shared by the others, and most, if not all, of them read the Bible with a tinge of apprehension born of a suspicion of the fact that it had been translated by White men. Yet their view of Scripture in no way detracted from or diminished their service as Christian pastors. In Humphrey, there was a profound respect for the Bible. All these ministers believed in Christ as the Savior for a fallen world and expected the Second Coming of Jesus to usher in a reign of peace and love.

These religious leaders, almost without exception, refused to see any cleavage between religion and politics, a fact that does not hold true for James K. Humphrey—that is, as far as political activism is concerned. Humphrey was not oblivious to events in the political world, but he never dabbled in or delved into politics like Richard Allen, Bishop Henry McNeal Turner, or Adam Clayton Powell Jr. Following in the pacifist tradition of the Seventh-day Adventist ministry,[134] Humphrey remained politically conservative all his life. This is not to say that the United Sabbath-Day Adventist leader discouraged engagement in politics, but although the other Black religious leaders extrapolated and forged political ideologies from their understanding of what it meant to be a Christian, Humphrey did not. What is certain is that all these men viewed the conditions of Black people as palpably unacceptable, struggled in their attempts to make sense of how a nation calling itself Christian could allow such conditions to exist in its midst, and were committed to challenging and changing the situation.

These were leaders of vision, resolve, and discernment who, more than anything, seized the opportunities placed before them to heighten the self-consciousness of the African American. To be sure, they were men whose temperaments ran the spectrum and whose ambitions provoked in others ire as well as admiration. Either way, they were symbols of the aspirations and struggles of their people and were products of a system that demanded of Black leaders a higher standard of moral behavior even as the system viewed people of color to be less than human. Because they were fully human, they were not without flaws and faults, and they did not try to deny or discount their shortcomings or glaring humanity as issues that were immaterial or irrelevant. Always painfully aware of their vulnerabilities, they nonetheless sensed the need to utilize their strengths in what they vowed was a worthy cause.

Although all these men were complex personalities whose lives reeked with contradictions and conundrum, their personalities are not difficult to understand when viewed against the backdrop of their social, economic, and political circumstances. Indeed, their personalities reflect the complexities and contradictions of their times, and when one considers that they were all religious leaders who had been taught that God had created all people equal, it is far from surprising that they experienced dissonance in attempting to reconcile the God of Scripture with the condition of the African American. The plight of Blacks in America left them conflicted, disturbed, and in some cases angry and made it utterly remarkable that they did not rise up to curse God and die.

SUMMARY

The Sabbath-Day Adventists emerged at one of the most ominous eras in American history. With the country caught up in the throes of the Great Depression, the new religious body experienced "Hard Times" economically and organizationally, and challenges without and within tested the will of Sabbath-Day Adventists to be a viable alternative to the Seventh-day Adventist denomination. Yet the energy and excitement that often accompany the creation or launch of a new organization propelled the group forward.

James Kemuel Humphrey, the first leader of the group, almost immediately assumed the title of bishop. Humphrey managed the new organization closely, superintending all facets of the group's operations. He is remembered as suave, intelligent, and visionary by members, and as a Bible-based, Christ-centered preacher. Throughout the 1930s, Sabbath-Day Adventists gave birth to congregations in the United States and the West Indies, hammering out a set of fundamental beliefs and a constitution and staging elaborate General Conference sessions along the way. The infant group succeeded in attracting middle-class individuals as well as the poor, and members state that it engendered among them a sense of community and belonging to do so. The group not only offered sanctuary and support to the African Americans from the South and Caribbean in search of meaning in the city but provided them with opportunities for self-expression and self-determination. It especially prized youth, creating contexts for nurture and professional growth for them.

James K. Humphrey's preaching remained, for the most part, mainstream Adventist after he splintered from the Seventh-day Adventist denomination. In addition, the structure and operation of the Sabbath-Day Adventist organization reflected that of its precursors. To be sure, Sabbath-Day Adventists promulgated a brand of the gospel that lifted up the Black presence in the Bible.

Yet Sabbath-Day Adventism did not exhibit a heightened sensitivity to the crucial social and political events that were its context. Humphrey's understanding of the Great Depression, World War II, the start of the cold war, and the Korean conflict reflected a conservative, even fundamentalist, interpretation. The bishop may not have been of the "pie-in-sky, sweet by-and-by" mindset, but he did encourage members to focus on the imminent Second Coming of Christ, when all injustices would be addressed and an age free of discrimination and segregation would be ushered in.

Chapter 6

The Sabbath-Day Adventist Church after Humphrey

Although James K. Humphrey gave up the leadership of the Sabbath-Day Adventist organization in 1947, five years before his death, almost from the moment they splintered attempts to reconcile Sabbath-Day Adventists with Seventh-day Adventists have been made by both groups.

One major factor that frustrated the early attempts at reconciliation was the property Sabbath-Day Adventists believed was rightfully theirs. Property ownership had played no small role in the break of 1929, and it was only after the local conference, union, and General Conference officials had agreed on the night of November 2, 1929, to turn over the title of First Harlem's building that they had been allowed to leave the premises unharmed. After temporarily getting the property back as the result of a lower court's ruling, Humphrey's group jealously guarded it. The new religious body fundamentally disagreed with the policy of Seventh-day Adventists that the local conference should hold the title to all property belonging to its constituent churches.

Attempts at Reconciliation

The attempts at reconciliation intensified after the death of Humphrey in 1952.[1] A couple of years after the bishop's death, William Samuels, Humphrey's successor as bishop, went so far as to invite a delegation from the Northeastern Conference of Seventh-day Adventists to make a case for reconciliation before his congregation.[2] The move was watershed in that it represented the first time a Seventh-day Adventist representative had met with Sabbath-Day Adventists to intentionally try to broker an agreement between the two religious bodies. Fully aware of the magnitude of the moment, the conference president himself appeared at New York United Sabbath-Day Adventist Church, delivering the sermon that Sabbath morning. In spite of his theme of love and forgiveness and an emphasis on disregarding past misunderstandings, the Sabbath-Day Adventist congregation opted to maintain the status quo.[3]

Samuels's attempts to return his group to the Seventh-day Adventist denomination were frustrated not because of theological differences but because of matters of church polity. A faction of the New York United Sabbath-Day congregation, still seething over the loss of the church's property almost two decades earlier, refused to accept Seventh-day Adventist policy on the issue of property ownership. A majority also disagreed with Seventh-day Adventist General Conference financial policies toward the local conference, holding that they were restrictive and perhaps even unfair. Yet the main reason United Sabbath-Day Adventists refused to return to the Seventh-day Adventist organization was their belief that Black conferences lacked the autonomy and power James K. Humphrey had envisioned they would have. The late bishop had pictured regional conferences as the answer to the absence of self-determination among African American Seventh-day Adventists, a dream Sabbath-Day Adventists believed had not come true with the establishment of regional conferences.[4]

Attempts to reconcile United Sabbath-Day Adventists with Seventh-day Adventists decreased after the former group rejected the plea of the local Seventh-day Adventist conference president, and any possibility of the merger happening was all but completely erased when the New York United congregation joined a small, fledgling Adventist organization in 1956. Together, they became the Unification Association of Christian Sabbath Keepers. Asserting that it had branches in the West Indies and as far away as West Africa, the organization was a loosely knit coalition struggling to achieve an identity and to convey a sense of mission. Samuels, bishop of the United Sabbath-Day Adventists when the merger occurred, immediately became its titular head and delivered the keynote addresses at several of the organization's yearly celebrations. Terminally optimistic, Samuels always preached Bible-based messages seasoned with hope and courage.[5]

In 2000, the pastor of New York United had as one of his major objectives the return of the congregation to the Seventh-day Adventist organization. A former Seventh-day Adventist minister and youth departmental director of the South

Central Conference of Seventh-day Adventists with headquarters in Nashville, Tennessee, Princeton Holt is a graduate of Oakwood College and a native New Yorker who grew up in Brooklyn hearing about the United Sabbath-Day Adventists. He accepted the invitation to pastor the church because of its strategic location in Harlem and his passion for urban ministry. Holt is a creative, visionary leader courageous enough to challenge members to focus on the future and unashamed to point out mistakes and flaws in the group's history. That in 2000 he desired to see the group once more a part of the Seventh-day Adventist organization was no secret. Yet Holt knew that he faced daunting challenges, not the least of which was the deep-seated attitudes of distrust and hostility a feisty minority still had for the Seventh-day Adventist denomination.[6]

POST-HUMPHREY SABBATH-DAY ADVENTIST LEADERSHIP

Humphrey's last days were difficult ones that are shrouded in uncertainty, conjecture, and suspicion. He succumbed to the encroachments of glaucoma, becoming legally blind toward the end of his life. Ermie Chandler remembers her husband, who was First Elder of the Ephesus Seventh-day Church at the time, taking Humphrey for medical attention on a few occasions, and says that one rumor making the rounds in Humphrey's twilight was that his family had threatened to terminate his pension if he were to return to the Seventh-day Adventist denomination.[7] At the very least, the rumor betrays the murkiness that covers Humphrey's last days.

Yet the challenges Humphrey's physical health presented paled in comparison to those he encountered in evaluating his life and accomplishments. Simply put, Humphrey died a sad man. His spouse of almost half a century died before him, and his daughter from that union had long ago terminated her association with the United Sabbath-Day Adventists. With his familial situation the subject of conjecture and allegation, Humphrey often felt alone and misunderstood. On occasions, he confessed that he felt he had not achieved his objective in establishing an independent religious organization that provided African Americans with the power and self-determination they lacked in ones run by Whites. Ironically, for reasons that are unclear, the bishop's funeral service did not take place at the New York United church facility.[8]

After Humphrey, New York United was led by William A. Samuels from 1947 to 1987. An Antiguan who had moved to New York City in the 1910s, Samuels was married by Humphrey in 1919 to Winifred Martin and was a member of First Harlem Seventh-day Adventist Church throughout the "Roaring Twenties." He was a carpenter who served the Seventh-day Adventist church in various capacities, including those of usher, Sabbath School teacher and superintendent, deacon, and local elder. He was ordained as an elder in 1944 and became assistant pastor shortly thereafter. Samuels aligned himself with Humphrey during the pastor's problems with the Seventh-day Adventists and became his "right-hand man" when Humphrey established the Sabbath-Day Adventist organization. The major accomplishment of Samuels's forty-year tenure as leader of the Sabbath-Day Adventists was the erection of New York United's present facility. Yet New York United lost a significant number of members over the move to 110th Street because tithe funds were used to build the property, which reportedly was built at a cost of $180,000. Allegedly, the congregation burnt the mortgage on the building in July 1961, a mere five years after it was constructed.[9]

A succession of "first day" ministers followed Samuels.[10] Not surprising, the organization has experienced difficulty bringing credentialed or licensed Seventh-day Adventist ministers to pastor Sabbath-Day Adventist congregations. The "first day" ministers were more preaching or pulpit pastors, fulfilling the need for the congregation to be spiritually fed. The day-to-day operation and strategic planning of the church remained in the hands of the Board of Trustees, made up in 2000 mostly of women. The arrangement may have worked for both entities, but it failed to engender a sense of belonging on the part of the "first day" clergy. In addition, it created problems in terms of their doctrinal and theological beliefs, not to mention their preaching at New York United.[11]

William Pointer Jr. was the first of these first day pastors, leading the New York United congregation from 1987 to 1992. A charismatic personality, Pointer sought to inject life into the worship service by introducing upbeat music and other elements that were averse to the taste of some conservative seniors, a sizeable number of whom comprised the congregation. The result was that the seniors balked, and Pointer, unable to effect a change in them, was muscled out. In the aftermath of his departure, attendance at New York United plummeted, and most of the youth left for various "Sunday keeping" churches.[12]

Following Pointer was Berwyn La Mar, who says he was an "interim" pastor for about a year and a half. Born in Georgia and with degrees from Faith Baptist Theological Seminary and Louisiana Baptist University, La Mar was an assistant pastor of another independent Seventh-day Adventist group in Brooklyn when he received the call to lead New York United. He says that he did not know about the history of the church until he began serving and that he found out information as he went along. La Mar states that attendance averaged thirty during his short stint and that he was able to baptize one individual, a young man from Africa. Pastor of the Greater Mt. Olive Missionary Baptist Church in Waycross, Georgia, in 2001, La Mar found the people at New York United loving and supportive, though not disposed to discourse about reconciliation with the Seventh-day Adventists. In addition, they were "Seventh-day Adventist" in every way but with respect to the writings of Ellen G. White. According to La Mar, one reason they believed Ellen G. White was not inspired was because the judge, in ruling on their property in the 1930s, had stated that Mrs. White was not a prophet.[13]

La Mar was asked to leave because his commuting back and forth to Georgia posed challenges the membership could not accept. His successor was Howard Brooks, formerly a Black Jew who wore and preached in ostensibly authentic Jewish religious garb. Brooks, who served from 1993 to 1996, ran up against opposition over the number of times the church wanted to have communion services. He wanted to celebrate the service annually, not quarterly as members desired, and when a compromise could not be brokered, Brooks departed.

When Kevin L. Jenkins was invited by the Trustee Board to serve as pastor in 1996, he met a congregation mired in the past and still furious because of the treatment Humphrey had received from the Seventh-day Adventist denomination. So strong was the anti-Seventh-day Adventist sentiment among the congregation that the first question posed to Jenkins at his job interview was whether he had any intentions of attempting a rapproachement between the Seventh-day Adventists and Sabbath-Day Adventists. Jenkins, himself a former Seventh-day Adventist minister was struck by the pall of death hanging over New York United, the mother—and in 2000, the only—Sabbath-Day congregation. When he assumed the pastorate of the congregation, weekly attendance averaged thirty to forty, peaking at one hundred for a Homecoming Celebration that saw many former members return to recount tales of the Humphrey era.[14] Jenkins found the stationery of the church "archaic looking," the carpeting in the sanctuary grey and dirty, and the membership unsure of its identity. The congregation was a classic example of sheep without a shepherd. The church seemed to have lost both its vision and mission. Yet what troubled the pastor the most were the exorbitant dues New York United was paying to the Unification Association of Christian Sabbath Keepers.[15]

Try as he might, Jenkins could see no substantive benefit coming to New York United as a result of its association with this group. To be sure, New York United served as the headquarters for the association and hosted at least one of the group's annual conclaves while Jenkins served as pastor. Yet the Sabbath School study guide that his congregation received from the association was a hodgepodge of Bible texts lacking a theme or focus. Certain that the time for a separation had come, Jenkins convinced the Trustee Board to opt out of membership in the Unification Association of Christian Sabbath keepers.[16]

An Oakwood College graduate with a doctor of ministry degree from United Theological Seminary, the young, visionary pastor plunged into his tenure with determination, seeking first to transform the sanctuary from a cold, uninviting room to a bright, cheery auditorium. New carpeting was installed, walls were painted, and, in keeping with his Afrocentrism, kinte cloth decorations were brought in to adorn the pulpit and rostrum. Jenkins's most significant accomplishment was convincing the membership to return to the Seventh-day Adventist Bible Lesson Study Guides as their source for small group interaction and study during the Sabbath School.

The twenty-first century brought with it new leadership to New York United. Princeton Holt arrived in January 2000 determined to effect a revival. Within a year he revamped the worship service, utilizing more music and audience participation, and early in 2001 he superintended a watershed event—the ordination of the church's first woman elder. On January 6, 2001, as church officers were installed and the communion service was conducted, Agatha Phillips was ordained as an elder. The spirit of celebration and worship was high that day, even though attendance was down because a snow storm had inundated the city a few days earlier. Members seemed to be genuinely in love with Holt and his family, whose wife and daughter preached the morning sermon that Sabbath. Holt's vision called for the church to implement an aggressive urban ministry that will transform the area, and he was optimistic that the greatest days of the church are before it.[17] In February 2001, seven individuals were baptized, evidence of the new life permeating New York United.

CONTEXTUALIZING THE SABBATH-DAY ADVENTISTS

Almost from the instant people of African descent in America began to appropriate the symbols of the Christian religion their European masters practiced and taught them, their brand of Christianity exhibited a conflicting strain and contradictory nature.[18] Eugene Genovese calls the phenomenon the "dialectic of accommodation and resistance."[19] On the one hand, their religion was a retooled Christianity that provided emotional and psychological strength to live in an alien, unfriendly world. On the other hand, their Christianity was a veritable form of self-expression and a vehicle of resistance to the discrimination of the White-dominated culture. African American religion did not oscillate between these two poles, holding them instead in dynamic, dialectical tension. Unarguably, United Sabbath-Day Adventists exhibited this contradictory nature of African American religion. In holding on to several of the doctrines of the Seventh-day Adventist denomination as well as elements of its organizational structure, Humphrey's group is an example of the juxtaposition of accommodation and activism characteristic of African American religion.

In his historical overview of ministry in the Black church, E. Forrest Harris Jr. offers the following division: (a) the pre–Civil War Black Church; (b) the Formative Period, from the Civil War through Reconstruction; (c) the Maturation Period, from Reconstruction to the beginning of the Great Migration; (d) the Expansion-Renaissance Period, from the Great Migration to World War II; (e) the Passive Protest Period, from World War II to 1955; and (f) the Radical-Reassertion Period, since 1955. The period during which Humphrey labored as a Seventh-day Adventist and later a Sabbath-Day Adventist minister was the Expansion-Renaissance Period.[20]

Describing a watershed era in the social history of ministry in Black churches, Gayraud S. Wilmore says that during this period people of African descent in America needed the church more than ever. Contending that by World War I Blacks were more segregated and discriminated against than they had been when the Fugitive Slave law was enacted, he cites an "unprecedented wave of lynchings, Ku Klux Klan and other anti-Negro hate groups, violence and dire poverty in the black community" as reasons for the deluge of Blacks seeking asylum in the North. As a consequence, Black churches were hard pressed to provide sanctuary to the newly arrived, some of whom turned up at their doorsteps with all their belongings.[21]

From the last decade of the nineteenth century to about World War II, African American religion, never a homogenous, monolithic phenomenon but a dynamic, creative force that expresses itself in a rich variety of ways, exploded in a number of forms. Mainstream Black denominations saw many of their members leave to join store front groups that seemed to meet the needs of the thousands of Blacks then pouring into America's cities, especially those in the North. The sheer diversity of these groups testify to their fierce independence, a fact that receives additional backing when the names of these groups are brought into focus.[22] Yet not all African Americans left predominantly White congregations to join or to form Black ones.

Why did some African Americans remain with predominantly White congregations? Why did some Blacks establish congregations affiliated with White-controlled religious groups? How did these Black congregations adapt the content of these White-controlled religious organizations to the African American experience? Baer and Singer pondered these questions but failed to come up with credible answers. Noting that Blacks belonging to White-controlled denominations fell into three broad categories—middle class who tended to join the mainstream denominations, new middle-class who tended to join unconventional religious groups, and working-class Blacks who tended to join White-controlled sects such as Jehovah's Witnesses and Seventh-day Adventists[23]—the authors stress that Blacks in these religious bodies were still predominantly members of all-Black congregations.[24] Citing Du Bois, Baer and Singer claim that in the early twentieth century most African American congregations of White-controlled denominations pitched their appeal to elite Blacks and that all-Black denominations catered more to the middle and lower middle class.[25] This was not the case with either First Harlem or the United Sabbath-Day Adventists. Yet First Harlem's giving patterns may have been due to the importance Seventh-day Adventists ascribe to stewardship, a concept the denomination views as encompassing much more than financial contributions. And Humphrey's independent movement struggled financially from its inception not because it catered to middle- to lower-class Blacks, many of whom were expatriates from the West Indies, but because Seventh-day Adventists look askance at independent movements. Do African Americans who belong to White-controlled religious bodies tend to be less activist than African Americans in Black-controlled ones? Not so, according to many scholars.[26]

In an attempt to understand the religious diversity evident in African American religion, Baer and Singer proposed a typology of Black sectarianism, coming up with a four-cell matrix. Each cell represents a different type of religious sect. Mainstream denominations accept the cultural norms of the broader society, aspire to obtain a piece of the American pie, and primarily draw members from the middle class who have achieved a measure of social legitimacy and stability. Messianic-Nationalist sects combine religious beliefs with a goal of achieving political, economic, social, and cultural autonomy. Founded by charismatic individuals whom followers tend to view as specially gifted leaders, messianic-nationalism touts a glorious Black past and a future age of accomplishment for Blacks. Conversionist sects lean toward an otherworldly apoliticalism, eschewing activism. They prize conversion and sanctification and are often criticized as being escapist. Thaumaturgical sects utilize the magical as a means of achieving such socially acceptable goals as wealth and health. Like mainstream denominations, they generally accept the cultural norms of the larger society.[27] In this typology, United Sabbath-Day Adventists fall into the messianic-nationalist category.

United Sabbath-Day Adventists, like their progenitor and counterpart, the Seventh-day Adventists, resist being identified as a cult, holding that they are in the mainstream of evangelical Christianity.[28] Yet one reason Sabbath-Day Adventists may have flourished during the 1930s was because of the social climate permeating Black America. According to Miles Mark Fischer, during the era "some unorthodox religious group which makes a definite appeal to Negroes" was to be found "almost in every center, particularly urban."[29] Exploiting the slowness of the organized Christian churches to address the spiritual, emotional, and social needs of the urban masses, these groups were led, for the most part, by unlettered individuals who eschewed the historical critical method of biblical interpretation popular at the time and appealed directly to Scripture in search of material for the proof-text kind of preaching for which they were known. C. Eric Lincoln and Lawrence Mamiya contend that this was an era characterized by "a relative quietism and an apparent vacuum of church leadership" into which cult leaders flowed with promises of utopia.[30] Cults and sects met in storefronts and other unpretentious assembly halls, often operating social ministries out of them.

Joseph R. Washington Jr. states that sectarianism is the response to power desired and denied, adding that the Black "cult-type" was not just a religious movement but a political, social, and economic force as well that spoke of ultimate Black triumph over principalities and powers. It was a "call to new life" and "a call to new power" in this present world. Though they created an abundance of myths, they themselves lived in a world devoid of myths. Their central and ultimate power was God, who empowered their leaders to transcend the immediate materiality of the world with transcendent, supernatural force.[31] And Howard Brotz asserts that for Black sects "communal power . . . in the sense of communal achievements and solidarity" was "a persistent standpoint" in the African American community. He explains that the Black sects pioneered in recasting the meaning of blackness, imputing immense value and meaning into the term while decrying the integrationist leanings of others in the African American community.[32]

Arthur Huff Fauset posits that people were drawn to the cults because of (a) a desire to be closer to the supernatural, (b) the charismatic personality of the leader, and (c) race consciousness. In addition, they wanted to rid themselves of physical and emotional illness.[33] The first three of Fauset's reasons seem to apply to the United Sabbath-Day Adventists. They desired "a closer walk with the Lord," the articles that appeared in the *Messenger* speaking to that desire and need, and race consciousness was a factor that drew people to the Sabbath-Day Adventists. After all, the group had splintered from the Seventh-day Adventists on that issue. Lastly, Humphrey's charismatic personality was no small draw to the group.

That Humphrey had had problems with the law and may have spent time in jail on charges that were ultimately dropped in no way detracted from his appeal or discounted his influence. Not a few of the cult leaders of the day had run afoul of the law. Yet, according to Fischer, it was uncommon for a cult leader to be "adjudged guilty of anything other than insanity." According to him, one cult leader was arrested twenty-six times, six times for insanity, and another, Father Chester Talliafero, founder of Saints' Rest in Philadelphia, was arrested three times for gross misconduct "only to be detained in an asylum from which he was released."[34] Cult leaders were charismatic personalities whose appeal depended in part on physical and psychological idiosyncracies, if not quirks. Humphrey's bearing helped set him apart as a specially chosen vessel of God, and his struggles with the Seventh-day Adventist denomination only added to his allure.

Arthur Huff Fauset also points out that the penchant of Black churches to split in the early part of the twentieth century was due in part to their nationalist tendencies. Especially when the groups existed as "cults," nationalism often eclipsed a focus on more traditional and widely accepted Christian tenets, including foundational doctrines such as the Trinity.[35] A distinguishing feature of these groups was the captivating, if not transfixing personality of the leader, an element that was true of the United Sabbath-Day Adventists.

The most celebrated Harlem religious leader during the 1930s was Father Divine, or George Baker, as he was named at birth. More than any other African American religious leader at the time, Father Divine personified and epitomized the "Black Gods of the Metropolis" tradition. Divine's Peace Mission achieved legendary, perhaps even mythical, status in New York City. Allegedly, a letter was once addressed simply to "God, Harlem, U.S.A.," and the United States Postal Service delivered the piece of correspondence to Father Divine.[36] Divine was also known as the Dean of the Universe; Master of Omnipotency; Beloved Savior; Master and King; Beloved Savior and Lord; Our Lord and Savior; King Sweet; Beloved King; Supreme Poet of the Universe; Author and Finisher of all Past, Present and Future Dispensations; Great Interpreter of all Creation; and Omnipotent Interpreter.[37]

A standout among the very few interracial religious organizations at the time, the Peace Mission Movement had as its cornerstone a three-fold ideology comprised of Americanism, Democracy, and Christianity, with Americanism being understood to mean an "amalgamation of all Races, Colors, Creeds." A distinguishing feature of Divine's movement was the ease with which Blacks and Whites related to each other. The organization boasted that there was no differentiation based on color within its ranks, and wore the antiracism that characterized it as a badge of honor, singing about it in hymns such as the following:

> *We shall have the Same Rights*
> *Not only Equal but the Same*
> *Side by Side, we shall ride*
> *The Same car, bus and train*
> *We shall play in the Same parks*
> *Study our lessons in the Same schools*
> *There shall be the Same Equal Rights*
> *For you, and you, and you!*[38]

The Peace Mission Movement had six fundamental requirements for anyone wanting to join, and all but one referenced a biblical text for warrant and backing. The requirements included an incomparable love for God; an acceptance of heaven "as a state of consciousness that can be attained in one's personal experience here on earth;" the acceptance that there can be no Fatherhood of God without the Brotherhood of Man; a belief in virginity and chastity; the belief that "misery, sickness and old age," as well as death, are not inevitable; and a willingness to adjust one's life in accordance with the aforementioned.[39] The Peace Mission staged no funeral services or weddings, and couples who joined the Movement became "religiously convicted of the necessity of ceasing to propagate until one has learned to perfect oneself," thus qualifying oneself to birth children. For Divine, self-control was the best birth control.⁴⁰

Divine's theology, if it can be called that, was a complex concoction. Though his followers viewed Divine as God, the Peace Mission Movement conceived of God as "the Creative Force of the Universe, the Universal Mind Substance, the Fundamental Principle and Source of all Goodness—Omnipotent, Omniscient, Omnilucent and Omnipresent." Humans were created by God, who endowed Adam and Eve with the power of choice, which they exercised in rebellion against God. Jesus was born to Mary, who "mentally and spiritually contacted God," and even though Jesus died and was resurrected, "He knew that He did not have the power to affect the universal emancipation of man." Thus, Jesus returned to his father, coming back to earth again in the person of Father Divine. Said Divine: "FATHER DIVINE is the Person of the Impersonal. He came in this expression for the purpose of lifting mankind out of the personal into the Impersonal."⁴¹

Father Divine not only made a foray into politics but claimed that he had as much right in politics as he had in religion. At a political convention held in 1936 to establish the Movement's Platform, Divine's Mission Movement adopted as its slogan "One for all and all for one, but not for one who's not for all." Divine invited the president of the United States to the convention and, even though neither Franklin Delano Roosevelt nor any other elected political figure of worth attended, some did offer their regrets for not being able to attend. The Convention unanimously adopted a resolution recognizing Father Divine as God, and delegates hammered out a platform of economic, political, and educational policies, all based on supposedly sound principles. Not surprising, the platform called for an end to the oppression of minorities and, appealing to the Holy Bible for support, asserted the oneness of the human race.⁴²

Accused of being sympathetic to the Communists, Divine asserted that he had no qualms about them, saying, "I stand for anyone who will deal justly between man and man." He claimed that because the Communists stood for "social equality, political and economic equality, and for justice in every issue," which were the very things for which he stood, he would cooperate with them. Yet he admitted that he found "fault with the Communist methods," though not necessarily their objectives. Even as he would cooperate with the Communists and any organization working to bring an "end to all oppression and suppression and race prejudice," he knew that he would have to bring about the end personally. In the end, Divine was not "representing religion" but "God on earth among men."[43]

Not surprising, Divine's influence among Harlem's masses caught the eye of many of the area's mainstream Black religious leaders.[44] Adam Clayton Powell Jr., Harlem's leading Black minister during the 1930s, was particularly chagrined by Divine's ministry and draw among Harlem's masses and never missed an opportunity to publicly lambast Divine. That Divine succeeded in provoking the ire of mainstream Black religious leaders and was regularly spoken about in the Black as well as the regular press, testifies to his influence. The regular clergy may have despised Divine, but his success in the Black community demonstrated to the mainstream Black religious leaders that, at the very least, "only by extending their commitments to racial equality and care for the soul could [they] maintain their stature in the black community."[45]

Divine should not be viewed or dismissed as an outlandish leader whose idiosyncratic tendencies and behavior resonated only with the lower-class masses. To be sure, Divine's claim that he was God was unprecedented among cult leaders at the time, putting him in a class all by himself. Divine's appeal transcended racial and economic lines; Whites, as well as the well-to-do, flocked to his gatherings in appreciable numbers. Divine succeeded in forging interracial, intercultural communication and bonds even as the nation struggled to define its racial soul. According to Henry Louis Gates Jr. and Cornel West, Divine left "his mark on the twentieth century as one who created extraordinary and untried new ways in which black people used religious imagination and business ingenuity" to ward off the discrimination they daily faced and to build their self-identity and race pride.[46]

Divine's fame and notoriety was challenged by Daddy Grace, the most flamboyant and controversial of the "Black Gods of the Metropolis." Grace, who was born in Cape Verde Islands, established the United House of Prayer For All People in Massachusetts in 1921. More messiah than nationalist, Grace held up himself as the liberator African Americans had been looking for, appealing to them to turn to him for salvation. Still, Grace never promoted himself as any deity. His penchant for flashy jewelry, shoulder-length flowing hair, and fancy suits did set him apart, as did the assortment of household goods and toiletries bearing his name that his organization promoted.

Born Charles Emmanuel, Daddy Grace refused to even admit he was African American in spite of his dark skin and incontrovertible Negroid features. He assumed the name "Daddy Grace" and declared himself a bishop, claiming that "every book in the Bible has been sealed by Grace" and that "all through the Bible there is Grace." Daddy Grace asserted that "Grace is the greatest thing in the world" and that "Grace will bring you through."[47]

Grace's legacy is that of being a master fund-raiser. His ability to get his followers to empty their pockets for his cause is legendary, as was his penchant for intimidating his followers. Ostensibly, Grace once told them: "If you sin against God, God can save you, but if you sin against Grace, God cannot save you." According to Daddy Grace, God had gone on vacation, leaving him in charge.[48]

A defining feature of the religious services of Daddy Grace was "extreme physical frenzy." Worshipers were whipped into this frenzy by those leading out, and many worshipers often lost consciousness during the ordeal. Daddy Grace would exploit this occurrence to the hilt, making off with large amounts of money, as people were prone to do whatever was requested of them in their state of ecstacy. The frenzy that characterized Grace's religious services was replete with sexual overtones; the dancing, crying, and moaning often engaged in by the women would lead to a conclusion that implied sexual congress. Whatever happened during one of Grace's religious service, and that included speaking in tongues, was often interrupted to collect offerings. Ushers would rush about to do so, calling out to worshipers to place their offerings in their plates so that they could win the prize as highest offering collector for that service. Yet for all the money Grace collected, he never engaged in any social ministry.[49]

Prophet Jones was another of the "Black Gods of the Metropolis." Jones, who asserted that he was the "Dominion Ruler of the Church of the Universal Triumph," was once invited to help dedicate a Peace Mission property in the vicinity of Philadelphia. Jones arrived towing a cadre of followers and attendants and carrying a collection of suitcases in which was an enviable wardrobe of expensive wear that included a mink coat purportedly costing in excess of ten thousand dollars. Jones may have been notorious for his opulence, but on meeting Daddy Grace once, Jones had to concede that Daddy Grace's opulence outshone his. What their encounter demonstrated is that Father Divine's allure and power eclipsed those of Jones. When they met, the two cult leaders were polite, cordial, and courteous and pledged to collaborate on some ventures that never really materialized.[50]

There are stark differences between Humphrey and these "Black Gods of the Metropolis," the most obvious being that at no time did Humphrey conceive of himself as a messiah or deliverer. Humphrey had no delusions of grandeur and never called himself God or the son of God in the theological sense. He eschewed the life of flamboyance and ostentation. He was never carried on the shoulders of followers, driven in a horse-drawn carriage, or chauffeured in a limousine. To be sure, Humphrey was urbane and suave, but empire building was never on his agenda. His book was the Bible, and he remained a Bible student and preacher to the end. He kept the attention of his members riveted on the Bible and lifted up Jesus Christ as the living word. As all conscientious clergy still do, Humphrey appealed for funds to keep his organization afloat, but the bishop never focused attention on finances to the exclusion of other critical organizational issues.

What kind of Black religious leadership did Humphrey provide? E. Forrest Harris Jr. has identified four styles or models of Black religious leadership relative to the "liberation praxis" in the African American church: pastoral, prophetic, reformist, and nationalistic. The pastoral model seeks to "comfort and to console those battered by life's adverse circumstances"; the prophetic seeks "to reveal the contradictions inherent in the life of the community and dominant culture and to clarify the ethical vision of justice in situations of human oppression"; the reformist is a "mix of politics and religion" on behalf of a disenfranchised Black community; and the nationalistic, who believes that self determination is a basic ethical and political right of people, advocates "some form of racial separation to allow blacks to gain a self-determined vision and control over their own destiny." The effectiveness of each model is tied to "moral accountability to the black community." Summing up, Harris says that ministry in the Black church "is an attempt to preach, teach, and live out the biblical message of freedom under God" so that it powerfully impacts "the realities of black existence in a context of cultural, social, political, and economic oppression." Yet this does not mean that Black religious leaders discount inner transformation. Indeed, they hold that inner renewal is both a prelude and postlude to social transformation.[51]

Using Harris's scheme, a reasonable conclusion is that Humphrey was prophetic and nationalistic as a Seventh-day Adventist minister and more pastoral as a United Sabbath-Day Adventist leader. To be sure, as Harris has allowed, African American religious leaders have seldom been exclusively one or the other, combining many elements of each model in their attempts to be self determining.[52]

An Assessment

Did Humphrey accomplish his objective of creating Black self-determination among Adventists? Are the United Sabbath-Day Adventists the autonomous religious organization its founder envisioned?

Viewed from the standpoint of numbers, the United Sabbath-Day Adventists are a failure, especially when compared to Black Seventh-day Adventist churches. In 2001, after seventy years of existence, New York United's attendance averaged sixty, and there were no branches of the group elsewhere. Most urban African American Seventh-day Adventist congregations, especially those in New York City, boast memberships in the hundreds, and the Ephesus Seventh-day Adventist Church, which grew out of the reorganized First Harlem, had a membership of approximately 2,200 in 2001. Yet success is not always a function of numbers. New York United may be small in numbers, but not in spirit or pride. Unbowed and indefatigable, the group forms an important chapter in the history of race relations in the Seventh-day Adventist Church. Humphrey's break with the Seventh-day Adventist Church set the tone for Black-White relations in the Seventh-day Adventist Church and was the catalyst that sparked the creation of a separate administrative structure for Blacks in the denomination in 1945. Thus, as far as Sabbath-Day Adventists are concerned, Humphrey's split helped modernize the Seventh-day Adventist Church.

Regrettably, not many African American Seventh-day Adventists know the name James K. Humphrey or the group he founded, and among those familiar with their history there is much confusion. Yet Humphrey's bold move in establishing an independent religious organization, replete with General Conference sessions modeled after those conducted by Seventh-day Adventists, inspired a generation of African Americans caught up in the throes of the Depression. To West Indians struggling to resonate with a new culture and to indigenous Blacks, many of them newly arrived from the South, his stance against an established power heralded a new day of resistance to and nonacceptance of unacceptable conditions and practices. Standing up to the Seventh-day Adventist denomination was a defining moment for African Americans.

Unable to reconcile Christianity's teaching of inclusion and community with what he considered the church's racist tendencies and behavior, Humphrey concluded that the independent church, founded and operated by Blacks, was the antidote to the lack of self determination and power among African Americans. Such a church would more effectively evangelize the Black community, meeting not just its spiritual but social, political, and economic needs as well. More important, it would be a visible monument to the Black theology of liberation.[53]

To be sure, Humphrey's brand of activist rhetoric did not approximate that of the nineteenth century Black liberator David Walker, whose cry to "awaken his afflicted brethren" struck a responsive strain in them.[54] Nor was his message a new interpretation of what some had been saying for a long time. Even his act of leaving the Seventh-day Adventist Church, a predominantly White religious denomination, was not unprecedented. Long before he established his independent organization, Richard Allen had walked out of the Methodist Church to do just that.[55] In fact, in its break from the Seventh-day Adventists, Sabbath-Day Adventists had seen history repeating itself, claiming that Richard Allen and James Humphrey broke from their denominations because of White mistreatment of Blacks.[56]

To the Sabbath-Day Adventists, launching an independent religious organization was a truly revolutionary act. They claimed that Christianity was steeped in revolution, having been founded by an individual who renounced the "ideas and ideals of the religious teachers of his day" in favor of the "practical and humane." Protestantism, too, had been born in revolution, the Protestant church developing and growing through the sacrifices of pioneers such as Huss, Jerome, Zwingli, Melanchton, Tyndale, Latimer, Knox, Ridley, and Cranmer. It was in the tradition of these men also that Humphrey had stood up to the Adventists. Inspired by their legacy of resistance to injustice and error, Humphrey and his supporters had "raised their voice against such enormities, realizing that all men are created equal." They had been compelled to create an institution "where all can serve the creator instead of the creature, and work in fairness and righteousness to all."[57]

Humphrey never claimed to be a deliverer of his people like the Old Testament biblical character Moses did. Instead, he chose to cast his struggle with the Seventh-day Adventist denomination within the broader framework of race relations. Yet one reason people embraced him was because of the mood of the times. A glut of migrants from the South and a stream of immigrants from the West Indies conspired with economic uncertainty to create the ideal conditions for a religious leader such as James K. Humphrey. As thousands of Blacks searched for meaning amid the limited material resources they encountered in American cities, they increasingly turned from the mainline church to the small, independent sects and groups with unique names and extraordinary leaders. Thus, Humphrey was but one in a generation of religious leaders who held themselves out as viable options, if not irrefutable answers, to the strange and new challenges of urban life.

Summary

The post-Humphrey Sabbath-Day Adventist Church has been beset by challenges that have seen its numbers reduced, and attempts at reconciliation with the Seventh-day Adventist denomination have been frustrated by long-held, deeply entrenched grudges and policies of the Seventh-day Adventist Church that Sabbath-Day Adventists will not accept. Sabbath-Day Adventists have experienced difficulty attracting clergy aware of its history and committed to its vision, with the result that pastoral tenures since Samuels have been marked by tension and apprehension, if not suspicion. Yet, the new millennium brought with it the hope and promise of a return to the "glory days," and the pastor of New York United in 2001 had connected with the congregation on levels the last three had been unable to, enjoying a collaborative partnership with the small but proud group. Together they hope to usher in a day of church growth and outreach that will bring transformation to the Harlem community.

Chapter 7

SUMMARY AND CONCLUSIONS

Scholars have stressed the dynamic role that religion has played in African American history. Robert T. Handy, for example, has stated that religion has been so important in African American history that any credible under-standing of African American history calls for careful attention to religion.[1] In a similar vein, C. Eric Lincoln avows that religion was from the beginning the organizing principle of the Black experience in America.[2] As such, a study of a group of African Americans that does not contemplate their religion is des-tined to be incomplete, if not problematic. In this study, an investigation of the Sabbath-Day Adventists, the history and religion of a population of African Americans come together in a particular social and political context—early twentieth century Harlem.

African Americans may have boasted that by 1930 Harlem was an empower-ment zone for Blacks, but it was more a colony of Black disenfranchisement. Beneath the surface of self-sufficiency were disturbing conditions that the Depression revealed. Yet long before the Great Depression those willing to look objectively at the situation of Blacks in Harlem admitted that alienation and powerlessness more accurately characterized African Americans in Harlem during the first three decades of the twentieth century. Exacerbating matters was the fact that indigenous African Americans and Black West Indians were coming together in large numbers for the first time.

The relationship between West Indians and indigenous African Americans was strained by distrust and suspicion, born in part by an ignorance of each other. Cultural differences gave rise to stereotypes, which in turn engendered a complex web of likes, dislikes, and division in the West Indian community. A civil war of sorts took place within Black America, with West Indians and indigenous African Americans arrayed against each other. Yet West Indians experienced another civil war within themselves. On the one hand, West Indians felt pulled toward the larger American culture; on the other, they wanted to retain their unique West Indian identity and culture. Amid this struggle, the myth of West Indian superiority developed, and West Indian hard work and achievement served to fuel the myth. The radicalism of the act of immigration, however, may have contributed to West Indian success more than any innate or cultural superiority on their part. In the end, West Indians and indigenous African Americans came together to combat common injustices and to pursue common goals. The result was a collaboration that may be termed intraracial progress.

James K. Humphrey was one of the West Indians who flooded Harlem in the early twentieth century. A Baptist minister from Jamaica, Humphrey was introduced by a layman to the Seventh-day Adventist church, a group that grew out of the Millerite movement of the early nineteenth century. Organized during the Civil War, the denomination demonstrated uncertainty in dealing with the Blacks who filtered into its tent meetings and churches. Ellen G. White, considered by the denomination as an inspired prophet, counseled the church as to how Blacks were to be evangelized and treated, and her son, Edson White, pioneered evangelistic efforts among Blacks in the South.

Humphrey began pastoring in New York City shortly after joining the Adventist church, quickly leading his Harlem congregation to a position of prominence and primacy. Blessed with presence and bearing, he commanded the admiration and respect of old and young alike and was a father figure to the youth, many of whom he mentored into adulthood. He was conservative in dress and impeccable in manners. Yet the minister was disturbed by what he perceived as a lack of self-determination among Blacks in the Seventh-day Adventist church. In an attempt to address the need, he began to promote a project called Utopia Park, which, denominational leaders argued, was outside of stated church policy. When Humphrey refused to alter his plans, he was defrocked, and his congregation, which overwhelmingly stood in solidarity with him, was expelled.

In the wake of his expulsion from the Seventh-day Adventist church, Humphrey established the United Sabbath-Day Adventists. A look at the history of this group shows that it struggled to survive financially, a fact that does not beg for explanation given the reality that it was born at the start of the Great Depression. Humphrey and the United Sabbath-Day Adventists certainly give the lie to the myth that during the Depression all Black preachers drove Cadillacs and all Black churches had plenty of money. His organization was poor, like most other small independent Black churches, and experienced the secularism that was beginning to inundate city churches.[3] Yet Sabbath-Day Adventists were able to establish congregations as far west as Omaha and in the West Indies.

Humphrey founded the Sabbath-Day Adventist organization because of the treatment people of color were experiencing in the Seventh-day Adventist church. Yet the bishop had no doctrinal disputation with the Seventh-day Adventists, unless, of course, his unclear position on Ellen G. White is counted. Doctrinally a Seventh-day Adventist to the end, his contention was that their theology was stained by discriminatory practices that betrayed an unacceptable dichotomy between the secular and the sacred, and, more important, led to powerlessness and disenfranchisement for African Americans. Like other African American religious leaders of his era, Humphrey's theology of service reflected a historic synthesis of pietism and pragmatism. He refused to drive a wedge between the spiritual and social needs of his people, instead combining moral regeneration and renewal with economic and educational self-help initiatives. His was a practical theology that saw no distinction between the cardinal Christian doctrine of grace and the Black need of self-worth and self-determination.[4] For Humphrey, any theology that failed to resonate with pressing, real-life issues such as social injustice was meaningless, and when it became clear to him that Seventh-day Adventist theology was not addressing Black issues, he reasoned that he could remain true to the essence of Adventism while repudiating its practices. Indeed, Humphrey may have aggressively pursued reconciliation with the Seventh-day Adventists if its leaders had hinted of a desire to redress the injustices meted out to Blacks.

Assessing Humphrey's career based on his personality is difficult. That he was part of a generation of ambitious West Indians who rose to leadership in Harlem is a tenable argument, but what motivated him psychologically is difficult to gauge. Admittedly, his immigrant status as well as his status as an African American in a segregated society shaped his thinking and ministry. In addition, what has been preserved of his writings and sermons offers clues to his personality. Based on these, Humphrey emerges as a complex individual, a study in paradox and ambiguity. That he was a gifted leader is certain. During his tenure as bishop of the Sabbath-Day Adventists, congregations were spawned and attendance at Sabbath-Day Adventist General Conference sessions was high. To be sure, Humphrey managed his organization closely, but he does not appear to have been a victim of megalomania. To the congregations spawned across the country he assigned and fostered indigenous leadership and autonomy.

Humphrey never pursued his dream of Utopia Park once he split with the Seventh-day Adventists. Undoubtedly, the struggle to keep a new religious organization afloat during economically difficult times as well as conflicts within the infant organization, consumed much of the bishop's time and energy. Still, that Humphrey aborted the project for which he gave up a successful career as a Seventh-day Adventist minister is noteworthy. More important, it does not appear that the United Sabbath-Day Adventists promoted or ran any coherent, comprehensive program for the economic uplift of its members or community. Admittedly, Humphrey encouraged youth to seek higher education, but he never entertained plans to operate a school on any level in New York City. United Sabbath-Day Adventists sponsored no benevolent or burial societies, as other Black religious groups did. Indeed, it appears that after his split with the Seventh-day Adventists Humphrey was far more conservative in this theology, and the group he established, to borrow Gayraud S. Wilmore's term, was a deradicalized church.[5]

The African Americans who remained with and joined Humphrey's group did so for several reasons, including the emotional and psychological benefits they received from a religious organization that to this day is misunderstood and miscast as a renegade cult that, at least in its early days, was woefully out of kilter with mainstream American values. Sabbath-Day Adventists of the Humphrey era speak fondly of the vibrant relationships that were nurtured and fostered within the infant group and of the sense of community and belonging it engendered. To them, being a part of the Sabbath-Day Adventist Church was like experiencing utopia on earth, and Humphrey, in spite of the legal issues and allegations of marital improprieties that dogged his tenure, is remembered positively by them as a courageous, visionary leader who wanted the best for his people.

Sabbath-Day Adventists tend to view their church history as one of resistance to, not one of domination by, an established, superior power. They are pleased about the stand Humphrey and they took against the Seventh-day Adventist church. Today, United Sabbath-Day Adventists are a proud, indefatigable group determined to perpetuate the legacy of their founding pastor and to fulfill his dream. To be sure, the New York congregation is all that is left of

Humphrey's religious organization, and the congregation numbers less than one hundred. Still, it occupies the building that is the only one ever built by Black Adventists in New York City, and the structure stands as a monument to the refusal of African Americans to accept discriminatory practices.

One reason the Sabbath-Day Adventist organization may have failed to attract new members is because of the premium the Seventh-day Adventist church places on loyalty to the organization and the unique perception it has of its place and role in world history. Individuals who join the church early understand that Seventh-day Adventists are a special people to whom have been bequeathed the task of disseminating the gospel in the context of the Three Angels' Messages of Revelation 14.

Sabbath-Day Adventists argue that their stance is the reason for the gains African Americans have made in the Seventh-day Adventist church. The real beneficiaries of Humphrey's stance are not so much Sabbath-Day Adventists, they believe, but the African Americans in the Seventh-day Adventist Church. As such, they view James Kemuel Humphrey as a pioneer in the struggle of people of African descent for autonomy and self-determination.

Appendix A. Fundamental Beliefs
of Sabbath-Day Adventists

Some Things We Believe

United Sabbath Day Adventists Believe

That the Bible is the word of God, and that all scripture was given by inspiration and is profitable for doctrine, reproof, correction, and instruction in righteousness, in order that believers may attain unto perfection. 2 Tim. 3:16.

That the Holy Scriptures are sufficient to impart unto us all the wisdom, knowledge and understanding necessary to salvation. 2 Tim. 3:15.

That the word of God should be studied and rightly divided by those who are seeking God's approval. 2 Tim. 2:15.

That prophecies were not given by the will or intelligence of men, but holy men wrote as they were moved upon by the Holy Spirit. 2 Peter 1:20, 21.

That the prophecies of the Bible are sure to be fulfilled, that, like a giant indistinguishable ray of light, they shine through the darkness of time until Jesus Christ returns. 2 Peter 1:19.

That those who follow the word of God will never walk in darkness. Psa. 119:105.

That God used Jesus Christ as the Creator of all things in heaven and earth. John 1:1–5; Col. 1:13–16; Heb. 1:1, 2.

That Jesus possessed a human and divine nature to successfully accomplish the work of redemption; that he had to be human and divine to make the connection (that was broken through the sin of our first parents) between fallen man and Jehovah. Phil. 2:8: Matt. 1:21, 23; Heb. 2:14–18.

That Christ is able to save the vilest sinner from sin and eternal death. Matt. 1:21; Acts 16:31; Rom. 5:1; John 3:16; Matt. 9:13.

That eternal life is a gift which was made possible through the death of Christ, and we also believe that the wages of sin is eternal death. Rom. 6:23.

That death came as a result of man's disobedience. Rom. 5:12–19.

That man was created a mortal being in a condition where death was possible. Gen. 2:16, 17; 3:22.

That the soul of man himself, that the term "Immortal soul" is contrary to the Scriptures, and that at death the soul dies. Gen. 2:7; Ezek. 18:4; Rom. 16:3.

That the dead are in their graves, and there they shall remain until Jesus comes. Job 14:7–15; 17:13.

That the righteous shall be rewarded at the Second Advent of Christ. Isa. 40:10; 62:11; Rev. 22:12.

That the wicked shall be punished with complete annihilation after the thousand years' reign of Christ and the saints. Rev. 20:7–9; Mal. 4:1; Psa. 37:10, 20, 38; 34:21, Prov. 2:22.

That the Judgment takes place after the coming of our savior Jesus Christ. Psa. 96:13; 50:3; 2 Tim. 4:1; Matt. 25: 31–40.

That the testimony of Jesus Christ is the spirit of prophecy; that it was the Spirit of Christ that prompted and actuated the prophets, and that, therefore, Christ was the directing intelligence behind every statement made, whether orally or in writing, by them. It was Christ who testified, through the prophets, therefore the testimony of Christ is the spirit of prophecy, and not the gift to prophesy. 1 Peter 1:10, 11; Rev. 1:9; 19:10.

That the martyrs throughout the Dark Ages had the testimony of Christ, and suffered for it. Rev. 20:4.

That the one hundred and forty-four thousand are not Gentiles, but Jews from the fleshly stock of Abraham, who shall be saved in God's kingdom; that they are not contaminated with popular false doctrines, hence they are considered virgins and are the first fruits of the gospel of Jesus Christ. We further believe that they form a special class, which follow the Lamb wherever He goes. Rev. 7:1–4; 14:1–5.

That the Holy Spirit is the seal of God and that we are sealed with that Spirit. Eph. 4:30; 1:13, 14; 2 Cor. 1:22. We believe that Christ was sealed with the Holy Spirit on the day of His baptism. John 6:27.

That the Holy Spirit is given for the purpose of leading and guiding God's people into all truth, and to glorify Christ in their lives. John 16:13, 14.

That the Holy Spirit is given as the Comforter, and abides with the Christian for ever. John 14:16, 17.

That whenever a man repents and is converted and baptized, he receives the gift of the Holy Ghost. Acts 2:38; 3:19.

That a man should be converted, or should be the recipient of the "new birth" to enter into the Kingdom of God. John 3:5; Matt. 18:3.

That those who are looking for the coming of Christ should live such lives as will make them worthy of being caught up to meet the Lord in the air. Titus 2:12, 14; 2 Pet. 3:11–14; 2 Thess. 4:14–18.

That the law of God is a transcript of His character, and is therefore as eternal as God Himself. Psa. 111: 7, 8. Psa. 89:34.

That the seventh day of the week, commonly called Saturday was sanctified and set apart as the Holy Sabbath, and should, therefore, be observed as the day of worship by all Christian. Gen. 2:1–3; Exod. 16:23, 28; 20:8–11.

That the Bible plan of tithing and the giving of offerings by its members is the proper means for the support of the Church. Mal. 3:8–11; Matt. 23:23.

That we are living in "the eleventh hour" of the history of the world, and that the call of the hour is to Negroes to preach the gospel to the world, since, through prejudice and race hatred, and in God's economy of grace, the Gentiles' (white race) time has been fulfilled. Matt. 20:6; 16:21–24.

That the Gentiles, as originally defined by the Bible, were Japethites, or the white race, and that the terms "Ethiopian," "Egyptian," "Hamite," and "Cushite" are applied to the Negro or black race. Gen. 10:5; Mark 10:33; Rom. 11:11, 25; Isa. 19:23–25; 11:11.

—R. Leo Soaries

Appendix B. Constitution and By-Laws of the New York Sabbath-Day Adventist Church

ARTICLE I—NAME

This church was incorporated under the laws of the State of New York, underthefollowingname:—NEWYORKUNITEDSABBATH-DAYADVENTISTCHURCH.

ARTICLE II—POLITY AND DOCTRINE

This Church acknowledges Jesus Christ as its head, and finds in the holy scriptures interpreted by the Divine Spirit through reason, faith and conscience, its guidance in matters of faith and discipline. This Church further recognizes the Bible as the sufficient rule of faith and practice, and firmly believes that living in accordance with the teachings of Jesus Christ is the true and revealed test of human fellowship.

ARTICLE III—OBJECT

Section 1. The primary objects and purposes of this Church are to promulgate the Christian Religion according to the Sabbath-Day Adventist Doctrine and to advance the spiritual understanding of all worshipers and followers thereof, and devotedly seek to diffuse and extend the knowledge and realization of the "Commandments of God" and the true and everlasting gospel of our Lord and Savior, Jesus Christ.

Section 2. As a secondary object we believe that in order to effectively carry out our primary objects and purposes it is and will be the duty of the officers, executives, elders, members, and the bodies constituted by them to personally perform and cooperate in all our activities to establish moral and evangelistic instruction and training and in all our other religious and secular activities especially those which may tend to improve, extend and place upon a sound and permanent foundation the tenets of the United Sabbath-Day Adventist Denomination and thereby to extend the general moral and religious interests of the worshipers and followers thereof.

ARTICLE IV—MEMBERSHIP

All persons who have been first taught the doctrines of our church and accept the covenants of the church and its authority and to subscribe to the following covenants:

1. To believe in the second coming of Jesus Christ
2. To keep the seventh day as the Sabbath
3. To pay one tenth of all income as a tithe to the church
4. To be baptized by complete immersion
5. To believe in the unconscious state of the dead
6. To believe in dress reform and health reform shall be eligible for membership in this Church.

Admission to membership in this church shall be made after presentation of an application for such membership made by the prospective member and such application shall be reported by the Board of Deacons, with its recommendation. The application and recommendation shall then be voted upon at the next meeting of the members. Before his election to membership the applicant shall publicly accept the covenants of the church and its authority. Members of the church may also be accepted on presentation of satisfactory letters of transfer from other churches, or if such letters are not available by reaffirmation of faith or confession of faith or by baptism if not previously baptized.

Persons recommended by the Board of Deacons who have been approved by vote of the members at a regular meeting or at a service of the Church shall be received after full baptism (if not previously baptized) at a regular service after public assent and acceptance of the covenant or after thoughtful and written acceptance of the covenant, or at such other times as the members of the Church shall order.

All persons shall continue to be such members and shall be bound by this constitution and by-laws and any amendments thereof.

Only such members who are in good standing may vote at any election, meeting or service of this Church.

Letters of dismission and recommendation to another Church may be granted by a vote of the members of the church upon request. This letter shall be valid as a recommendation for one year only unless renewed, and the letter of recommendation shall so state. The right of any member requesting such letter to vote at any meetings of this Church shall be terminated upon notice of acceptance into another church or at the end of one year if inquiry shall determine such letter shall not be renewed. No letter shall be granted except one addressed to a particular church, named by the applicant.

If a member desires to join another religious body this church may present to the applicant a certificate of his standing in this church and his membership shall cease.

Should a member become an offense to the Church and to its good name by reason of immoral or unchristian conduct or by consistent breach of his covenant vows, this Church on recommendation of its Board of Deacons may censure such members, or member, and by a two-thirds vote of a duly elected called meeting, suspend or terminate his or her membership; but only after due notice and hearing and after faithful efforts have been made to bring such members to amendment in accordance with the law of Christ and the Church.

If, because of change of faith or for other reasons not involving Christian conduct, a member in good standing ceases his obligations, the Church shall patiently endeavor to secure his continuance in its fellowship but failing such efforts after a reasonable time, the Church may grant his request and terminate such membership, but no member shall receive any letter of transfer to a church of another faith.

Any former membership by a vote of the Church taken at a duly constituted meeting after notice of such restoration application has been given to the members, if such application is made after an offense, evidence must be given of reformation, and if, for any other cause, upon satisfactory explanation by the former member, and acceptance by the Board of Deacons. The Board of Deacons will report upon its resolution with its recommendations for approval or disapproval.

ARTICLE V—SERVICES AND MEETINGS

Section 1. Service of worship shall be held at given hours each Sabbath except when temporarily suspended by a vote of the members of the Church.

The ordinance of the Lord's Supper shall be celebrated on the first Sabbath of each quarter. Baptism of adults and Blessing of Children shall be administered at such time and times as the elders may appoint or designate. The annual meeting of the members shall be held on the first Sabbath in February at which meeting the annual reports of officers, organizations, and departments shall be given, and at this meeting there shall be elected the officers for the ensuing term, the adoption of the annual budget, and the consideration and adoption of plans for the new year.

The regular Sabbath and mid-week services of the Church shall be considered competent in case of necessity to transact the business of the Church if a quorum is present; except for corporate actions requiring legal notices and except for business specifically referred to other meetings.

Special meetings for the transaction of business may be called by the elder, the officers, deacons and trustees, and shall be called by the clerk of the Church on written request of twenty five (25) adult members of the church, provided that the nature of the business to be transacted shall be stated in the notice calling the special meeting.

Any changes in the constitution, by-laws, or rules and regulations of the Church shall be made at a meeting of the members called for that purpose and nature of the change shall be stated in the notice of meeting.

A quorum shall consist of twenty five (25) members in good standing.

Any meeting involving elections of officers, trustees, or elders shall be by standing vote, unless the majority of the members present at such meeting shall decide to vote by ballot. In which case election shall be by ballot only. The President of the Church shall preside at all meetings of the members at which business is to be transacted, including meetings of the Board of Trustees. The presence of the Elder of the Church may be requested at any meeting.

Election of officers shall take place after nominations are made in the following manner. Officers shall be nominated for their respective offices upon the meeting of the members held on the first Sabbath in December of each year. Election of all officials shall take place at the meeting of the members, upon the first Sabbath in January and upon their election, they shall be immediately installed in office. Nomination and election of members of the Board of Trustees shall take place the first Sabbath in February of each year.

ARTICLE VI—OFFICERS AND BOARD

The activities of the Church shall be divided into two parts, namely, (a) Business and Administrative, (b) Spiritual.

The Spiritual division of the church shall be presided over by the Elder and assistant Elder of Elders, elected by the members as hereafter set forth and the Business and Administrative officers shall be as follows:

1. The President
2. The Vice President
3. The Treasurer
4. The Clerk
5. Financial Secretary
6. The Board of Deacons
7. The Board of Trustees

The duties of the various officers and boards shall be set forth in the by-laws and any amendments thereof.

The members may also at each annual meeting elect an Executive Committee composed of the Board of Trustees, the President, Clerk of the Church, the Chairman of the Board of Deacons, the Chairman of the Board of Deaconesses, and three lay members of the church. It shall be the duty of the Executive Committee to act in any emergency which cannot await the calling of a regular or special meeting of the members called after notice containing the reason and purpose of calling such special meeting. A vote of approval or disapproval shall be by 75% of a quorum of the members in good standing attending such meeting, or a majority thereof, whichever is greater in number.

A Board of Missions shall be elected at each annual meeting consisting of five (5) lay members. The Elder shall be a member of the missions board, ex-officio. This Board shall take the responsibility of spreading the gospel in such areas and places as the members shall approve at the annual meeting or at any special meetings called for that purpose. The budget of the missions board shall be submitted at the same time at the annual meeting as the budget for all other activities of the church.

At the annual meeting members shall vote upon a choir master, assistant choir master, organist and secretary of the choir.

At the annual meeting there shall be elected the officers of the Sabbath School, namely, Superintendent, Secretary, and Pianist in such number as the members shall approve.

ARTICLE VII—TITHES AND DUTIES

The Board of Trustees shall levy and assess all tithes and other payments to the church as they shall deem proper subject to the approval of the membership at the annual meeting or at any special meeting called for that specific purpose.

ARTICLE VIII—COMMITTEES

Committees shall be appointed by the President or Board of Trustees in such number and composition as the work of the church may from time to time find necessary. All committees shall report to the authority appointing the committee, for such action as may be found necessary. All such committees connected with the church and using its equipment shall be regarded as an integral part of the church and under the supervision and control of the Board of Trustees and shall be generally supervised by them.

ARTICLE IX—PROVISION IN CASE OF CONFLICT

In the event that any disagreement or conflict shall arise between the Pastor or Elder and the officers, or between the members of the church and any elected or appointed official, the point of issue shall be formulated in writing signed by at least five (5) members and the matter shall be submitted to the Board of Trustees and to the General Membership at a special meeting called for that purpose after due notice to all the members, which notice shall state the reason and purpose of calling the meeting and the issue to be determined by the membership. The vote of the membership shall be final and binding upon all parties. The action taken by the members at such meeting shall be by not less than $\frac{2}{3}$ vote.

ARTICLE X—AMENDMENTS

This constitution may be amended at any time at an annual meeting or at any special meeting called for that purpose, the notice of which shall contain the reason and object of calling the meeting and the votes of 75% of the members shall be necessary to pass any amendment to this constitution.

By-Laws

ARTICLE I—OFFICERS

PRESIDENT: The President shall preside at all business and secular meetings of the members of the members, and shall conduct all of the business affairs of the church, subject to the approval of the Board of Trustees. He shall sign all checks for the withdrawal of funds. He is authorized to sign all contracts, agreements, or order of the church. He shall carry out all orders and decisions of the Board of Trustees.

THE VICE PRESIDENT: The Vice President shall do any and all things in the absence of the President which are delegated to the President.

CLERK OF THE CHURCH: The church clerk shall keep a faithful record of the proceedings of the church and of the Board of Trustees of which he shall be a member ex-officio and its secretary. He shall keep a register of addresses of members of the church, together with dates and modes of their reception and removal and also a record of baptisms and marriages. He shall issue letters of transfer voted by the church and notify the church to which such letters are addressed. He shall preserve on file all communication and written official reports; notify all persons elected to offices and committees; send out legal notices of all meetings when such notices are required or necessary; he shall conduct all correspondence in so far as the same is not otherwise provided for, and shall perform such other duties as are prescribed by law or as usually pertain to the office of the clerk or secretary of a church or assembly.

THE TREASURER: The Treasurer shall receive all monies from the financial secretary and all other monies of the church and give receipt for the same. He shall deposit funds received in such depository as the Trustees shall order. Under direction of the Board of Trustees he shall have custody of all papers relating to the property of the church. He shall pay all the bills of the church upon the order of the Board of Trustees or their properly appointed agent. He shall keep accurate and correct accounts of all receipts and disbursements and shall be required to give such bond as the Board of Trustees shall prescribe. He shall keep a separate account of benevolence funds in accordance with the order of the church.

FINANCIAL SECRETARY: The financial secretary shall be elected at the annual meeting. He shall receive all payments of current expenses and benevolence subscriptions and shall take charge of all offerings and special collections. He shall keep an accurate and correct account with each subscriber; he shall pay all monies received to the proper treasurer taking receipts for the same, and he shall furnish subscribers with quarterly statements of their accounts.

THE ELDER: The Elder shall be called or elected for an indefinite term by a $\frac{2}{3}$ vote of the members of the church at an annual meeting or at a special meeting called for that purpose. The Elder shall have charge of the spiritual welfare and work of the church and shall conduct his duties with the assistance of the Board of Deacons and under the supervision of the Board of Trustees. He shall seek to enlist men and women as followers of Jesus Christ, preach the gospel, administer the ordinances of the church and have under his chair all services of public worship and the spiritual activities of the church. He shall preside at all meetings of the church at which spiritual matters are to be discussed or voted upon except when matters concerning himself are to be considered or when another moderator is chosen by the meeting. The members of the church shall at any time by a majority vote, at a meeting called for that purpose, request the resignation of the Elder. The Elder shall have the right to give to the church sixty (60) days previous notice that he desires to leave of his own volition, except that in case of loss of ministerial standing on the part of the Elder, his right of office shall cease at once.

Whenever a vacancy occurs in the pastorate of the church, the members at a meeting specifically called for that purpose upon due notice, shall elect a pulpit committee; such committee after seeking the guidance of the Divine Spirit shall, with the cooperation of the Board of Trustees, and of the Board of Deacons, make a canvass of available ministers and settle upon the one who, in their judgment, should be called to the Eldership and introduce him to the church and propose his election as Elder or Pastor at a meeting duly called on notice for such purpose. When he has been so elected, and has accepted the call to the church, the Elder shall become a member of the church and subscribe to the constitution and by-laws of the church and be bound thereby.

ARTICLE II—ADMINISTRATIVE BOARD

THE BOARD OF TRUSTEES: The Board of Trustees shall consist of a minimum of nine (9) or a maximum of twelve (12) members elected at the annual meeting in accordance with the laws of the State of New York. There shall be three (3) categories of members of the Board of Trustees. Three (3) shall be elected for a term of three years, three (3) shall be elected for a term of two years, and three (3) shall be elected for a term of one year. At following annual meetings, vacancies in the board shall be filled by the election of three members for three year periods, so that three new members of the Board shall be voted upon at each annual meeting. If any other vacancies occur in the board, such vacancies may be filled at an annual meeting or at a special meeting called for that purpose for the unexpired term of the vacancy. The Board shall elect its own officers and committees and shall determine its own mode of procedure. There shall be a chairman of the Board of Trustees and the Clerk of the Church shall act as its secretary ex-officio, without right to vote. Under the direction of the church and except as otherwise provided for, the Board of Trustees shall have the case of and the custody of the property of the church and shall have charge of its financial affairs subject to rules and regulations prescribed by the membership and by the laws of the State of New York. The Board shall have no power to buy, sell, or mortgage, lease or transfer property without the specific authority given by a ⅔ vote of the church.

THE BOARD OF DEACONS: The Board of Deacons shall consist of (12) members. It shall be the duty of the Board of Deacons to cooperate with the Elder in ministering to the spiritual interests of the church and community.

They shall assist in preparation and administration of the ordinances in caring for the poor, sick, sorrowing, the indifferent, and strangers. They shall give attention to the discipline as found in the by-laws. They shall receive applications by letter or otherwise for admission to church membership and shall examine all applicants for membership on confession of faith with respect to their fitness therefore. They shall provide for the supply of the pulpit in case of a vacancy, or in case of the absence of the elder.

THE BOARD OF DEACONESSES: The Board of Deaconesses shall be composed of five (5) members of the church. The Deaconesses shall visit the sick and needy, especially of their own sex, call upon new members, introduce new families into the life of the church, and cooperate with the Pastor or Elder in promoting the spiritual life of the church.

The deacons and deaconesses shall hold joint meetings whenever such meetings are deemed necessary to the development of the spiritual life of the church.

THE BOARD OF MISSIONS: The Board of Missions shall be composed of five (5) members who shall all be members of the church. They shall undertake such missions both at home and abroad as they shall be advised by the Board of Deaconesses acting jointly as to plans for such missions. They shall prepare a budget to be submitted at each annual meeting and report on their work at such meetings.

THE SABBATH SCHOOL: The Sabbath School shall be composed of as many members as the annual meeting shall deem necessary. The annual meeting shall also elect such superintendents, secretaries, and pianists as they may deem necessary and proper to carry out the work of the church. The officers of the Sabbath School shall prepare a budget to be submitted at the annual meeting and shall make their report upon their work at the annual meeting or at such other meetings as may be called for that purpose.

THE CHOIR: The choir shall assemble themselves to practice so that they might sing to the honor and glory of God. They shall open their practice with prayer and close with prayer so that God might be well pleased. Members of the choir must be members of the church and prospective members of the church who are of good behavior. All members of the choir will be expected to attend practice except in case of sickness or matter over which they have no control, and in the latter cases, a note of excuse must be presented to the Choir Master. Perfect behavior will be expected of all members of the choir. Any member of the choir who is absent from choir practice for three consecutive practice nights without having reasonable cause therefore, shall be excused from the choir.

The choir shall be comprised of a Choirmaster, and Assistant Choirmaster, an Organist and a Secretary. The Choirmaster shall have full control of the choir and in his absence, the assistant Choirmaster shall have such control. The secretary will keep the necessary records of the choir and attend to all of their correspondence.

DISMISSAL OF A MEMBER: All members of the church are required to bear their share of the responsibility for the upkeep of the church according to their ability, to so conduct themselves as to be a credit to the church and God.

A member of the church may be dismissed from the church in accordance with the rules laid down by the Master Himself (See Matthew 18:15–19).

Any member who violates the principles of our faith and the doctrines of the church as we teach them, will be liable to dismissal by a vote of the members at an annual meeting or at a meeting specially called for that purpose.

Upon paying his tithe to the treasurer of the church, a member shall request and receive from the treasurer a receipt therefore.

Notes

Introduction

1. *General Conference Bulletin*, Fortieth Session, vol. 9, no. 11, Mountain View, California, May 25, 1922, 253.

2. For an impartial account of the work of the United States Sanitation Commission, impaneled on June 13, 1861, by President Abraham Lincoln to conduct scientific research on the physical, mental, and moral powers of people of African descent, see John S. Haller Jr., *Outcasts from Evolution: Scientific Attitudes of Racial Inferiority, 1850–1900* (Urbana: University of Illinois Press, 1971), 19–34.

3. The names and terms with which people of African descent living in North America have resonated, or by which they have preferred to be called, have changed over the years. *Negro, Afro-American, Colored, Black, African-American,* and *African American* have all been used. Today, the preferred term is *African American*, with or without the hyphen. In the first half of the twentieth century, the period that is the focus of this book, *Negro* was the term in vogue, but in this book I have elected to use the terms *African American* and *Black*, at times using them interchangeably. Of course, direct quotes shall reflect the term used by the source referenced. Not surprising, some West Indians are ambivalent about the term *African American*, believing that it excludes them. Those who subscribe to this view see themselves as being *Afro-Caribbean*.

4. In this book, the words *Black* and *White* are capitalized, even when they are used as adjectives, as in the case of Italian, German, Irish, Jewish, etc.

5. Charles E. Bradford argues that when White European slave traders landed on the African continent, they found people who knew of Christianity. See Charles E. Bradford, *Sabbath Roots: The African Connection* (Barre, VT: L. Brown and Sons, 1999).

6. R. W. Schwarz, *Lightbearers to the Remnant* (Washington, D.C.: Review and Herald Publishing Association, 1979), 477–79.

7. Bernice Samuel, interview by author, Jamaica, New York, Apr. 17, 2000.

8. Seventh-day Adventist churches in a particular geographical area are grouped together and governed by an entity called a conference. Ostensibly, a conference, sometimes referred to as a local conference, is a united body of churches, which are themselves united bodies of believers. The next level of the denomination's organizational structure is the union, which is a united body of conferences in a region. For example, during Humphrey's pastoral

tenure in the Greater New York Conference, the churches in the New York City area were a part of the Greater New York Conference, and those in upstate New York were a part of the New York Conference. Both conferences were a part of the Atlantic Union, headquartered in Massachusetts. Local conferences supervise Adventist mission and ministry in the churches, whereas the union supervises the work in the local conferences. Both the local and union conference have executive committees that assist their presidents in planning and executing their responsibilities. The organizational structure of the Seventh-day Adventist church consists of five administrative and four constituent levels. Members form the constituency of a local church, a group of churches form the constituency of a local conference, a group of conferences form the constituency of a union, and a group of unions form the constituency of the General Conference. Yet there are five levels to the administrative structure of the denomination: (1) the local church, (2) the local conference, (3) the local union, (4) the division, and (5) the General Conference. World divisions are simply the General Conference operating in a particular part of the world, and in 2005 there were thirteen world divisions.

9. *General Conference Bulletin*, vol. 6, no. 16, Thirty-Seventh Session (Washington, D.C.: The General Conference of Seventh-day Adventists, 1909), 243. The Negro Department of the General Conference of Seventh-day Adventists was established with a view to strengthening and superintending work among African Americans.

10. Ibid., 286.

11. *General Conference Bulletin*, Thirty-Eight Session, vol. 7, no. 20 (Washington, D.C.: The General Conference of Seventh-day Adventists, 1913), 309.

12. Greater New York Conference of Seventh-day Adventists, *Minutes of the Biennial Session of the Greater New York Conference of Seventh-day Adventists*, Feb. 24, 1920, Greater New York Conference Archives, Manhasset, New York.

13. Adventist church polity calls for churches to be voted into a local conference at a duly called meeting of the conference.

14. Greater New York Conference of Seventh-day Adventists, *Minutes of the Seventeenth Session of the Greater New York Conference of Seventh-day Adventists*, June 20–24, 1922, Greater New York Conference Archives, Manhasset, New York.

15. Ibid.

16. Greater New York Conference of Seventh-day Adventists, *Minutes of the Eighteenth Session of the Greater New York Conference of Seventh-day Adventists*, Mar. 12–14, 1924. Greater New York Conference of Seventh-day Adventist Archives, Manhasset, New York.

17. Donald L. Vanterpool, "A Study of Events Concerning the First Harlem Church," unpublished term paper (Berrien Springs, MI: Andrews University School of Graduate Studies, 1979), 12.

18. *Minutes of the Eighteenth Session of the Greater New York Conference of Seventh-day Adventists*, Mar. 12–14, 1924.

19. Until recently, the Harvest Ingathering campaign was conducted annually in Seventh-day Adventist churches around the world. A humanitarian venture aimed at alleviating pain and suffering worldwide, it called for church members to canvass their neighbors and friends for financial contributions to help in a worthy cause.

20. Greater New York Conference of Seventh-day Adventists, *Minutes of the Twentieth Session of the Greater New York Conference of Seventh-day Adventists*, Mar. 20–24, 1928, Greater New York Conference Archives, Manhasset, New York.

21. *Minutes of the Eighteenth Session of the Greater New York Conference of Seventh-day Adventists*, Mar. 12–14, 1924.

22. No one is sure who the individual referred to by Humphrey is, though speculation has centered on Louis C. Sheafe and not J. W. Manns, who also visited with Humphrey. Formerly pastor of the Northwest Washington, D.C. Church at 10th and V streets, Sheafe and his congregation defected from the denomination in 1907, returning to it some years later. Subsequently, Sheafe left again, never to return. See Jacob Justiss, *Angels in Ebony* (Toledo, OH: Jet Printing Services, 1975), 45.

23. *General Conference Bulletin*, Fortieth Session, vol. 9, no. 11, May 25, 1922, 253–54.

24. Although Humphrey used Peter as the springboard for his sermon, he appealed to the apostle Paul for warrant and backing for his main thesis. Quoting profusely from Paul's letter to the Romans and Corinthians, Humphrey claimed that suffering is the inevitable experience of people who became Christians. More topical than expository, the sermon demonstrates that Humphrey was at least a biblical preacher, if not a theologian, at this point in his ministry.

25. *General Conference Bulletin*, Fortieth Session, 253–54.

26. Humphrey's exposition appears to lack theological depth and does not reflect the historic African American perspective on pain and suffering. Two excellent studies of the African American theology of pain and suffering are James H. Cone, *God of the Oppressed* (San Francisco: Harper and Row, 1975), and Anthony B. Pinn, *Why, Lord? Suffering and Evil in Black Theology* (New York: Continuum, 1995).

27. *General Conference Bulletin*, Fortieth Session, 253–54.

28. Ibid.

29. Though allusion is made to Humphrey's leadership role in the Greater New York Conference and Adventist church, he is conspicuously absent when Black leaders are surveyed by some indigenous African American writers. For example, in *A Star Gives Light: Seventh-day Adventist African American Heritage*, Humphrey is named as one of three Blacks who were disenchanted with the denomination's proposal that the Black work be organized on a mission basis because such an arrangement would not facilitate Black representation on all levels of church organization. Humphrey is also mentioned as one of the evangelists responsible for the growth of the Black membership to 3,500 by 1918. Yet, Humphrey is not mentioned in the book's history of the Black Seventh-day Adventist ministry. See Norwida A. Marshall, ed., *A Star Gives Light: Seventh-day Adventist African American Heritage* (Decatur, GA: Southern Union Conference of Seventh-day Adventists, 1989), 43–44.

30. A Bible Worker or Bible Instructor is a licensed missionary who assists a minister in his or her work. Bible Workers follow up on people interested in having Bible studies, either for their own edification or as a prelude to their becoming baptized members of the church. In addition, Bible Workers function full or part time and may or may not be remunerated for their services.

31. Greater New York Conference of Seventh-day Adventists, *Comparative Reports for the Years 1920–1927,* Twentieth Session, Mar. 20–24, 1928, Greater New York Conference Archives, Manhasset, New York.

32. Greater New York Conference of Seventh-day Adventists, *Minutes of the Nineteenth Biennial Session of the Greater New York Conference,* Mar. 24–26, 1926, Greater New York Conference Archives, Manhasset, New York.

33. Among the useful works of the Progressive era are Richard Hofstadter, *The Age of Reform* (New York: Alfred A. Knopf, 1956); John W. Chambers, *The Tyranny of Change: America in the Progressive Era, 1900–1917* (New York: St. Martin's Press, 1980); Robert M. Cruden, *Ministers of Reform: The Progressives' Achievement in American Civilization, 1889–1920* (New York: Basic Books, 1982); John Milton Cooper, *Pivotal Decades: The United States, 1900–1920* (New York: Columbia, 1990); Gabriel Kolko, *The Triumph of Conservatism: A Reinterpretation of American History, 1900–1916* (New York: Free Press of Glencoe, 1963). The lives and policies of the two American presidents who dominated the era are adequately covered in John Milton Cooper, *The Warrior and the Priest: Woodrow Wilson and Theodore Roosevelt* (Cambridge: Harvard University Press, 1983).

34. James Cone says that their African heritage and existential situation in America have always caused Black clergy to stop short of bifurcating the material and spiritual needs of their people (*Speaking the Truth: Ecumenism, Liberation, and Black Theology* [Grand Rapids: William B. Eerdmans Publishing Company, 1986], 92).

35. Regional conferences or Black conferences are not constituted as regular local conferences. Each regional conference covers the area of a union, and the membership of each Regional Conference is composed principally of the African Americans in that region or union. In 2005, there were nine Regional Conferences in the North American Division of Seventh-day Adventists. In the Pacific and North Pacific Unions of the North American Division, as well as in the Seventh-day Adventist Church in Canada, there are no Regional Conferences, although there are all-Black churches. In those places, the affairs of Blacks are looked after by Regional Affairs directors. Most Seventh-day Adventist churches in Bermuda, also a part of the North American Division, are all-Black, and the president and officers of the Bermuda Conference are Black. To date, no book-length, comprehensive, or concise history of regional conferences has been written. In-depth accounts of the development of the phenomenon that seek to plumb and explore its rationale and, more important, implications for the future are yet to be researched. However, one is able to arrive at an understanding of how regional conferences came into being from a reading of the following: W. W. Fordham, *Righteous Rebel* (Washington, D.C.: Review and Herald Publishing Association, 1990); Delbert Baker, *The Unknown Prophet* (Washington, D.C.: Review and Herald Publishing Association, 1987); Ronald Graybill, *Ellen G. White and Church Race Relations* (Washington, D.C.: Review and Herald Publishing Association, 1970); Ronald Graybill, *Mission to Black America* (Washington, D.C.: Review and Herald Publishing Association, 1971); Louis B. Reynolds, *We Have Tomorrow: The Story of Adventists with an African American Heritage* (Washington, D.C.: Review and Herald Publishing Association, 1984); *Seventh-day Adventist Encyclopedia* (Washington, D.C.: Review and Herald Publishing Association, 1976); *Regional Voice: A Commemorative Issue,* Summer 2005.

36. The 13th Fundamental Belief of Seventh-day Adventists reads: "The church is one body with many members, called from every nation, kindred, tongue, and people. In Christ we are a new creation; distinctions of race, culture, learning, and nationality, and differences between high and low, rich and poor, male and female, must not be divisive among us. We are all equal in Christ, who by one Spirit has bonded us into one fellowship with Him and with one another; we are to serve and be served without partiality or reservation. Through the revelation of Jesus Christ in the Scriptures we share the same faith and hope, and reach out in one witness to all. This unity has its source in the oneness of the triune God, who has adopted us as His children." See *Seventh-day Adventists Believe . . . A Biblical Exposition of 27 Fundamental Doctrines* (Hagerstown, MD: Review and Herald Publishing Association, 1988), 171.

Chapter 1. The Utopia Park Affair

1. To "talk over" a matter connotes open dialogue. Yet less than five minutes into his presentation Dickson stated that Humphrey's attitude and actions had caused the organization to take "decided action," which church leaders had come "to *announce* to you as a church" (italics mine). Later, toward the end of his presentation, Dickson said that the meeting had been requested so that "we might inform you as a church of our decision." Whether church leaders were there to announce or inform the church of their decision, it seems certain that they were not there to "talk over" the matter. See James L. McElhany, ed., *Statement Regarding the Present Standing of Elder J. K. Humphrey* (Washington, D.C.: General Conference of Seventh-day Adventists, 1930), 5.

2. Ibid., 5–6. What exactly did Seventh-day Adventist church leaders have in mind with their references to unity? Were they talking about unity of purpose, uniformity of polity and policy, control by the denomination, or something else? Undoubtedly, unity was a central theme of theirs, though it is uncertain exactly what they had in mind. That they looked with disfavor on independent, "self-supporting" ventures is a reasonable conclusion, and their nonacceptance of such was only heightened when race was involved. Adventist leadership has always placed a premium on loyalty, desiring members to press together even if it meant subjugating their own desires. Years later, when he was president of the General Conference, Neal Wilson was still holding up church unity as a higher value than that of self-determination and equality of access and opportunity for any one racial group. In rebutting calls by Black church leaders for Black Unions, Wilson appealed to the metaphor of a family remaining together in spite of differences "that the ultimate good of the whole family can be realized and protected." See Neal C. Wilson, "Black Unions," Oct. 12, 1978.

3. McElhany, *Statement*, 6–10.

4. Ibid., 11.

5. Ostensibly, the membership that night voted 695 to 5 to sever its relationship with the Greater New York Conference and to support James K. Humphrey.

6. Legend has it that about 1,000 people were present at the meeting, that a riot would have erupted but for the quick intervention of Humphrey, and that denominational

leaders were ushered out to safety only after agreeing to return the title of its property to First Harlem.

7. McElhany, *Statement*, 20.

8. Ibid., 11, 13.

9. Ibid., 12.

10. "Seventh-day Adventists Break with White Governing Body Over Minister: Harlem Church Severs Ties with Conference on Grounds that Parent Group Practices Racial Discrimination," *New York Amsterdam News*, vol. XX, no. 49, Nov. 6, 1929, 1.

11. "Adventist Pastor Slams Broadsides at Fraud Charges," *New York Amsterdam News*, vol. XX, no. 50, Nov. 13, 1929, 1, 3.

12. "Rev. J. K. Humphrey loses 25-year Pastorate in 7th Day Adventist Church in New York," *New York Age*, vol. 43, no. 10, Nov. 16, 1929, 1.

13. "Minister Cleared in Resort Project: Kelly Denies His Office Persecuted Sponsor of Venture," *New York Amsterdam News*, vol. XXI, no. Dec. 4, 1929, 1, 2.

14. McElhany, *Statement*, 21–22.

15. Greater New York Conference of Seventh-day Adventists, *Minutes of the Twenty-First Biennial Session of the Greater New York Conference of Seventh-day Adventists*, Jan. 27–29, 1930, Greater New York Conference Archives, Manhasset, New York. This small group would later become the nucleus of the Ephesus Seventh-day Adventist church, which at the end of the twentieth century was the largest Seventh-day Adventist congregation in New York City. Interestingly, Louis Dickson made no mention of Humphrey to the delegates of the session, vis-a-vis the changes in the working force of the Conference.

16. W. A. Spicer, "New Memorials in Greater New York," *Advent Review and Sabbath Herald*, vol. 106, no. 51, Dec. 19, 1929, 22.

17. *Advent Review and Sabbath Herald*, vol. 107, no. 9, Feb. 27, 1930, 22.

18. J. L. McElhany, "The Greater New York Conference Session," *Advent Review and Sabbath Herald*, vol. 107, no. 11, Mar. 13, 1930, 20.

19. Delbert W. Baker, "Regional Conferences: 50 Years of Progress," *Adventist Review*, Nov. 1995, 12.

20. Charles Kinney is considered the "Father of Black Adventism." He was the first person of color to receive credentials from the Seventh-day Adventist Church and was instrumental in the spread of Adventism among African Americans. Yet Kinney early encountered what he thought was racism in the Seventh-day Adventist Church when his members were segregated on the day of his ordination. Kinney was the first African American Seventh-day Adventist minister to come out for a separate administrative structure for Blacks.

21. See George Knight, *Organizing to Beat the Devil* (Hagerstown, MD: Review and Herald Publishing Association, 2001), 146.

22. See George Knight, *From 1888 to Apostasy: The Case of A. T. Jones* (Hagerstown, MD: Review and Herald Publishing Association, 1987), 242.

23. Alven Makapela, *The Problem with Africanity in the Seventh-day Adventist Church* (Lewiston/Queenston/Lampeter: Edwin Mellon Press, 1996), 210–18

24. Knight, *From 1888 to Apostasy*, 242.

25. *Advent Review and Sabbath Herald*, vol. 86, no. 23, June 10, 1909, 13.

26. Ibid.

27. Ibid.

28. *Advent Review and Sabbath Herald*, vol. 86, no. 24, June 17, 1909, 8.

29. Ibid.

30. *Advent Review and Sabbath Herald*, vol. 86, no. 23, June 10, 1909, 13.

31. Knight, *Organizing to Beat the Devil*, 146–47.

32. *Yearbook of the Seventh-day Adventist Denomination* (Washington, D.C.: Review and Herald Publishing Association, 1922), 263.

33. Makapela, *Problem with Africanity*, 223.

34. According to Seventh-day Adventist policy, all deeds/titles to real property must be held by the local conference, ostensibly to safeguard the property from the whims and fancies of the local congregation.

35. J. W. Manns, "Why Free Seventh-day Adventists?" (n.p., n.d.: Banner Publishing Association), 1–3. The Adventist Heritage Center, Andrews University, Berrien Springs, MI.

36. Ibid., 16.

37. Ibid., 3–4.

38. Ibid, 13–14.

39. Manns supplied 12 reasons for choosing to call his group "Free," saying it is "the privilege of all men to be free from fear of their fellow men." Reasons 9 through 12 are as follows: "Ninth. We are free because the white leaders of the Seventh-day Adventist denomination discriminate against colored people. They do this abominable, most detestable, discriminating in the organization, the Church, the office, the school and sanitarium, notwithstanding the Negro membership must make great sacrifices to aid in building up these wonderful institutions now owned by the S. D. A. denomination. Tenth. We are free because Negro Seventh-day Adventists, as a rule, are barred from Seventh-day Adventist Northern and Western schools, where schools of the world make no distinction of races. Eleventh. We are free because the white leaders of the Seventh-day Adventist denomination bar even Negro Seventh-day Adventist patients from their sanitariums, when the worldly institutions of the same kind, accept colored people of every walk of life. Twelfth. We are free, because Negro Seventh-day Adventists are barred from holding any clerical position in the Seventh-day Adventist Publishing houses, tract societies and conference offices" (Ibid., 12–13).

40. Ibid., 9, 11.

41. Ibid., 17, 18.

42. Arthur L. White, letter to Mrs. Hedy Jemison, June 20, 1972, Adventist Research Center, James White Library, Andrews University, Berrien Springs, MI.

43. Although Ellen G. White died in 1915, she left boxes of manuscripts that first her family and later the Ellen G. White Estate, a department/subsidiary of the General Conference of Seventh-day Adventists, have published as books, pamphlets, and magazine articles. Publication of previously unpublished material continues to this day.

44. Ellen G. White, *Testimonies to the Church* (Mountain View, CA: Pacific Press Publishing Association, 1948), 9:195–98.

45. Ibid., 206.

46. Ibid, 214–15, 223.

47. Ibid., 195–97.

48. Ibid., 199.

49. Manns, "Why Free Seventh-day Adventists?" 4–5, 8–9.

50. Ibid., 7–10.

51. E. G. White, *Testimonies to the Church*, 9:206–8.

52. Knight, *Organizing to Beat the Devil*, 145.

53. The twelve Seventh-day Adventist colleges in North America are strategically located across the country to primarily serve the constituency where they are located. Ideally, they do not market themselves or recruit students beyond their individual union territory. Exempted from this guideline are Loma Linda University, the denomination's premiere medical institution, located in Loma Linda, California; and Andrews University, the organization's flagship educational institution and primary graduate school, located in Berrien Springs, MI.

54. Letter, Union College, Aug. 22, 1919, as it appears in *"?"* (n.p.: The Russworm Publishing Company, n.d.), 19.

55. Ibid.

56. One of the three individuals who authored the obituary of W. H. Green, who died on Oct. 21, 1928, was J. K. Humphrey. Humphrey was at Green's funeral services, which were held in Detroit, MI, and were presided over by General Conference president W. A. Spicer, who delivered the eulogy. *Advent Review and Sabbath Herald*, vol. 105, no. 52, Dec. 27, 1928, 22.

57. "Report of the Autumn Council of the General Conference Committee," *Advent Review and Sabbath Herald*, vol. 106, no. 46, Nov. 14, 1929, 7–8.

58. J. W. Christian, "Our Colored Work in Chicago," *Advent Review and Sabbath Herald*, vol. 107, no. 11, Mar. 13, 1930, 24–25.

59. The concept of regional conferences had been mentioned as early as 1889 by Charles Kinney. Seventh-day Adventist Archives, General Conference of Seventh-day Adventists, Silver Springs, MD.

60. *"?,"* 7.

61. Makapela, *Problem with Africanity*, 229–31.

62. Ibid., 231. See also W. W. Fordham, *Righteous Rebel* (Washington, D.C.: Review and Herald Publishing Association, 1990), 79.

63. *The Utopia Park Health Benevolent Association* (n.p.: n.d.).

64. Ibid.

65. Joe Mesar and Tom Dybdahl, "The Utopia Park Affair and the Rise of Northern Black Adventists," *Adventist Heritage*, vol. 1, no. 1, 37.

66. See William H. Pease and Jane H. Pease, *Black Utopia: Negro Communal Experiments in America* (Madison, WI: The State Historical Society of Wisconsin, 1963).

67. Letter, Louis K. Dickson to Elder J. K. Humphrey, Aug. 13, 1929, in McElhany, *Statement*, 6.

68. Letter, J. K. Humphrey to Elder Louis K. Dickson, Aug. 20, 1929, in McElhany, *Statement*, 7.

69. Letter, Louis K. Dickson to Elder J. K. Humphrey, Aug. 26, 1929, in McElhany, *Statement*, 7–8.

70. McElhany, *Statement*, 8.

71. Seventh-day Adventist clergy do not use the title "Reverend," but "Pastor." The use of the latter term helps to distinguish Seventh-day Adventist clergy from "first day" ministers. In addition, the contradistinction is replete with theological significance.

72. McElhany, *Statement*, 8–9.

73. Ibid., 9.

74. Ibid., 10.

CHAPTER 2. ASSESSING THE UTOPIA PARK AFFAIR

1. McElhany, *Statement*, 5–6.

2. Maurice Roy Jordine, *Reflections on J. K. Humphrey and the First Harlem Church*, unpublished term paper, James White Library, Andrews University, Berrien Springs, MI, Spring 1972, 12.

3. For an enlightening account of the historic role of African American clergy persons in the Black community, see Charles V. Hamilton, *The Black Preacher in America* (New York: William Morrow and Company, 1972); H. Beecher Hicks Jr., *Images of the Black Preacher* (Valley Forge, PA: Judson Press, 1977); and Emerson Boddie, *God's "Bad Boys"* (Valley Forge, PA: Judson Press, 1972). See also James H. Harris, *Preaching Liberation* (Minneapolis: Fortress Press, 1995), in which the author asserts that the Black preacher/pastor is "the most visible, listened-to spokesman in the black community," and this in spite of the fact that the Black preacher has not always been the most formally educated (3).

4. Tunde Adeleke, *UnAfrican Americans* (Lexington, KY: University Press of Kentucky, 1998), 8, 10. Adeleke, a Nigerian, writes about Black nationalism from an African perspective, decrying the failure of American Blacks to view it from that perspective. Even as Adeleke writes about Black nationalism from an African perspective, he holds up three African Americans—Martin Robison Delany, Alexander Crummell, and Henry McNeal Turner—as the individuals who pioneered in the development of the concept, which he equates with Pan-Africanism.

5. Although Black nationalism, as a concept, "is more easily described than defined," the phenomenon has been defined as "the belief of a group that it shares, or ought to share, a common heritage of language, culture and religion, and that its heritage, way of life and ethnic identity are distinct from those of other groups." Furthermore, the group "ought to rule themselves and shape their own destinies." In a nutshell, Black nationalism "was a rejection of the American status quo." See Edwin S. Redkey, *Black Exodus: Black Nationalist and Back-to-Africa Movements, 1890–1910* (New Haven: Yale University Press, 1969), 10, 15. See also Essien U. Essien-Udom, *Black Nationalism: A Search for an Identity in America* (Chicago: University of Chicago Press, 1962), 20.

6. Redkey, *Black Exodus*, 290.

7. Among the valuable works on Marcus Garvey and the UNIA are Edmund Moses Cronon, *Black Moses: The Story of Marcus Garvey and the Universal Negro Improvement Association* (Madison: University of Wisconsin Press, 1969); Cary D. Wintz, ed.,

African American Political Thought, 1890–1930: Washington, Du Bois, Garvey, and Randolph (Armonk, NY: M. E. Sharpe, 1966); John Henrik Clarke, ed., *Marcus Garvey and the Vision of Africa* (New York: Random House, 1974); Robert A. Hill, ed., *Marcus Garvey: Life and Lessons* (Berkeley, CA: University of California Press, 1987); and Marcus Garvey, *Philosophy and Opinions of Marcus Garvey* (New York: Arno Press, 1968). See also Tony Martin, *Marcus Garvey, Hero* (Dover, MA: The Majority Press, 1983); *Marcus Garvey, Message to the People* (Dover, MA: The Majority Press, 1986); and *The Pan-African Connection: From Slavery to Garvey and Beyond* (Dover, MA: The Majority Press, 1983).

8. American-born Blacks and Black West Indians have always existed in creative tension, at best. The reasons for their less than optimum relationship run the gamut from the sublime to the ludicrous. An extended analysis of the relationship between these two cultural groups that share a common racial heritage is provided in Chapter 3.

9. The published objectives of the forerunner of the UNIA, the Universal Negro Improvement and Conservation Association and African Communities League, established by Garvey in 1914 in Jamaica, were: "To establish a Universal Confraternity among the race; to promote the spirit of race pride and love; to reclaim the fallen of the race; to administer to and assist the needy; to assist in civilizing the backward tribes of Africa; to strengthen the imperialism of independent African states; to establish commissionaires or agencies in the principal countries of the world for the protection of all Negroes, irrespective of nationality; to promote a conscientious Christian worship among the native tribes of Africa; to establish universities, colleges and secondary schools for the further education and culture of the boys and girls of the race; to conduct a world-wide commercial and industrial intercourse." Neil Hickey and Ed Edwin, *Adam Clayton Powell and the Politics of Race* (New York: Fleet Publishing, 1965), 27.

10. Was racism new or shocking to Caribbean immigrants? Had they not experienced racial discrimination in the Caribbean? Indeed, had not racial discrimination played a role in their immigration to the United States? West Indian Blacks were prone to reflect wistfully of their countries, making believe that there was little, if any, racism there. Garvey was more realistic, refusing to bury his head in the sand or gloss over the stark reality of race prejudice that existed in the West Indies. He bemoaned the lack of civil liberties and structures that facilitated protest in the Caribbean and was happy that in the United States he had the opportunity to launch a race-conscious movement.

11. See Robert A. Hill, ed., *The Marcus Garvey and Universal Negro Improvement Association Papers,* vol. 1, 1826–Aug. 1919 (Berkeley, CA: University of California Press, 1983).

12. Ibid., xl.

13. Roi Ottley and William Weatherby, *The Negro in New York* (New York: Oceana, 1967), 211–13.

14. Ibid., 212.

15. Roi Ottley, *New World A-Coming* (New York: Arno Press and New York Times, 1968), 73. Scholars are divided over whether Garveyism was a religion or not, or as to its religious elements and dimensions. Arthur Huff Fauset did not include the movement in his study of Black cults in the urban North. See *Black Gods of the Metropolis: Negro Religious Cults of*

the Urban North (New York: Octagon Books, 1970). Yet other scholars could not help but see religious elements in the movement. See, for example, Randall K. Burkett, *Garveyism as a Religious Movement* (Metuchen, NJ: Scarecrow Press, 1978), in which Garvey is examined as a Black theologian. See also Henry J. Young, *Major Black Religious Leaders, 1755–1940* (Nashville: Abingdon, 1977); Gayraud Wilmore, *Black Religion and Black Radicalism* (Garden City, NY: Doubleday, 1972), in which Wilmore argues that Garveyism was "in the best tradition of the Black Church in America"; and Randall K. Burkett, *Black Redemption: Churchmen Speak for the Garvey Movement* (Philadelphia: Temple University Press, 1978), in which the author posits that the Garvey movement cannot be fully understood apart from its religious dimensions.

16. Mesar and Dybdahl, "Utopia Park Affair," 22–35.

17. Claude McKay, "Like a Strong Tree," in "?," 22.

18. Makapela, *Problem with Africanity*, 248, 262.

19. McElhany was vice president of the General Conference when he authored the explanation of events. See McElhany, *Statement*.

20. Ogden's article was reprinted in its entirety in McElhany's *Statement*, 22–24.

21. "?," 3–4.

22. Allegedly, the small, fledgling group had remitted $12,000 over a five year period to the Greater New York Conference, with nothing to show for it. Ibid., 8.

23. Seventh-day Adventists believe that the tithe, which is 10 percent of income, is holy, belongs to God, and is to be used solely for the support of the gospel ministry, that is, for the remuneration of clergy persons.

24. "?," 8.

25. Ibid.

26. W. W. Fordham, *Righteous Rebel* (Washington, D.C.: Review and Herald Publishing Association, 1990), 158.

27. One year after Kinney had called for the establishment of regional conferences, a White Seventh-day Adventist worker seemed to give tacit endorsement to the idea. In 1890, R. M. Kilgore, the newly appointed director of Seventh-day Adventist efforts in the South, called for the establishment of Adventist churches along racial lines, believing that the separation of the races in worship would greatly facilitate the numerical growth of both groups. See Kilgore's full report of his early evangelistic journeys in the South in *Advent Review and Sabbath Herald*, vol. 66, no. 43, Oct. 29, 1889, 683.

28. *New York Amsterdam News*, June 18, 1944.

29. See Delbert W. Baker, "Regional Conferences: 50 Years of Progress," *Adventist Review*, Nov. 1995, 11–15.

30. Calvin B. Rock, "A Better Way," *Spectrum*, Spring 1970, 21–22. Not all people of African descent in North America worship in congregations belonging to a regional conference. For any number of reasons, some African Americans hold membership in White congregations that belong to state conferences. In addition, not all Black churches in the North American Division belong to regional conferences, for any number of reasons opting not to be a part of the regional conference covering their territory but to belong to the local state conference. One issue plaguing regional conferences is a lack of appreciation of their

history. Even among Black Seventh-day Adventists there exists a tragic ignorance about how regional conferences came about, and many Whites view the phenomenon as a power play on the part of Blacks.

31. Mesar and Dybdahl, "Utopia Park Affair," 41, 53.

CHAPTER 3. THE TENOR OF THE TIMES

1. For a trenchant treatment of the period, see Geoffrey Perrett, *America in the Twenties* (New York: Simon and Schuster, 1982). See also William Leutenberg, *The Perils of Prosperity, 1914–1932*, 2nd ed. (Chicago: University of Chicago Press, 1993).

2. Gilbert Osofky, *Harlem: The Making of a Ghetto* (New York: Harper and Row Publishers, 1963), 3–34; Jervis Anderson, *This Was Harlem: A Cultural Portrait, 1900–1950* (New York: Farrar Straus Giroux, 1981), 3–12.

3. Not surprising, the Harlem of today is not the Harlem of the 1920s. At first, Black Harlem ran from 135th Street to the south to 145th Street to the north, and from Eight Avenue to the west to the East River to the east. Few Blacks ventured beyond those boundaries at the start of the 1920s. Yet by the end of the decade Black Harlem had expanded to 110th Street to the south and 155th Street to the north, and from St. Nicholas Avenue to the west to the East River to the east.

4. Bureau of the Census, *Fifteenth Census, 1930: Population* (Washington, D.C., 1933), II, 216–218; Adam Clayton Powell Sr., *Against the Tide: An Autobiography* (New York: Richard R. Smith, 1938), 70–71.

5. Alain Locke, " Harlem," *Survey Graphic*, vol. VI, no. 6, Mar. 1925, 630.

6. James Weldon Johnson, *Black Manhattan* (New York: Arno Press and New York Times, 1968), 146.

7. Alain Locke, *The New Negro: An Interpretation* (New York: Arno Press and New York Times, 1968), 7.

8. Rudolph Fisher, "The City of Refuge" in Locke, *New Negro*, 57–59.

9. Langston Hughes, "My Early Days in Harlem," in *Harlem: A Community in Transition*, ed. John Henrik Clarke (New York: The Citadel Press, 1963), 62–63.

10. Paul Robeson, *Here I Stand: An Autobiography* (Boston: Beacon Press, 1958), 1–2.

11. Konrad Bercovici, "The Black Blocks of Manhattan," *Harper's Magazine*, Oct. 1924, 617.

12. "Twenty-four Hundred Negro Families in Harlem: An Interpretation of Living Conditions of Small Wage Earners" (New York: Urban League, 1927), 23.

13. Bercovici, "Black Blocks," 623.

14. *New York Amsterdam News*, Feb. 28, 1923, 9.

15. *New York Amsterdam News*, vol. XVII, no. 20, May 16, 1923, 1.

16. The "numbers" was a ubiquitous practice in Harlem. More than pastime, it dominated life and was played on Harlem's street corners, back alleys, and dwellings. Bets were given to "runners" on slips of paper. Dream books, the numbers of hymns, dates, prices paid for merchandise, license plates, and a host of other sources supplied hopeful players with

the numbers they played. "Bankers" received all bets and paid out all winnings. Often, they failed to do so, though at the risk of their lives.

17. Hughes, "My Early Days," 63.

18. Claude McKay, *A Long Way From Home: An Autobiography* (New York: Harcourt Brace and World, 1970), 49.

19. John C. Walter, *The Harlem Fox: J. Raymond Jones and Tammany, 1920–1970* (Albany: State University of New York Press, 1989), 37–44.

20. *New York Amsterdam News*, Dec. 20, 1922, 8.

21. Roi Ottley and William Weatherby, *The Negro in New York* (New York: Oceana, 1967), 231; *Daily News*, Nov. 4, 1929, 2, 11.

22. Ottley and Weatherby, 230–31.

23. Winthrop D. Lane, "Ambushed in the City: The Grim Side of Harlem," *Survey Graphic*, vol. VI, no. 6, Mar. 1925, 692–694; *New York Age*, vol. 36, no. 21, Feb. 10, 1923, 1.

24. Bercovici, "Black Blocks," 617.

25. Ibid.

26. Ibid., 620.

27. Lane, "Ambushed," 714, 715.

28. Ibid.

29. Henry O. Harding, M.D., "Health Opportunities in Harlem," *Opportunity*, vol. 4, no. 48, Dec. 1926, 8.

30. For an incisive look at Harlem politics during this period, see Thomas M. Henderson, "Harlem Confronts the Machine: The Struggle for Local Autonomy and Black District Leadership," *Afro-Americans in New York Life and History*, vol. 3, no. 2, July 1979, 51–68.

31. *New York Age*, vol. 32, no. 7, Nov. 9, 1918, 1; vol. 33, no. 8, Nov. 15, 1919, 1; vol. 34, no. 7, Nov. 6, 1920, 1; vol. 35, no. 8, Nov. 12, 1921, 1.

32. Edwin R. Lewinson, *Black Politics in New York City* (New York: Twayne Publishers, 1974), 64–65.

33. Ibid, 34–35.

34. Ibid., 59.

35. *Negro World* was the official organ of the UNIA. Calling itself "The Voice of the Awakened Negro" and "The Peerless Paper," it was dedicated solely to the "interests of the Negro race." The paper was published weekly and boasted a circulation of 50,000.

36. *Negro World*, vol. X, no. 6, Mar. 26, 1921, 3.

37. Adam Clayton Powell Jr., *Adam by Adam: The Autobiography of Adam Clayton Powell Jr.* (New York: The Dial Press, 1971), 51.

38. James Weldon Johnson, "After Garvey—What?" *Opportunity*, vol. I, no. 8, Aug. 1923, 231–233.

39. A. F. Elmes, "Garvey and Garveyism—An Estimate," *Opportunity*, May 1924, 139–141.

40. For an excellent analysis of the impact of the phenomenon, see Vann Woodward, *The Strange Career of Jim Crow*, 2nd ed., rev. (New York: Oxford University Press, 1966).

41. See Arthur Link, *Woodrow Wilson and the Progressive Era, 1910–1917* (New York: Harper and Brothers, 1954).

42. Adam Clayton Powell Sr., *Against the Tide*, 67–70.

43. *New York Age*, vol. 33, no. 29, Apr. 10, 1920, 1.

44. *New York Age*, vol. 40, no. 23, Feb. 19, 1927, 5.

45. For an incisive look at the historic role of the African American church in the Black community, see E. Franklin Frazier's *The Negro Church in America* (New York: Schoeken Books, 1976).

46. *New York Age*, vol. 40, no. 19, Jan. 22, 1927, 5.

47. Walter, *Harlem Fox*, 36.

48. As stated earlier, religion has always been a central force in Black life, and nowhere was it more so than in early twentieth century Harlem, where it was expressed in a vast array of religious organizations. Some of these manifestations were established and structured, and others were loose, ever evolving and moving, and transient. Cults and sects abounded in Harlem, and spiritualists found the area fertile ground to peddle the accessories of their trade. Harlem had churches bearing names such as "The Metaphysical Church of the Divine Investigation," "St. Matthew's Church of the Divine Silence and Truth," and "Tabernacle of the Congregation of the Disciples of the Kingdom" (Johnson, *Black Manhattan*, 163–66).

49. James Weldon Johnson, "The Question of Too Many Churches," *New York Age*, vol. 33, no. 26, Mar. 20, 1920, 4.

50. *New York Age*, vol. 33, no. 24, Mar. 6, 1920, 1.

51. Ibid.

52. Adam Clayton Powell Sr., "The Church in Social Work," *Opportunity*, vol. 1, no. 1, Jan. 1923, 15.

53. Anderson, *This Was Harlem*, 145–51.

54. Bercovici, "Black Blocks," 618.

55. Frank Dolan, "Harlem Breakfast Caps Gotham Night," *Daily News*, vol.11, no. 109, Oct. 31, 1929, 2.

56. Johnson, *Black Manhattan*, 161.

57. Ibid., 161–62.

58. Poet, songwriter, essayist, novelist, and literary critic, James Weldon Johnson (1871–1938) was an extremely talented and versatile African American. Initially a school principal who went on to earn a law degree, Johnson passed the Florida bar exam in spite of the racist behavior of the examiner. He became a United States diplomat, serving as consul general at the U.S. Embassy in Venezuela and Nicaragua, where his fluency in Spanish served him well. Known as the first *modern* African American, he also served as professor of Creative Literature at Fisk University and as the general secretary of the NAACP from 1920 to 1930.

59. Claude McKay, *A Long Way From Home: An Autobiography* (New York: Harcourt, Brace and World, 1970), 27.

60. "Harlem—1920's Mecca for West Indians," *New York Amsterdam News*, Sept. 6, 1980, 9.

61. Ibid.

62. Ira de Augustine Reid, *The Negro Immigrant: His Background, Characteristics and Social Adjustment, 1899–1937* (New York: Columbia University Press, 1939), 133.

63. Thomas Sowell, *Ethnic America: A History* (New York: Basic Books, 1981), 219.

64. W. A. Domingo, "Gift of the Black Tropics," in Locke, *Negro World*, 345.

65. Roi Ottley and William Weatherby, eds., *The Negro in New York* (New York: Oceana Publications, 1967), 192.

66. Ibid.

67. *New York Amsterdam News*, Sept. 6, 1980, 9.

68. Lennox Raphael, "West Indians and Afro-Americans," *Freedomways*, vol. 4, no. 3, Summer 1964, 442.

69. Orde Coombs, "West Indians in New York: Moving Beyond the Limbo Pole," *New York*, vol. 3, no. 28, July 13, 1970, 28–32.

70. Ransford W. Palmer, *Pilgrims from the Sun: West Indian Migration to America* (New York: Twayne Publishers, 1995), 31–43.

71. For an enlightening and provocative discussion of slavery, see Orlando Patterson's *Slavery and Social Death: A Comparative Study* (Cambridge, MA: Harvard University Press, 1982), in which the author, a Jamaican historian/sociologist on the faculty of Harvard University, argues that slavery is without honor.

72. Sowell, *Ethnic America*, 218.

73. Coombs, "West Indians in New York," 28–32.

74. "A Caribbean Issue," editorial, *Opportunity*, vol. 4, no. 47, Nov. 1926, 334.

75. Ransford W. Palmer, "In Search of a Better Life: Caribbean Migration to America," in *U.S.–Caribbean Relations: Their Impact on People and Culture*, ed. Ransford W. Palmer (Westport, CT: Praeger, 1998), 65.

76. Ibid., 65–66.

77. Philip Kasinitz, *Caribbean New York: Black Immigrants and the Politics of Race* (Ithaca, NY: Cornel University Press, 1992), 94–95.

78. To be sure, neither do immigrants completely hold on to their old customs and folkways wholescale. Inevitably and invariably, time modifies, blunts, and softens the old ways of doing things. Moreover, even as the immigrant adapts to the new environment he or she invents and creates other ways, almost always of a defensive nature, to help him or her survive the special conditions under which life must now be lived.

79. Reid, *Negro Immigrant*, 26, 35.

80. Mulatto or light skinned West Indian women advertised themselves as such for work in Harlem. Chester T. Crowell, "The World's Largest Negro City," *Saturday Evening Post*, Aug. 8, 1925, 97.

81. Raphael, "West Indians and Afro-Americans," 438–45.

82. Crowell, "World's Largest Negro City," 93–94.

83. Parsram Sri Thakur, *A Comparison of West Indian and American Undergraduates on Selected Cognitive Factors* (New York: New York University Press, 1975). Thakur argues that the West Indian dialect does not serve their cognitive needs, adversely affecting them in the areas of verbal comprehension, general reasoning, spatial scanning, and inductive thinking.

84. Reid, *Negro Immigrant*, 130–31.

85. Ibid., 135–36.

86. Bert J. Thomas, "Historical Functions of Caribbean-American Benevolent/ Progressive Associations," *Afro-Americans in New York Life and History*, vol. 12, no. 2, July 1988, 45–58; Ottley and Weatherby, 193.

87. Clarence G. Contee, "Du Bois, the NAACP, and the Pan African Congress of 1919," *Journal of Negro History*, vol. LVII, no. 1, Jan., 1972, 18.

88. Kasinitz, *Caribbean New York*, 112.

89. Ibid., 212.

90. Calvin B. Holder, "The Rise of the West Indian Politician in New York City, 1900–1952," *Afro-Americans in New York Life and History*, vol. 4, no. 1, Jan. 1980, 45–59.

91. Walter, *Harlem Fox*, 51.

92. For a scholarly treatment of Hubert H. Harrison, particularly as it relates to Black uplift ideology, see Kevin Gaines, *Uplifting the Race: Black Leadership, Politics, and Culture in the Twentieth Century* (Chapel Hill: The University of North Carolina Press, 1996), 234–60.

93. John C. Walter and Jill Louise Ansheles, " The Role of the Caribbean Immigrant in the Harlem Renaissance," *Afro-American in New York Life and History*, vol, I, no. 1, Jan. 1977, 56–58.

94. John C. Walter, "Black Immigrants and Political Radicalism in the Harlem Renaissance," *Western Journal of Black Studies*, vol. 1, no. 2, June 1977, 131–41. In his analysis of the Harlem Renaissance, Walker points out that it was not all about art and artists. Included in his analysis is a look at the immigrant impulse, the distinctive elements of its rhetoric, and its role and legacy. See also, "Frank Crosswaithe: Pioneering Pullman Porter," *West Indian-American*, vol. 1, no. 4, Jan. 1928.

95. Reid, *Negro Immigrant*, 122.

96. For an intelligent and balanced discussion of the issue, see Keith Henry's "Caribbean Migrants in New York: The Passage from Political Quiescence to Radicalism," *Afro-Americans in New York Life and History*, vol. 2, no. 2, July 1978, 29–46. Henry argues that the Caribbean immigrant lacked credible modes of protest in the Caribbean, where sedition charges were frequently made after World War I. He cites the punitive and preemptory measures against Garvey on his return to Jamaica as evidence of the lack of personal and political freedom in the West Indies during this time.

97. *Western Journal of Black Studies*, 131–41.

98. Kasinitz, *Caribbean New York*, 209–22.

99. Reid, *Negro Immigrant*, 107–108; Locke, *New Negro*, 345–46.

100. Carter Godwin Woodson, *The Negro Professional Man and the Community* (Washington, D.C.: The Association for the Study of Negro Life and History, 1934), 83.

101. Johnson, *Black Manhattan*, 153. See also Oscar Handlin, *The Newscomers: Negroes and Puerto Ricans in a Changing Metropolis* (Cambridge: Harvard University Press, 1959) in which the author contends that West Indians were better prepared for urban life and were more aggressive.

102. Ottley, *New World A-Coming*, 47.

103. Ibid., 45–46.

104. Kasinitz, *Caribbean New York*, 48.

105. W. E. B. Du Bois, *The Souls of Black Folk* (Chicago: A. C. McClurg and Co., 1931), 4–5.

106. Lennox Raphael, "The West Indian Syndrome: To be or not to be an American Negro," *Negro Digest*, vol. XIII, no. 1, Nov. 1963, 30–34.

107. David A. Baptiste Jr., Kenneth V. Hardy, and Laurie Lewis, "Clinical Practice with Caribbean Immigrant Families in the United States: The Intersection of Emigration, Immigration, Culture, and Race," in *Caribbean Families, Diversity Among Ethnic Groups*, ed. by Jaipaul L. Roopnarine and Janet Brown (Greenwich, CT: Ablex Publishing, 1997), 275–303.

108. Ottley, *New World A-Coming*, 45–47; Joyce Toney, "Exporting Culture: Caribbean Americans in New York City" in *U.S—Caribbean Relations: Their Impact on Peoples and Cultures*, ed. Ransford W. Palmer (Westport, CT: Greenwood Press, 1998), 87–96.

109. Locke, *New Negro*, 349.

110. According to Du Bois, it was the West Indian immigrant who inspired free Blacks in the North to press for full assimilation and amalgamation with the society on the same basis as other people after 1830, when slavery appeared to be irretrievably mired in the South. He says that their agitation and leadership led to a new era of self-determination and self-development, and that West Indians were largely responsible for the emphasis on manhood that defined nineteenth century Black protest. Du Bois also did not lose sight of the West Indian's practice of blazing new trails, citing as evidence the accomplishment of the Antiguan John W. A. Shaw, who became deputy commissioner of taxes for Queens County in New York in the early 1890s. See DuBois, *The Souls of Black Folk*, 48. Carter G. Woodson adds that in proportion to their numbers in the United States, West Indians made a much larger contribution to the advancement of the race than native Blacks. W. A. Domingo asserted that as an inexorable army of destiny seekers who had left the verdant hills and luxurious beaches of the West Indies, West Indians had not only brought to America the "gift of the tropics" but had enriched Black life here. In Harlem they had become a "factor and a figure," not only because of their idiosyncrasies and unique accents but because of their spirit. See W. A. Domingo, "The Gift of the Tropics," in Locke, *New Negro*, 341–42.

111. Kasinitz, *Caribbean New York*, 52.

112. Reid, *Negro Immigrant*, 123.

113. Langston Hughes, *The Big Sea: An Autobiography* (New York: Hill and Wang, 1949), 247.

114. Johnson, *Black Manhattan*, 153–54; David Levering Lewis, *When Harlem Was in Vogue*, (New York: Alfred A. Knopf, 1981), 109–13.

115. Johnson, *Black Manhattan*, 281.

116. James Weldon Johnson, *Along This Way: The Autobiography of James Weldon Johnson* (New York: The Viking Press, 1933), 381.

117. Reid, *Negro Immigrant*, 226–27.

118. Woodson, *The Negro Professional Man and the Community*, 233.

Chapter 4. The Black Experience in
Adventism, 1840–1930

1. Douglas Morgan, *Adventism and the American Republic: The Public Involvement of a Major Apocalyptic Movement* (Knoxville: University of Tennessee Press, 2001), 3.

2. Makapela, *Problem With Africanity*, 1–2.

3. Withrop S. Hudson, "A Time of Religious Ferment," in *The Rise of Adventism*, ed. Edwin S. Gaustad (New York: Harper and Row, 1974), 1–17.

4. Ibid., 4, 7. According to Calvin B. Rock, Adventism was forged in a socio-political context ideal for its novelty and uniqueness. The time period was dubbed "The Era of Good Feelings" and was characterized by a fierce and pervasive optimism based on American idealism and a sense of determinism. Resilient and irrepressible, Americans believed that the nation had been raised up by God for a specific, special purpose, and that citizens had it within themselves to vault from misery to new levels of achievement, self-determination, and greatness. Attending this mood was a belief that Americans did not have to tarry until Christ's second coming to achieve these ends in heaven. Such ends were both possible and probable in the here and now. See Calvin B. Rock, *Institutional Loyalty vs Racial Freedom: The Dilemma of Black Seventh-day Adventists* (Nashville: Vanderbilt University, 1984), 7–9.

5. According to Francis D. Nichol, a Seventh-day Adventist historian and former editor of the official organ of the church, *Adventist Review*, Miller had read George S. Faber but no other British author on the subject. For a concise summary of the types of millennialism that have existed, if not thrived, in the United States, see Morgan, *Adventism and the American Republic*, 4–8.

6. Trenchant treatment of William Miller may be found in *The Seventh-day Adventist Encyclopedia*, vol. 10 (Washington, D.C.: Review and Herald Publishing Association, 1976), 889–91. See also LeRoy E. Froom, *The Prophetic Faith of Our Fathers* (Washington, D.C.: Review and Herald Publishing Association, 1954); Robert Gale, *The Urgent Voice: The Story of William Miller* (Washington, D.C.: Review and Herald Publishing Association, 1975); Everett Newfon Dick, *William Miller and the Advent Crisis, 1831–1844* (Berrien Springs, MI: Andrews University Press, 1994); David L. Rowe, "Thunder and Trumpets: The Millerite Movement and Apocalyptic Thought in Upstate New York, 1840–1845," Ph.D. dissertation, University of Virginia, 1974; Ruth Alden Doan, *The Miller Heresy, Millennialism, and American Culture* (Philadelphia: Temple University Press, 1987). For a Seventh-day Adventist perspective of the Great Disappointment, see Mervyn C. Maxwell, *Magnificent Disappointment* (Boise, ID: Pacific Press Publishing Association, 1994). For a look at the social and political context of the Millerite movement, see Reuben Elmore Ernest Harkness, "Social Origins of the Millerite Movement," Ph.D. dissertation, University of Chicago, 1927.

7. Beginning on Feb. 28, 1840, Himes published a periodical called *Signs of the Times* (Boston). Later, he added *The Midnight Cry* (New York City). Together, these two periodicals were the vehicle that disseminated information among Adventists and the medium that facilitated the exchange of their ideas. A valuable study of Joshua V. Himes is David

Tallmadge Arthur, "Joshua V. Himes and the Cause of Adventism, 1839–1845," master's thesis, University of Chicago, 1961.

8. The first general conference was held in Oct. 1840. General conferences brought believers together for edification and unification.

9. Jonathan M. Butler, "Adventism and the American Experience" in Gausted, *Rise of Adventism*, 175.

10. George Knight, *A Search for Identity: The Development of Seventh-day Adventists Beliefs* (Hagerstown, MD: Review and Herald Publishing Association, 2000), 50.

11. Charles E. Dudley Sr., *Thou Who Hast Brought Us: The Story of the Growth and Development of the Seventh-day Adventist Denomination as it Relates to African-Americans* (Brushton, N.Y.: Teach Services, 1997), 77; Louis B. Reynolds, *We Have Tomorrow: The Story of American Seventh-day Adventists with an African Heritage* (Washington, D.C. and Hagerstown, MD: Review and Herald Publishing Association, 1984), 19. See also Walter L. Pearson Jr., "Bound for Glory," *Adventist Review*, vol. 171, no. 48, Dec. 1994, 8–10, in which the author calls Blacks in the Millerite Movement "unsung heroes" who not only received hope from the movement but gave voice to the cry "the Bridegroom in coming!" In addition, Pearson says that Blacks' acceptance of Miller's views and teaching was "the logical response to people seeking an end to injustice." George Knight balks at including Charles Bowles among the Blacks who played key roles in the Millerite Movement. He claims that even though Adventist historian L. E. Froom first identified Bowles as such, and even though others, such as Louis B. Reynolds, followed Froom in doing so, his thorough research of primary documents did not turn up any evidence that a Black named Charles Bowles figured in the Millerite Movement. Knight's conclusions may be on target, since both Froom and Reynolds merely identify Bowles as a Black who was instrumental in the Millerite Movement, failing to elaborate or expand on how instrumental he was.

12. Delbert W. Baker, "William Foy: Messenger to the Advent Believers," *Adventist Review*, vol. 165, no. 2, Jan. 14, 1988, 8–10. For a full treatment of William Foy, see Delbert Baker, *The Unknown Prophet* (Washington, D.C.: Review and Herald Publishing Association, 1987).

13. George Knight, *Millennial Fever and the End of the World: A Study of Millerite Adventism* (Boise, ID: Pacific Press, 1993), 117–19.

14. Ronald D. Graybill, "The Abolitionist-Millerite Connection," in *The Disappointed: Millerism and Millenarianism in the Nineteenth Century*, ed. Ronald L. Numbers and Jonathan M. Butler (Bloomington: Indiana University Press, 1987), 139–50.

15. Knight, *Millennial Fever*, 117.

16. Ibid., 75, 116, 69, 117.

17. Ibid., 69–70, 107–8.

18. Joseph Bates, *The Autobiography of Elder Joseph Bates* (Battle Creek, MI: Steam Press, Seventh-day Adventist Publishing Association, 1868), 262.

19. Malcolm Bull and Keith Lockhart, *Seeking a Sanctuary: Seventh-day Adventism and the American Dream* (San Francisco: Harper and Row Publishers, 1989), 194–95.

20. Seventh-day Adventists believe that the gift of prophecy was resident in Ellen Gould Harmon White. A frail 17-year-old from Gorham, Maine, when she began to receive visions,

White became the guiding force in the Seventh-day Adventist church, bequeathing to the denomination a body of writing and verbal counsels that continue to shape and inform the church's theology, polity, and ministry. The 17th Fundamental Belief of Seventh-day Adventists reads: "One of the gifts of the Holy Spirit is prophecy. This gift is an identifying mark of the remnant church and was manifested in the ministry of Ellen G. White. As the Lord's messenger, her writings are a continuing source of truth which provide for church comfort, guidance, instruction, and correction. They also make clear that the Bible is the standard by which all teaching and experience must be tested." *Seventh-day Adventists Believe*, 217. Illuminating works on Ellen G. White include, Arthur L. White, *Ellen G. White: Messenger to the Remnant* (Hagerstown, MD: Review and Herald Publishing Association, 1969); Herbert E. Douglass, *Messenger of the Lord: The Prophetic Ministry of Ellen G. White* (Nampa, ID: Pacific Press Publishing Association, 1998); George R. Knight, *Meeting Ellen White: A Fresh Look at her Life, Writings, and Major Themes* (Hagerstown, MD: Review and Herald Publishing Association, 1996); George R. Knight, *Reading Ellen White: How to Understand and Apply Her Writings* (Hagerstown, MD: Review and Herald Publishing Association, 1997); George R. Knight, *Walking with Ellen White: The Human Interest Story* (Hagerstown, MD: Review and Herald Publishing Association, 1999).

21. For a concise account of the theological development of Sabbatarian Adventism, see George Knight, *A Search for Identity: The Development of Seventh-day Adventist Beliefs* (Hagerstown, MD: Review and Herald Publishing Association, 2000), 17–89.

22. Morgan, *Adventism and the American Republic*, 26.

23. According to Reynolds, Sojourner Truth was baptized by Adventist pioneer Uriah Smith in the Kalamazoo River in Battle Creek, MI. See Reynolds, *We Have Tomorrow*, 22–27. One of the best works on Sojourner Truth is Nell Painter's *Sojourner Truth: A Life, A Symbol* (New York: W.W. Norton and Company, 1995). George Knight, although admitting that Sojourner Truth "attended one of Miller's lectures and at least two Adventist camp meetings," states that the primary evidence shows that Sojourner Truth thought Millerism was a hoax (*Millennial Fever*, 118).

24. Bull and Lockhart argue that Adventists not only had no coherent strategy to evangelize Blacks but that they may even have gone to great lengths to avoid contact with them. Whenever African Americans joined the Seventh-day Adventist church, the authors contend, they did so on their own initiative, often stumbling upon or simply showing up at Adventist meetings. Yet the authors most scathing commentary is that the Adventist church endorsed segregation, "first by expediency, and then by choice." See Bull and Lockhart, *Seeking a Sanctuary* (San Francisco: Harper and Row Publishers, 1989), 194.

25. *Advent Review and Sabbath Herald*, vol. 45, no. 14, Apr. 1, 1875, 110; *Advent Review and Sabbath Herald*, vol. 50, no. 17, Oct. 25, 1877, 135; *Advent Review and Sabbath Herald*, vol. 51, no. 2, Jan. 10, 1878, 15.

26. *Advent Review and Sabbath Herald*, vol. 58, no. 10, Aug. 30, 1881, 155.

27. Seventh-day Adventist pioneers believed that William Miller and his followers had delivered the messages of the two angels of Revelation 14:6–8 and that they were sounding the message of the angel of Revelation 14:9–11. The prophetic messages recorded in Revelation 14: 6–11 form the foundation of Seventh-day Adventist doctrine and theology. See

Seventh-day Adventist Encyclopedia, rev. ed.(Washington, D.C.: Review and Herald Publishing Association, 1976), 1483–84.

28. *Seventh-day Adventist Encyclopedia*, 1192.

29. *Advent Review and Sabbath Herald*, vol. 47, no. 21, May 25, 1876, 166.

30. *General Conference Daily Bulletin*, vol. 1, no. 1, Oakland, California, Nov. 14, 1887, 2.

31. "Regional Affairs, Office of, and Regional Conferences," *Seventh-day Adventist Encyclopedia* (Washington, D.C.: Review and Herald Publishing Association, 1976), 1193.

32. *Advent Review and Sabbath Herald*, vol. 66, no. 43, Oct. 29, 1889, 683.

33. Adventist polity calls for a group to be organized as a "company" first. On demonstrating numerical and financial strength, the "company" is then organized and recognized as a church.

34. Arthur W. Spalding, *Origin and History of Seventh-day Adventists*, vol. 2 (Washington, D.C.: Review and Herald Publishing Association, 1962), 188.

35. Nathine Washington, *Charles M. Kinney: The Man*, unpublished term paper, James White Library, Andrews University, Berrien Springs, MI, Spring, 1975.

36. Charles M. Kinney, "Statement on the Concept of Regional Conferences," Oct. 2, 1889, Seventh-day Adventist church, General Conference Archives, Silver Spring, MD.

37. *General Conference Bulletin*, vol. 1, no. 1, Nov. 14, 1887, 2–3.

38. Ibid.

39. *Advent Review and Sabbath Herald Extra, Daily Bulletin of the General Conference*, vol. 4, no. 5, Mar. 11, 1891, Battle Creek, Mich., 70.

40. Calvin B. Rock, *Go On!* (Washington, D.C.: Review and Herald Publishing Association, 1994), 101–102. See also letter of Charles M. Kinney to John N. Loughborough, General Conference Archives, Silver Spring, MD.

41. A tithe is 10 percent of one's earnings and is used by the church to remunerate its clergy.

42. *General Conference Bulletin*, vol. 5, no. 9 (Oakland, CA: Review and Herald Publishing Association, 1903), 131.

43. Rock, *Go On!*, 102.

44. *Advent Review and Sabbath Herald*, vol. 49, no. 8, Feb. 22, 1877, 59.

45. *Advent Review and Sabbath Herald*, vol. 49, no. 21, May 24, 1877, 166.

46. One of the best histories of Oakwood College is Mervyn Warren's *Oakwood: A Splendid Vision: 1896–1996* (Huntsville, AL: Oakwood College, 1996).

47. *General Conference Bulletin*, vol. 5, no. 9, Thirty-Fifth Session (Oakland, CA: Review and Herald Publishing Association, 1903), 130.

48. For the most authoritative work on Knight, see Patricia Maxwell's *Journey to Freedom* (Boise, ID: Pacific Press, 1987).

49. According to Solomon Ben David, O. O. Fransworth and E. E. Franke began Seventh-day Adventist work in New York City in the mid-1890s, with both of them pitching tents in Harlem. By 1901, Franke was claiming 225 followers in three churches, $3,000 annually in tithe, and "liberal donations." In Dec. of that year the Greater New York Conference was organized as an arm of the Atlantic Union Conference, becoming fully operational on Jan. 1, 1902, with offices at 400 W. 57th Street. Solomon Ben David, *The History of the Seventh-day*

Adventist Church in New York City (Jerusalem, Israel: The Palestine Printing Press, 1995), 16–17, 30.

50. *Advent Review and Sabbath Herald*, vol. 79, no. 23, June 10, 1902, 18; *Advent Review and Sabbath Herald*, vol. 79, no. 45, Nov. 11, 1902, 18; *Advent Review and Sabbath Herald*, vol. 80, no. 8, Feb. 24, 1903, 17.

51. *Seventh-day Adventist Encyclopedia* (Washington, D.C.: Review and Herald Publishing Association, 1976), 1195.

52. Delbert W. Baker, "In Search of Roots: Adventist African-Americans: Part Two: The Turning Point," *Adventist Review*, vol. 170, no. 6, Feb. 11, 1993, 9.

53. Roy Branson, "Ellen G. White–Racist or Champion of Equality?" *Review and Herald*, vol. 147, no. 15, Apr. 9, 1970, 2.

54. For an excellent analysis of the connecting linkages Adventists saw between slavery and prophecy, see Roy Branson's "Slavery and Prophecy" (*Review and Herald*, Apr. 16, 1970), in which the author argues that far from having little to do with their views on moral and social issues, Adventist theology was a reflection of national problems. Branson avers that Adventist pioneers such as James and Ellen White, Uriah Smith, and John Nevins Andrews believed that a correct understanding of Scripture and doctrines was intimately and inextricably linked to "proper attitudes" regarding race relations and that, more than anything else, the oppression of Blacks in the United States unambiguously identified America and the role it would play in the span of Bible prophecy. In short, slavery was an indicator and barometer of the times.

55. In 1888 Adventists convened a council in Minneapolis to debate the merits and utility of righteousness by faith, a theological notion championed by Martin Luther that is a hallmark of the Reformation, and its relationship to obedience. Up to 1888, Adventists had been known to emphasize obedience to God's Ten Commandment law, several of them holding that obedience to the law was the way an individual procured salvation. The matter came to a head in 1888, when the church went on record as recognizing the primacy of righteousness by faith. Enlightening studies of the conference include, The Ellen G. White Estate, comp., *Manuscripts and Memories of Minneapolis* (Boise, ID: Pacific Press Publishing Association, 1988); George R. Knight, *A User Friendly Guide to the 1888 Message* (Hagerstown, MD: Review and Herald Publishing Association, 1998); Donald K. Short and Robert J. Wieland, *1888 Re-Examined* (Paris, OH: The 1888 Message Study Committee, 1989).

56. The *General Conference Bulletin* of Oct. 24, 1889 neither documents nor reflects any resolution on the race issue, ostensibly because none was ever voted.

57. Ellen G. Whites's statements, articles, letters, and excerpts on the race issue were compiled by church leaders and published as *The Southern Work* (Hagerstown, MD: Review and Herald Publishing Association, 1966). To this day, *The Southern Work* remains Ellen White's most definitive and authoritative work on the issue.

58. E. G. White, *Southern Work*, 11, 14, 15, 55.

59. Ibid., 15.

60. Ellen G. White, "Lift up Your Eyes and Look on the Field," *Advent Review and Sabbath Herald*, vol. 73, no. 4, Jan. 28, 1896, 50.

61. E. G. White, *Southern Work*, 15.

62. Ibid., 35.

63. Ellen G. White, "An Example in History," *Advent Review and Sabbath Herald*, vol. 72, no. 51, Dec. 17, 1895, 801.

64. *Advent Review and Sabbath Herald*, vol. 73, no. 4, Jan. 28, 1896, 50.

65. *Advent Review and Sabbath Herald*, Jan. 21, 1896, 33.

66. "The Southern Work," *General Conference Bulletin*, Fifty-Fifth Session, vol. 5, no. 13, Oakland, CA., Apr. 14, 1903, 203.

67. Ibid., 204.

68. E. G. White, *Testimonies for the Church*, 1:202, 264.

69. Delbert Baker, "In Search of Roots: Adventist African-Americans: Part Three: The Ministry Begins," *Adventist Review*, vol. 170, no. 7, Feb. 18, 1993, 16–17.

70. E. G. White, *Southern Work*, 15.

71. Ibid.

72. "The Southern Work," *General Conference Bulletin*, Thirty-Fifth Session, vol. 5, no. 113, Oakland, CA., Apr. 14, 1903, 202.

73. Ibid., 205.

74. E. G. White, *Testimonies for the Church*, 9:206–7.

75. Bull and Lockhart, *Seeking a Sanctuary*, 195–97.

76. Roy Branson, "Slavery and Prophecy," *Review and Herald*, vol. 147, no. 16, Apr. 16, 1970, 9.

77. Ibid.

78. Roy Branson, "The Crisis of the Nineties," *Review and Herald*, vol. 147, no. 17, Apr. 23, 1970, 4–6.

79. Ellen White had once encouraged African Americans not to "urge that they be placed on an equality with white people." See *Testimonies for the Church*, 9:214.

80. Ron Graybill, *Ellen G. White and Church Race Relations* (Washington, D.C.: Review and Herald Publishing Association, 1970), 117–18.

81. Ibid., 118.

82. It was on *The Morning Star* that the first issue of *Gospel Herald* was printed in 1898. Geared toward the African American community, this magazine would later become *Message Magazine*, which today continues to be the premiere Seventh-day Adventist magazine aimed at Blacks.

83. A full and detailed account of James Edson White's efforts to bring African Americans into the Seventh-day Adventist church is contained in Ronald D. Graybill's *Mission to Black America: The True Story of Edson White and the Riverboat Morning Star* (Mountain View, CA: Pacific Press Publishing Association, 1971).

84. R. W. Schwarz, *Light Bearers to the Remnant* (Mountain View, CA: Pacific Press Publishing Association, 1979), 238.

85. Ibid., 236–39.

86. There has been an ongoing debate about the persistence of Africanisms in African American culture, especially in Black religion, for some time. Illustrative, if not representative, of the opposing factions are Franklin Frazier and Melville Herskovits. Frazier contends that the brutal Middle Passage and slavery conspired to all but completely erase whatever

African culture there was in the slaves. See E. Franklin Frazier, *The Negro Church in America* (New York: Schocken Books, 1964), 1–6. Melville Herskovits argues that even today there is much in the way of Africanisms, parallelisms, and retentions in African American culture (*The Myth of the Negro Past* [Boston: Beacon Press, 1964]). A credible middle ground is Albert Raboteau's *Slave Religion: The Invisible Institution in the Antebellum South* and Eugene Genovese's *Roll, Jordan, Roll: The World the Slaves Built*, in which the authors contend that African American religion is a syncretism or blending of the African and European into a new and uniquely American religion.

87. James E. White, "Report of Southern Missionary Society," *General Conference Bulletin*, Thirty-Fifth Session, vol. 5, no. 13, Oakland, CA, Apr. 14, 1903, 200–1.

88. "In the Regions Beyond," *General Conference Bulletin*, Thirty-Fourth Session, vol. IV, no. 3, Apr. 5, 1901, 85.

89. Letter to Ellen G. White, Ellen G. White Estate, General Conference of Seventh-day Adventists, Silver Spring, MD.

90. Ibid.

91. *Gospel Herald*, vol. II, no. 10, Battle Creek, MI, Oct. 1900, 85–87.

92. Ibid., 85.

93. *General Conference Bulletin*, Thirty-Fifth Session, vol. 5, no. 13, Oakland, Calif., Apr. 14, 1903, 202.

94. E. G. White, *Testimonies for the Church*, 9:204–5.

95. Norman K. Miles, "Tension Between the Races," in *The World of Ellen G. White*, ed. Gary Land (Washington, D.C.: Review and Herald Publishing Association, 1987), 47–60.

96. A canvasser was an individual who went door to door selling church literature. No longer known as such, they are now called literature evangelists.

97. *Advent Review and Sabbath Herald*, vol. 86, no. 23, June 10, 1909, 13.

98. *General Conference Bulletin*, Thirty-Fourth Session, vol. IV, no. 17, Apr. 22, 1901, 389.

99. *Advent Review and Sabbath Herald*, vol. 106, no. 46, Nov. 14, 1929, 7–8.

100. W. W. Fordham, *Righteous Rebel*, 139.

101. H. D. Singleton, "Eighty Years of Adventism," in *Telling the Story: An Anthology on the Development of the Black SDA Work*, comp. Delbert W. Baker (Loma Linda, CA: Loma Linda University Press, 1996), 4:82.

102. It was not until 1961, approximately three decades after Humphrey's split from the Seventh-day Adventist denomination, that the church issued its first public statement on human relations in the context of race. It read, in part, "(1) That we continue to encourage the employment of workers in our institutions without regard to race, color, or national origin, and on the basis of qualifications and merit. (2) That we continue the service of regional workers in overseas fields, and that we explore the possibility of finding further overseas territories in which they can serve. (3) That when circumstances require, committees be set up within the union conferences to study the problem of human relations, and that workshops be conducted to give guidance and instruction in dealing with local racial problems. (4) That a representative standing committee in the General Conference be appointed on human relations. (5) That normal church channels be used in dealing with all racial and human relations problems" (*Actions of the Autumn Council Pertaining to the North American*

Division, Oct. 1961, 6–7). Four years later, the denomination again publicly went on record on the issue, saying: "(1) Membership and office in all churches and on all levels must be available to anyone who qualifies without regard to race. (2) In our educational institutions there should be no racial bias in the employment of teachers or other personnel nor in the admission of students. (3) Hospitals and rest homes should make no racial distinction in admitting patients or in making their facilities available to physicians, interns, residents, nurses, and administrators who meet the professional standards of the institution. It is further recommended that these recommendations be given serious consideration and that every effort be put forth to implement them as rapidly as is consistently possible" (*Actions of the Spring Council Pertaining to the North American Division*, Apr. 1965, 1–2).

103. Rock, *Institutional Loyalty*, 27–28.

104. Ibid., 49.

105. Ibid., 42.

106. Ibid., 43.

107. Rock, "A Better Way," *Spectrum*, Spring 1970, 24.

108. *Institutional Loyalty versus Racial Freedom: The Dilemma of Black Seventh-day Adventist Leadership*, 54–57.

109. Ibid., 61.

110. See Revelation 18:4, "Then I heard another voice from heaven say: 'Come out of her, my people, so that you will not receive any of her plagues; for her sins are piled up to heaven, and God has remembered her crimes.'"

111. Rock, "A Better Way," 22, 25, 30.

112. Frank W. Hale Jr., "Commitment vs Capitulation," *Spectrum*, Spring 1970, 31. Says Hale: "As a church, we are plagued by the critical gap that exists between the nature of our witness and the caliber of our actions. Nowhere does this gap yawn more dangerously than when we try to face, or try not to face, the question of our living as brothers, black and white, within our own churches. The not-too-remote analogy between the Seventh-day Adventist church organization and the American political organization, from local to national levels, is inescapable. At virtually every point where there are obstacles to desegregation within the church, one sees a parallel to familiar obstacles he has encountered in the fabric of his own community. . . . Because of the many, many inequities that are apparent, we have opened the floodgates on ourselves. In short, the patterns of racism are so obvious in so many areas of church life and thought that many black Seventh-day Adventists are losing confidence in the commitments of the church to healthy human relations. Many black Seventh-day Adventists feel that the overt and covert support of a substantial number of white Adventists given to the philosophies projected by such men as Eric Hoffer, David Lawrence, and Paul Harvey make racism endemic to the Adventist way of life. Consequently, the philosophy of separatism is gaining within our church as it has in secular circles. When we must admit to ourselves that we do not have the spiritual courage to come to grips with the problems that make mockery of our faith, then we may be admitting that our faith is a mockery" (Hale, "Commitment vs Capitulation" 34).

113. *Institutional Loyalty*, 39–40.

114. Ibid., 4.

115. D. W. Baker, "In Search of Roots: Adventist African-Americans, Part Two: The Turning Point," *Adventist Review*, vol. 170, no. 6, Feb. 11, 1993, 10.

116. One of the best analyses of Black religion during slavery is Albert Raboteau's *Slave Religion: The "Invisible Institution" in the Antebellum South* (Oxford and New York: Oxford University Press, 1978). For a credible view of the ways in which the Black church has historically functioned in the African American community, see E. Franklin Frazier's *The Negro Church in America* (New York: Schocken Books, 1964).

117. Delbert Baker, "In Search of Roots: Exploring the History of Adventist African-Americans in the United States," *Adventist Review*, vol. 170, no. 5, Feb. 4, 1993, 13–14.

CHAPTER 5. THE CHURCH HISTORY OF THE SABBATH-DAY ADVENTISTS

1. Some useful studies of the time period are Michael Parrish, *Anxious Decades: America in Prosperity and Depression* (New Haven: Yale University Press, 1992); Robert S. McElvaine, *The Great Depression in America, 1929–1941* (Boston: Beacon Press, 1984); T. H. Watkins, *The Great Depression: America in the 1930s* (New York: Henry Holt, 1993); Richard Pells, *Radical Visions and American Dreams: Culture and Social Thought in the Depression Years* (New York: Harper and Row, 1973); and John B. Kirby, *Black Americans in the Roosevelt Era: Liberalism and Race* (Knoxville: University of Tennessee Press, 1980).

2. In utilizing oral history as a methodology, I am indebted to the following: Eva M. McMahon, ed., *Interactive Oral History Listening* (Hillsdale, NJ: L. Erlbaum Associates, 1994); Robert Perks and Alistair Thomson, eds., *The Oral History Reader* (New York: Routledge, 1998); and Studs Terkel, *Hard Times: An Oral History of the Great Depression* (New York: Pantheon Books, 1970).

3. A bishop is "a rank in the ordained Christian ministry. The bishop oversees the affairs of the church in a particular area, and only bishops can ordain others to the ministry." Albert J. Raboteau, *African-American Religion* (New York and Oxford: Oxford University Press, 1999), 133.

4. Ucilla La Condre, interview by author, tape recording, Bronx, NY, June 11, 2000.

5. According to the Old Testament, God told Moses that when Pharaoh asked who had sent him to demand the release of the children of Israel, Moses was to inform the Egyptian leader that "I Am" had sent him. See Exodus 3:14.

6. Irene Jarvis, interview by author, tape recording, Brooklyn, New York, Aug. 15, 2000.

7. An insightful and valuable contribution on some of these individuals, including some who are not as well known, is Randall K. Burkett and Richard Newman's *Black Apostles: Afro-American Clergy Confront the Twentieth Century* (Boston: G. K. Hall, 1978).

8. Hans A. Baer and Merrill Singer, *African-American Religion in the Twentieth Century: Varieties of Protest and Accommodation* (Knoxville: The University of Tennessee Press, 1992), 124, 125.

9. Bernice Samuel, interview by author, tape recording, St. Albans, New York, Apr. 17, 2000.

10. La Condre, interview.

11. Because of their more conservative orientation, initially West Indian pastors in the United States seldom preached in robes. Today, more of them do.

12. Olga La Beet, interview by author, tape recording, New York, NY, June 12, 2000. The New York United Sabbath-Day Adventist Church was made up mostly of West Indians, and many of its indigenous African American members had West Indian roots. The two cultural groups got along reasonably well, although incidents did occur that revealed an underlying tension. For example, Irene Jarvis says that once a West Indian member uttered some disparaging remarks about indigenous African Americans, claiming that West Indian parents were better at raising children. The statement created much confusion at the church, almost splitting it. Jarvis, interview.

13. Dorothy Simmonds, interview by author, tape recording, Mt. Vernon, NY, June 11, 2000; La Condre, interview.

14. Simmonds, interview.

15. Miriam Flatts, interview with the author, tape recording, Huntington, NY, June 10, 2000.

16. Ermie Chandler, telephone conversation with the author, Mar. 26, 2001.

17. Simmonds, interview; Jarvis, interview.

18. One member alleges that Humphrey's vast knowledge and depth was the main reason she later earned an A in one of her literature courses in college. Olga La Beet, interview with the author, tape recording, New York, NY, June 12, 2000.

19. La Condre, interview. One 1930s religious leader whom Humphrey shunned was Father Divine, the Harlem cult leader who wielded a powerful influence on thousands of Blacks at the time. La Condre, interview.

20. Jarvis, interview.

21. La Condre, interview.

22. Aileen Hunter, telephone conversation with the author, Mar. 4, 2001.

23. Samuels, interview.

24. Agatha Phillips, interview by author, New York, NY, Jan. 6, 2001.

25. Samuels, interview. Samuels belonged to the first group, having purchased a policy for her entire family.

26. La Condre, interview.

27. Simmonds, interview.

28. Jarvis, interview.

29. E. Forrest Harris Jr., *Ministry for Social Crisis: Theology and Praxis in the Black Church Tradition* (Macon, GA: Mercer University Press, 1993), 24–25.

30. See Lawrence Levine, *Black Culture and Black Consciousness: Afro-American Folk Thought from Slavery to Freedom* (New York: Oxford University Press, 1977), xi.

31. *United Sabbath-Day Adventist Messenger*, vol. II, no. 11, Nov., 1931, 5.

32. Ibid., 4.

33. Ibid., 6.

34. Ibid., 12.

35. Ibid., 9.

36. Ibid., 1, 15.

37. Ibid., 8.

38. Ibid.

39. Ibid., 9.

40. Ibid., 13.

41. Ibid., 14.

42. *United Sabbath-Day Adventist Messenger*, vol. III, no. 8, Aug. 1932, 3.

43. Ibid., 7.

44. Ibid., 10–11.

45. Ibid., 11–12.

46. Ibid., 8, 10.

47. The extent of the relationship between the Seventh-day Baptists and the United Sabbath-Day Adventists is unclear.

48. Ibid., 15.

49. Ibid., 9.

50. *United Sabbath-Day Adventist Messenger*, vol. 10, no. 2, June 1939, 3.

51. *General Conference Bulletin*, vol. 7, no. 20 (Washington, D.C.: Review and Herald Publishing Association, 1913), 309.

52. *United Sabbath-Day Adventist Messenger*, Nov. 1931, 3.

53. Ibid., 5.

54. *United Sabbath-Day Adventist Messenger*, Aug. 1932, 4–5.

55. Ibid., 4, 15.

56. Ibid., 12.

57. Ibid., 13.

58. Peter J. Paris, *The Social Teaching of the Black Churches* (Philadelphia: Fortress Press, 1985), 129.

59. Ibid., 46, 133.

60. Seventh-day Adventists do not have a creed but a "fundamental" set of beliefs. See *Seventh-day Adventists Believe . . . A Biblical Exposition of 27 Fundamental Doctrines* (Silver Spring, MD: General Conference of Seventh-day Adventists, 1988).

61. *United Sabbath-Day Adventist Messenger*, Aug. 1932, 9–10.

62. Given Humphrey's love of young people and his ministry to and mentorship of them, it is surprising that the document does not mention an entity or department specifically aimed at the youth.

63. *Constitution and By-Laws of the New York United Sabbath Day Adventist Church*, n.p., n.d. See Appendix B.

64. *United Sabbath Day Adventist Messenger*, vol. 10, no. 2, June 1939, 8.

65. Ibid., 7.

66. Ibid., 7–10.

67. Humphrey fought an array of charges throughout his ministry, including allegations of marital infidelity and financial mismanagement. None of the charges have ever been proven true.

68. *United Sabbath Day Adventist Messenger*, June 1939, 11. Traditionally, these licenses have been reserved for women functioning as Bible Instructors.

69. Ibid., 4, 5.

70. Ibid., 8, 9.

71. Ibid., 8.

72. Mesar and Dybdahl, "Utopia Park Affair," 41.

73. Olga La Beet, interview.

74. *United Sabbath-Day Adventist Messenger*, June 1939, 2.

75. *United Sabbath-Day Adventist Messenger*, vol. VI, no. 1, Jan., 1935, 8.

76. Ibid.

77. See *United Sabbath-Day Adventist Messenger*, vol. 28, no. 4, Jan.–Mar., 1953, 3.

78. *United Sabbath-Day Adventist Messenger*, June 1939, 3, 4.

79. Dybdahl and Mesar, "Utopia Park Affair," 54.

80. La Beet, interview.

81. *United Sabbath-Day Adventist Messenger*, vol. II, no. 11, Nov. 1931, 2.

82. *United Sabbath-Day Adventist Messenger*, June 1939, 7.

83. Felix Murray, interview with the author, tape recording, New York, New York, June 10, 2000. Murray, whom Ruth predeceased, was Ruth's second husband. Her first husband was named Spencer. Born in Harlem in 1919, Murray married Ruth in 1972, twenty years after her father, James K. Humphrey, had died. Murray remembers her speaking fondly of her father and cherishing pictures and objects of his. Ruth Humphrey, who was childless, died in 1997. With her death the known Humphrey legacy ended.

84. Albert Raboteau, "Richard Allen and the African Church Movement," in *Black Leaders of the Nineteenth Century*, ed. by Leon Litwack and August Meir (Urbana and Chicago: University of Illinois Press, 1988), 11–12.

85. *United Sabbath-Day Messenger*, Aug. 1932, 3.

86. The biblical passage Humphrey was alluding to is Ecclesiastes 3:1, which states: "To everything there is a season, A time for every purpose under heaven." See *United Sabbath-Day Messenger*, Aug. 1932, 2.

87. Ibid.

88. Ibid.

89. Ibid.

90. *United Sabbath-Day Adventist Messenger*, vol. 11, no. 11, Nov. 1931, 3.

91. *United Sabbath-Day Adventist Messenger*, vol. 16, no. 3, July–Sept. 1944, 1–5.

92. World War II did have an impact on United Sabbath-Day Adventists operations. Among other things, it led to the cancellation of their 1944 General Conference Session. Ibid., 6.

93. La Condre, interview.

94. *United Sabbath-Day Adventist Messenger*, June 1939, 5.

95. Melchizedek was an Old Testament priest to whom Abraham, the first Jew and father of the faithful, remitted tithes of all he earned. See Genesis 14:20.

96. *United Sabbath-Day Adventist Messenger*, June 1939, 5.

97. La Condre, interview.

98. *United Sabbath-Day Adventist Messenger*, June 1939, 5.

99. *United Sabbath-Day Adventist Messenger*, Nov. 1931, 11.

100. Indeed, many members of Humphrey's United New York congregation have maintained cordial relations with members of the Ephesus Seventh-day Adventist church. Throughout the history of the two congregations, some individuals from the same family attended one church, and other family members attended the other. In addition, especially up until the late 1970s, many youth would attend the divine worship service at one church in the morning and the youth meeting at the other church in the afternoon. La Condre, interview.

101. Kevin L. Jenkins, telephone conversation with the author, Nov. 20, 2000.

102. Given Humphrey's involvement on many of the denomination's conference, union, and General Conference committees, it is reasonable to assume that he may have seen her.

103. La Condre, Simmonds, and La Beet interviews.

104. Ibid.

105. Glossolalia is the term used for speaking in tongues.

106. *United Sabbath-Day Adventist Messenger*, November 1931, 3.

107. Ibid., 2, 3.

108. *United Sabbath-Day Adventist Messenger*, June 1939, 4. Speaking more on the issue, Humphrey claimed that former Seventh-day Adventists made "bad members."

109. *United Sabbath-Day Adventist Messenger*, Nov. 1931, 14.

110. Like Seventh-day Adventists, Sabbath-Day Adventists divided the calendar into four quarters, the last Sabbath of each quarter being designated Thirteenth Sabbath. On this Sabbath, a special offering was collected for missionary endeavors around the world.

111. *Sabbath School Tutor*, vol, 16, no. 3, July–Sept. 1944, 7–14.

112. La Condre, interview.

113. Ibid.

114. Samuels, interview. The bishop was jolted when his daughter showed up at church one day with her ears pierced. Thereafter, their relationship suffered. In time, Ruth stopped attending church altogether, even though she lived across the street.

115. The fact that Sabbath-Day Adventists abbreviate their name as Seventh-day Adventists do (SDA) has contributed to the confusion. There is no evidence that Sabbath-Day Adventists have done so precisely for this purpose.

116. La Beet, interview.

117. Carol V. R. George, *Segregated Sabbaths* (New York: Oxford University Press, 1973), 5, 7–8. For a poignant portrayal of Allen's life history, see Marcia M. Matthews, *Richard Allen* (Baltimore: Dublin, 1963).

118. Albert J. Raboteau, "Richard Allen and the African Church Movement," in *Black Leaders of the Nineteenth Century*, ed. Leon Litwack and August Meier (Urbana and Chicago: University of Illinois Press, 1988), 18.

119. For an excellent biography of Turner, see Stephen Ward Angell, *Bishop Henry McNeal Turner and African American Religion in the South* (Knoxville: University of Tennessee Press, 1992). See also M. M. Ponton, *Life and Times of Henry M. Turner* (New York: Negro

Universities Press, 1970), in which tributes to Bishop Turner by colleagues in ministry are particularly poignant and eloquent. All eulogize Turner as a credit to African Americans and their struggle to achieve a measure of self-determination in the United States.

120. Henry McNeal Turner, quoted in *Autobiography of a People: Three Centuries of African American History Told By Those Who Lived It*, ed. by Herb Boyd, (New York: Doubleday, 2000), 165.

121. John Dittmer, "The Education of Henry McNeal Turner," *Black Leaders of the Nineteenth Century*, ed. by Leon Litwack and August Meier (Urbana and Chicago: The University of Illinois Press, 1988), 260–61.

122. Darryl M. Trimview, *Voices of the Silenced: The Responsible Self in a Marginalized Community* (Cleveland: Pilgrim Press, 1993), 21–35.

123. Adeleke, *UnAfrican Americans*, 95, 97, 99. Turner had a strange view of the races, believing that the Black race was the "junior race of the world." He stated: "But while I accept the doctrine of the unity of the human race, I believe the negro division of it is the junior race of the world, and that this boy race has a long and mighty future before it, and that an enslavement here, while actuated by the cupidity of whites, is intended to be in the order of Providence, the culmination of glorious results. What we will do, no earthly creature can divine; but one thing is sure, we must be put in full possession of every right and privilege here, or this nation must pay us $40,000,000,000 for our 200 years' service, and let us go where we can have unconditional manhood. I have calculated how much this nation owes the negro, and it figures out to just $40,000,000,000. We must have it and will have it, or full manhood here, and we are not going to receive full manhood recognition here. The whites will not concede it. Therefore as soon as these old slave dwarfs, slave mannikins, and slave fools die out, our children and their children will play a new deal in the programme of the future." See Herb Boyd, *Autobiography of a People* (New York: Doubleday, 2000), 167.

124. Trimview, *Voices of the Silenced*, 49–62.

125. Ibid.

126. Francis J. Grimke, "A Resemblance and a Contrast," in *American Sermons: From the Pilgrims to Martin Luther King, Jr.*, ed. by Michael Warner (New York: The Library of America, 1999), 723–41.

127. Neil Hickey and Ed Edwin, *Adam Clayton Powell and the Politics of Race* (New York: Fleet Publishing, 1965), 21.

128. Adam Clayton Powell Jr., *Adam by Adam: The Autobiography of Adam Clayton Powell, Jr.* (New York: Dial Press, 1971), 43–44.

129. Peter J. Paris, *Black Leaders in Conflict: Joseph H. Jackson, Martin Luther King, Jr., Malcolm X, Adam Clayton Powell, Jr.* (New York: Pilgrim Press, 1978), 108.

130. Powell, *Adam by Adam*, 42.

131. Paris, *Black Leaders in Conflict*, 138.

132. Powell, *Adam by Adam*, 42. See also, V. P. Franklin, *Living Our Stories, Telling Our Truths: An Autobiography and the Making of the African American Intellectual Tradition* (New York: Scribner, 1995), 391–417.

133. Paris, *Black Leaders in Conflict*, 138

134. For an insightful analysis of how Seventh-day Adventists have historically dealt with politics, see Morgan, *Adventism and the American Republic*.

CHAPTER 6. THE SABBATH-DAY ADVENTIST CHURCH AFTER HUMPHREY

1. Before his death, Humphrey visited Seventh-day Adventist churches. Worshiping at the Ephesus SDA Church one Sabbath, he was invited to the rostrum. Why Humphrey was at Ephesus and not New York United that Sabbath is unknown. Was he thinking of or nursing thoughts of returning to the Seventh-day Adventist denomination? Probably not. Humphrey was retired and had given up the leadership of New York United at the time he worshiped at Ephesus. Still, Humphrey's presence at Ephesus shows that at the very least he was still open to worshiping in an African American Seventh-day Adventist congregation.

2. The Northeastern Conference is the regional conference comprising the states of New York, New Hampshire, Vermont, Maine, Massachusetts, and Connecticut.

3. Mesar and Dybdahl, "Utopia Park Affair," 53.

4. Ibid., 80.

5. Ibid., 54.

6. Princeton Holt, interview with author, tape recording, New York, NY, Aug. 11, 2000.

7. Chandler, telephone conversation.

8. La Condre, interview.

9. Hunter, interview.

10. A "first day" minister is a pastor of a different religious persuasion, usually one that does not hold that Saturday is the Bible Sabbath. Like the majority of Protestants, these ministers accept Sunday, the first day of the week, as the Bible Sabbath, professedly in honor of the resurrected Christ.

11. Kevin Jenkins, telephone conversation with the author, Nov. 10, 2000.

12. Hunter, interview.

13. Berwyn La Mar, telephone conversation with the author, Mar. 4, 2001.

14. A gospel concert held in conjunction with the Homecoming Celebration attracted almost 300 people.

15. Jenkins, interview.

16. Jenkins argued that getting out of the Association would save the church money it could not afford to waste, and the congregation accepted his argument. Ibid.

17. Princeton Holt, conversation with the author, Jan. 6, 2001.

18. The contradictory nature of African American religion is given full treatment by Hans A. Baer and Merrill Singer in *African-American Religion in the Twentieth Century: Varieties of Protest and Accommodation* (Knoxville: University of Tennessee Press, 1992).

19. Genovese, *Roll, Jordan, Roll*, 659.

20. Forrest E. Harris Jr., *Ministry for Social Crisis: Theology and Praxis in the Black Church Tradition* (Macon, GA: Mercer University Press, 1993), 19.

21. Gayraud S. Wilmore, *Black and Presbyterian: The Heritage and the Hope* (Philadelphia: Geneva Press, 1983), 43.

22. Gayraud Wilmore, *Black Religion and Black Radicalism* (Maryknoll, NY: Orbis, 1983), 152.

23. The debate on whether Seventh-day Adventistism is a cult has raged for years, with church leaders vigorously denying the charge. Walter Martin has given extensive study to the issue in *The Truth about Seventh-day Adventism* (Grand Rapids: Zondervan Publishing House, 1960) and *The Kingdom of the Cults* (Minneapolis: Bethany House Publishers, 1997). In the latter, Martin devotes a chapter to "The Puzzle of Seventh-day Adventism," saying "it is perfectly possible to be a Seventh-day Adventist and be a true follower of Jesus Christ despite certain heterodox concepts" (517). See also Richard Kyle, *The Religious Fringe: A History of Alternative Religions in America* (Downers Grove, IL: InterVarsity Press, 1993), in which the author says that Seventh-day Adventists are "an established, institutionalized sect that is set off from society by certain peculiar beliefs and practices." Included in those beliefs are the Sabbath and dietary practices (151). For Kyle, Seventh-day Adventism is a sect, though one that possesses cultic characteristics. H. J. Bergman, *The Religious Fringe: Cults, Cultists and Seventh-day Adventists* (College Place, WA: Walla Walla College, 1991) argues that whether Seventh-day Adventists are a cult or sect is not as important as why cults exist and the reasons people join them.

24. Baer and Singer, *African American Religion in the Twentieth Century*, 103.

25. Ibid., 49.

26. Ibid., 108. See also, August Meier, *Negro Thought in America, 1880–1915: Racial Ideologies in the Age of Booker T. Washington* (Ann Arbor: University of Michigan Press, 1966), 222.

27. Ibid., 55–64. See also Hans A. Baer and Merrill Singer, "Toward a Typology of Black Sectarianism as a Response to Racial Stratification," in *African-American Religion: Interpretive Essays in History and Culture*, ed. Timothy E. Fulop and Albert J. Raboteau (New York and London: Routledge, 1997), 257–76.

28. The terms cult and sect are used pejoratively. Yet, As Joseph Washington Jr. reminds us, historically religions were cults before they evolved into sects and then churches. Christianity itself began as a Jewish cult. It then became a persecuted sect before growing into a denomination and finally into a triumphant church. Joseph R. Washington Jr., *Black Sects and Cults* (New York: University Press of America, 1986), 1, 2. A recent contribution on the phenomenon of cults is James R. Lewis, *Cults in America* (Santa Barbara, CA: ABC–CLIO, 1998). For an excellent and insightful analysis of the sect or church debate, including whether Seventh-day Adventists are a sect, cult, or mainstream denomination, see Rock, *Institutional Loyalty*, 11–20. Rock, after weighing the evidence, pro and con, concludes that the Seventh-day Adventist denomination is an "established sect." Such a group is "somewhat more inclusive, less alienated, and more structured than the sect." Unlike true sects which either disappear in time or morph into the established church, the "established sect" does neither.

29. Miles Mark Fischer, "Organized Religion and the Cults," in *Afro-American Religious History: A Documentary Witness*, ed. Milton C. Sernett (Durham, NC: Duke University Press, 1985), 392.

30. C. Eric Lincoln and Lawrence H. Mamiya, *The Black Church in the African American Experience* (Durham, NC: Duke University Press, 1990), 121.

31. Washington, *Black Sects and Cults*, 140, 13–15.

32. Howard Brotz, *The Black Jews of Harlem: Negro Nationalism and the Dilemmas of Negro Leadership* (New York: Schocken Books, 1970), 64.

33. Arthur Huff Fauset, *Black Gods of the Metropolis* (New York: Octagon Books, 1944), 76.

34. Fischer, "Organized Religion and the Cults," 397.

35. Fauset, *Black Gods of the Metropolis*, 9, 76, 107–9.

36. Two excellent works on Father Divine are Robert Weisbrot's *Father Divine and the Struggle for Racial Equality* (Urbana, Chicago and London: University of Illinois Press, 1983), and Jill Watts's *God, Harlem, U.S.A.: The Father Divine Story* (New York: Columbia University Press, 1995).

37. Charles Samuel Braden, *These Also Believe: A Study of Modern American Cults and Minority Religious Movements* (New York: Macmillian, 1957), 44.

38. Ibid., 18–19.

39. M. J. Divine, *The Peace Mission Movement* (Philadelphia: Imperial Press, 1982), 46–47.

40. Ibid., 51–53.

41. Ibid., 44–45.

42. John Hoshor, *God in a Rolls Royce: The Rise of Father Divine, Madman, Menace, or Messiah* (New York: Hillman-Curl, 1936), 236–39.

43. Ibid., 252.

44. For a detailed account of Divine's impact on the masses, see Sara Harris, with the Assistance of Harriet Crittenden, *Father Divine: Holy Husband* (New York: Doubleday, 1953). The authors' prose is vivid, graphic, and sometimes raw.

45. Weisbrot, *Father Divine*, 181.

46. Henry Louis Gates Jr. and Cornel West, *The African-American Century: How Black Americans Have Shaped Our Country* (New York: Free Press, 2000), 125.

47. Fauset, *Black Gods of the Metropolis*, 23.

48. Ibid., 26.

49. Ibid., 22–30.

50. Weisbrot, *Father Divine*, 215–16.

51. Harris, *Ministry for Social Crisis*, 93–98.

52. Ibid., 93.

53. According to James H. Cone, the establishment of independent Black churches is a "visible manifestation of Black Theology." See James H. Cone, *A Black Theology of Liberation* (Philadelphia: Lippincott, 1970), 59.

54. See Peter J. Hinks, *To Awaken My Afflicted Brethren: David Walker and the Problem of Antebellum Slave Resistance* (University Park, PA: Pennsylvania State University Press, 1997).

55. See Carol V. R. George, *Segregated Sabbath: Richard Allen and the Emergence of Independent Black Churches, 1760–1840* (New York: Oxford University Press, 1973).

56. *United Sabbath-Day Adventist Messenger*, Aug. 1932, 14–15.

57. Ibid., 13–14.

CHAPTER 7. SUMMARY AND CONCLUSIONS

1. Robert T. Handy, "Negro Christianity and American Church Historiography," in ed. Jerald C. Brauer, *Reinterpretation in American Church History*, (Chicago: University of Chicago Press, 1968), 111.

2. C. Eric Lincoln, Foreward, In Cone, *A Black Theology of Liberation*, 10.

3. See Gayraud Wilmore, *Black Religion and Black Radicalism*, 161.

4. Cone says that the organizing of Black church is a visible manifestation of Black Theology (*A Black Theology of Liberation*, 59). Other works that deftly explore the phenomenon known as Black Theology include James H. Cone, *Risks of Faith: The Emergence of a Black Theology of Liberation, 1968–1998* (Boston: Beacon Press, 1999); Will Coleman, *Tribal Talk: Black Theology, Hermeneutics, and African American Ways of Telling the Story* (University Park: Pennsylvania State University Press, 2000); James H. Evans, *We Have Been Believers: An African-American Systematic Theology* (Minneapolis: Fortress Press, 1992); and Dwight N. Hopkins, *Introducing Black Theology of Liberation* (Maryknoll, NY: Orbis, 1999).

5. Cone, *Black Religion and Black Radicalism*, 135–66.

BIBLIOGRAPHY

Adeleke, Tunde. *UnAfrican Americans: Nineteenth Century Black Nationalists and the Civilizing Mission.* Lexington, KY: The University Press of Kentucky, 1998.

Anderson, Jervis. *This Was Harlem: A Cultural Portrait, 1900–1950.* New York: Farrar Straus Giroux, 1981.

Angell, Stephen Ward. *Bishop Henry McNeal Turner and African-American Religion in the South.* Knoxville: University of Tennessee Press, 1992.

Arthur, David Tallmadge. "Joshua V. Hines and the Cause of Adventism, 1839–1845." Master's thesis, University of Chicago, 1961.

Baer, Hans A., and Merrill Singer. *African-American Religion in the Twentieth Century: Varieties of Protest and Accommodation.* Knoxville: University of Tennessee Press, 1992.

———. "Toward a Typology of Black Sectarianism as a Response to Racial Stratification." In *African-American Religion: Interpretive Essays in History and Culture,* ed. Timothy E. Fulop and Albert J. Raboteau. New York and London: Routledge, 1997.

Baker, Delbert W. "In Search of Roots: Exploring the History of Adventist African-Americans in the United States." *Adventist Review* 170, no. 5 (Feb. 5, 1993): 12–14.

———. "In Search of Roots: Adventist African-Americans, Part Two: The Turning Point." *Adventist Review* 170, no. 6 (Feb. 11, 1993): 8–10.

———. "In Search of Roots: Adventist African-Americans, Part Three: The Ministry Begins." *Adventist Review* 170, no. 7 (Feb. 18, 1993): 16–18.

———. *The Unknown Prophet.* Washington, D.C.: Review and Herald Publishing Association. 1987.

———. "William Foy: Messenger to the Advent Believers." *Adventist Review* 165, no. 2 (June 14, 1988): 8–10.

———. "Regional Conferences: 50 Years of Progress." *Adventist Review* (Nov. 1995): 11–15.

Baptiste, David A., Jr., Kenneth V. Hardy, and Laurie Lewis. "Clinical Practice with Caribbean Immigrant Families in the United States: The Intersection of Emigration, Immigration, Culture, and Race." In *Caribbean Families, Diversity among Ethnic Groups,* ed. Jaipaul L. Roopnarine and Janet Brown, 275–303. Greenwich, CT: Ablex Publishing, 1997.

Bates, Joseph. *The Autobiography of Elder Joseph Bates.* Battle Creek, MI: Steam Press, 1868.

Ben David, Solomon. *The History of the Seventh-day Adventist Church in New York City.* Jerusalem, Israel: Palestine Printings Press, 1995.

Bercovici, Konrad. "The Black Blocks of Manhattan." *Harper's Magazine*, Oct. 1924, 613–623.

Bergman, H. J. *The Religious Fringe: Cults, Cultists and Seventh-day Adventists.* College Place, WA: Walla Walla College, 1991.

Billingsley, Andrew. *Mighty Like a River: The Black Church and Social Reform.* New York: Oxford University Press, 1999.

Boddie, Emerson. *God's Bad Boys.* Valley Forge, PA: Judson Press, 1972.

Bontemps, Arna. *The Harlem Renaissance Remembered.* New York: Dodd, Mead and Company, 1971.

Boyd, Herb. *Autobiography of a People.* New York: Doubleday, 2000.

Braden, Charles Samuel. *These Also Believe.* New York: Macmillan, 1957.

Bradford, Charles E. *Sabbath Roots: The African Connection.* Barre, VT: L. Brown and Sons, 1999.

Branson, Roy. "The Crisis of the Nineties." *Review and Herald* 147, no. 17 (Apr. 23, 1970): 4–6.

———. "Ellen G. White–Racist or Champion of Equality." *Review and Herald* 147, no. 15 (Apr. 9, 1970): 2–3.

———. "Slavery and Prophecy." *Review and Herald* 147, no. 17 (Apr. 16, 1970): 7–9.

Brotz, Howard M. *The Black Jews of Harlem.* New York: Schocken Books, 1970.

Bull, Malcolm, and Keith Lockhart. *Seeking a Sanctuary: Seventh-day Adventism and the American Dream.* San Francisco: Harper and Row, 1989.

Burkett, Randall K. *Black Redemption: Churchmen Speak for the Garvey Movement.* Philadelphia: Temple University Press, 1978.

———. *Garveyism as a Religious Movement: The Institutionalization of a Black Civil Religion.* Metuchen, NJ: Scarecrow Press and the American Theological Library Association, 1978.

Burkett, Randall K., and Richard Newman. *Black Apostles: Afro-American Clergy Confront the Twentieth Century.* Boston: G. K. Hall, 1978.

Butler, Jonathan. "Adventism and the American Experience." In *The Rise of Adventism*, ed. Edwin Gaustad, 173–206. New York: Harper and Row, 1974.

"A Caribbean Issue." Editorial. *Opportunity* 4, no. 47 (Nov. 1926): 334.

Chambers, John W. *The Tyranny of Change: America in the Progressive Era, 1900–1917.* New York: St. Martin's Press, 1980.

Christian, J.W. "Our Colored Work in Chicago." *Advent Review and Sabbath Herald* 107, no. 11 (Mar. 13, 1930): 24–25.

Clarke, John Henrik, ed. *Marcus Garvey and the Vision of Africa.* New York: Random House, 1974.

Coleman, Will. *Tribal Talk: Black Theology, Hermeneutics, and African American Ways of "Telling the Story."* University Park, PA: Pennsylvania State University Press, 2000.

Cone, James H. *Black Theology and Black Power.* New York: Seabury Press, 1969.

———. *A Black Theology of Liberation.* Philadelphia: J. B. Lippincott, 1970.

———. *For My People: Black Theology and the Black Church.* New York: Orbis Books, 1984.

———. *God of the Oppressed.* San Francisco: Harper and Row, 1975.

———. *Risks of Faith: The Emergence of a Black Theology of Liberation, 1968–1998.* Boston: Beacon Press, 1999.

————. *Speaking the Truth: Ecumenism, Liberation, and Black Theology.* Grand Rapids: William B. Eerdmans Publishing Company, 1986.

Cone, James H., and Gayraud S. Wilmore. *Black Theology: A Documentary History, Volume One: 1966–1979.* Maryknoll, NY: Orbis Books, 1993.

Contee, Clarence G. "Du Bois, the NAACP, and the Pan African Congress of 1919." *Journal of Negro History* 57, no. 1 (Jan. 1972): 13–28.

Coombs, Orde. "West Indians in New York: Moving Beyond the Limbo Pole." *New York* 3, no. 28 (July 13, 1970): 28–32.

Cooper, John Milton. *Pivotal Decades: The United States, 1900–20.* New York: Columbia, 1990.

————. *The Warrior and the Priest: Woodrow Wilson and Theodore Roosevelt.* Cambridge, MA: Harvard University Press, 1983.

Cooper, Wayne F. *Claude McKay: Rebel Sojourner in the Harlem Renaissance.* New York: Schocken Books, 1987.

Cronon, Edmund Moses. *Black Moses: The Story of Marcus Garvey and the Universal Negro Improvement Association.* Madison, WI: University of Wisconsin, 1969.

Crowell, Chester T. "The World's Largest Negro City." *Saturday Evening Post,* Aug. 8, 1925, 8–9, 93–94, 97.

Cruden, Robert M. *Ministers of Reform: The Progressives' Achievement in American Civilization, 1889–1920.* New York: Basic Books, 1982.

Dick, Everett Newfon. *William Miller and the Advent Crisis, 1831–1844.* Berrien Springs, MI: Andrews University Press, 1994.

Dittmer, John. "The Education of Henry McNeal Turner." In *Black Leaders of the Nineteenth Century,* ed. by Leon Litwack and August Meier, 253–72. Urbana and Chicago: University of Illinois Press, 1988.

Divine, M. J. *The Peace Mission Movement.* Philadelphia: Imperial Press, 1982.

Doan, Ruth Alden. *The Miller Heresy, Millennialism, and American Culture.* Philadelphia: Temple University Press, 1987.

Dolan, Frank. "Harlem Breakfast Caps Gotham Night." *Daily News* 2, no. 109, Oct. 31, 1929, 2, 4.

Domingo, W. A. "Gift of the Black Tropics." In *The New Negro,* ed. Alain Locke, 341–49.

Du Bois, W. E. B. *The Souls of Black Folk.* Chicago: A. C. Mc Clurg, 1931.

Dudley, Charles E. *Thou Who Hast Brought Us.* Brushton, NY: Teach Services, 1997.

Elmes, A. F. "Garvey and Garveyism–An Estimate." *Opportunity* (May 1924): 139–41.

Essien-Udom, Essien U. *Black Nationalism: A Search for an Identity in America.* Chicago: University of Chicago Press, 1962.

Evans, James. *We Have Been Believers: An African-American Systematic Theology.* Minneapolis: Fortress Press, 1992.

Fauset, Arthur Huff. *Black Gods of the Metropolis: Negro Religious Cults of the Urban North.* New York: Octagon Books, 1970.

Fischer, Miles Mark. "Organized Religion and the Cults." In *Afro-American Religious History: A Documentary Witness,* ed. Milton C. Sernett, 390–98. Durham, NC: Duke University Press, 1985.

Fisher, Rudolph. "The City of Refuge." In *The New Negro*, ed. Alain Locke, 57–74.

Fordham, W. W. *Righteous Rebel*. Washington, D. C.: Review and Herald Publishing Association, 1990.

Franklin, V. P. *Living Our Stories, Telling Our Truths*. New York: Scribner, 1995.

Frazer, Trevor. *The Emergence of the Black Conference in the Seventh-day Adventist Church*. Senior thesis, Atlantic Union College, 1972.

Frazier, E. Franklin. "The Garvey Movement." *Opportunity* 4, no. 47 (Nov. 1926), 346.

———. *The Negro Church in America*. New York: Schoeken Books, 1976.

Froom, LeRoy E. *The Prophetic Faith of Our Fathers*. Washington, D.C.: Review and Herald Publishing Association, 1954.

Gaines, Kevin. *Uplifting the Race: Black Leadership, Politics, and Culture in the Twentieth Century*. Chapel Hill: The University of North Carolina, 1996.

Gale, Robert. *The Urgent Voice: The Story of William Miller*. Washington, D.C.: Review and Herald Publishing Association, 1975.

Garvey, Marcus. *Philosophy and Opinions of Marcus Garvey*. New York: Arno Press, 1968.

Gates, Henry Louis, Jr., and Cornel West. *The African-American Century*. New York: The Free Press, 2000.

Genovese, Eugene. *Roll, Jordan, Roll: The World the Slaves Built*. New York: Pantheon Books, 1974.

George, Carol V. R. *Segregated Sabbaths: Richard Allen and the Emergence of Independent Black Churches, 1760–1840*. New York: Oxford University Press, 1973.

Graybill, Ronald D. "The Abolitionist-Millerite Connection." In *The Disappointed: Millerism and Millenarianism in the Nineteenth Century*, ed. Ronald L. Numbers and Jonathan Butler, 139–150. Bloomington: Indiana University Press, 1987.

———. *Ellen G. White and Church State Relations*. Washington, D.C.: Review and Herald Publishing Association, 1970.

———. *Mission to Black America: The True Story of Edson White and the Riverboat Morning Star*. Mountain View, CA: Pacific Press Publishing Association, 1971.

Grimke, Francis J. "A Resemblance and a Contrast." In *American Sermons*, ed. Michael Warner, 723–41. New York: Library of America, 1999.

Hale, Frank W., Jr. "Commitment vs Capitulation." *Spectrum* (Spring 1970): 31–34.

Haller, John S. *Outcasts from Evolution: Scientific Attitudes of Racial Inferiority, 1850–1900*. Urbana: University of Illinois Press, 1971.

Hamilton, Charles V. *The Black Preacher in America*. New York: William Morrow, 1972.

Handlin, Oscar. *The Newcomers: Negroes and Puerto Ricans in a Changing Metropolis*. Cambridge: Harvard University Press, 1959.

Handy, Robert T. "Negro Christianity and American Church Historiography." In *Reinterpretation in American Church History*, ed. Jerald C. Brauer, 91–112. Chicago: University of Chicago Press, 1968.

Harding, Henry O. "Health Opportunities in Harlem." *Opportunity* 4, no. 48 (Dec. 1926): 8.

Harkness, Elmore Ernest. "Social Origins of the Millerite Movement." Ph.D. dissertation, University of Chicago, 1967.

"Harlem–1920's Mecca for West Indians." *New York Amsterdam News* (Sept. 1980): 9.

Harris, Forrest E. *Ministry for Social Crisis: Theology and Praxis in the Black Church Tradition*. Macon, GA: Mercer University Press, 1993.

Harris, James H. *Preaching Liberation*. Minneapolis: Fortress Press, 1995.

Harris, Sara, with the assistance of Harriet Crittenden. *Father Divine: Holy Husband*. New York: Doubleday, 1953.

Harvey, Edward. *Historical Sketches of Blacks in the Seventh-day Adventist Church in America*. Term paper, Andrews University, 1974.

Haynes, George E. "The Church and the Negro Spirit." *Survey Graphic* 6, no. 6 (Mar. 1925): 695–97, 708–9.

Henderson, Thomas M. "Harlem Confronts the Machine: The Struggle for Local Autonomy and Black District Leadership." *Afro-Americans in New York Life and History* 3, no. 2 (July 1979): 51–68.

Henry, Keith. "Caribbean Migrants in New York: The Passage from Political Quiesence to Radicalism." *Afro-Americans in New York Life and History* 2, no. 2 (July 1978): 29–46.

Herskovits, Melville. *The Myth of the Negro Past*. Boston: Beacon Press, 1964.

Hickey, Neil, and Ed Edwin. *Adam Clayton Powell and the Politics of Race*. New York: Fleet Publishing, 1965.

Hicks, H. Beecher, Jr. *Images of the Black Preacher*. Valley Forge, PA: Judson Press, 1977.

Hill, Robert A., ed. *The Marcus Garvey and Universal Negro Improvement Association Papers*. 3 vols. Berkeley, Los Angeles, London: University of California, 1983.

———, ed. *Marcus Garvey: Life and Lessons*. Berkeley: University of California Press, 1987.

Hinks, Peter P. *To Awaken My Afflicted Brethren: David Walker and the Problem of Antebellum Slave Resistance*. University Park, PA: Pennsylvania State University Press, 1997.

Hofstadter, Richard. *The Age of Reform*. New York: Alfred A. Knopf, 1956.

Holt, Princeton. Interview by author. New York, Aug. 11, 2000.

Hopkins, Dwight N. *Introducing Black Theology of Liberation*. Maryknoll, NY: Orbis Books, 1999.

Hoshor, John. *God in a Rolls Royce: The Rise of Father Divine, Madman, Menace or Messiah*. New York: Hillman-Curl, 1936.

Hudson, Winthrop S. "A Time of Religious Ferment." In *The Rise of Adventism*, ed. Edwin S. Gaustad, 1–17. New York: Harper and Row, 1974.

Hunter, Aileen. Telephone conversation with author. New York, Mar. 4, 2001.

Hughes, Langston. *The Big Sea: An Autobiography*. New York: Hill and Wang, 1940.

———. "My Early Days in Harlem." In *Harlem: A Community in Transition*, ed. John Henrik, 62–64. New York: The Citadel Press, 1963.

"In the Regions Beyond." *General Conference Bulletin*, Thirty-Fourth Session, 6, no. 3 (Apr. 5, 1909): 83–86.

Jarvis, Irene. Interview by author. Tape Recording. Brooklyn, New York, Aug. 15, 2000.

Jenkins, Kevin. Telephone conversation with author, Nov. 20, 2000.

Johnson, James Weldon. "After Garvey—What?" *Opportunity*, 1, no. 8 (Aug. 1923): 231–33.

———. *Along This Way: The Autobiography of James Weldon Johnson*. New York: Viking Press, 1933.

———. *Black Manhattan*. New York: Arno Press and New York Times, 1968.

———. "The Question of Too Many Churches." *New York Age* 33, no. 26 (Mar. 20, 1924): 4.

Jordine, Maurice Roy. *Reflections on J. K. Humphrey and the First Harlem Church.* Term paper, Andrews University, 1978.

Justiss, Jacob. *Angels in Ebony.* Toledo: Jet Printing Services, 1975.

Kasinitz, Philip. *Caribbean New York: Black Immigrants and the Politics of Race.* Ithaca and London: Cornell University Press, 1992.

Kinney, Charles M. *Letter to John N. Loughborough.* Seventh-day Adventist church General Conference Headquarters. Silver Spring, MD.

———. *Statement on the Concept of Regional Conferences.* Seventh-day Adventist Church General Conference Headquarters. Silver Spring, MD.

Kirby, John B. *Black Americans in the Roosevelt Era: Liberalism and Race.* Knoxville: University of Tennessee Press, 1980.

Knight, George R. *Millennial Fever and the End of the World: A Study of Millerite Adventism.* Boise, ID: Pacific Press, 1993.

———. *A Search for Identity: The Development of Seventh-day Adventist Beliefs.* Hagerstown, MD: Review and Herald Publishing Association, 2000.

———. *From 1888 to Apostasy: The Case of A.T. Jones.* Hagerstown, MD: Review and Herald Publishing Association, 1987.

———. *Organizing to Beat the Devil.* Hagerstown, MD: Review and Herald Publishing Association, 2001.

Kolko, Gabriel. *The Triumph of Conservatism: A Reinterpretation of American History, 1900–1916.* New York: Free Press of Glencoe, 1963.

Kyle, Richard. *The Religious Fringe: A History of Alternative Religions in America.* Downers Grove, IL: InterVarsity Press, 1993.

Land, Gary. *Adventism in America.* Grand Rapids, MI: William B. Eerdmans Publishing Company, 1986.

Land, Winthrop D. "Ambushed in the City: The Grim Side of Harlem." *Survey Graphic* 6, no. 6 (Mar. 1925): 692–94, 713–15.

Leutenberg, William. *The Perils of Prosperity, 1914–1932.* 2nd edition. Chicago: University of Chicago Press, 1993.

Levine, Lawrence. *Black Culture and Black Consciousness: Afro-American Folk Thought from Slavery to Freedom.* New York: Oxford University Press, 1977.

Lewinson, Edwin R. *Black Politics in New York City.* New York: Twayne Publishers, 1974.

Lewis, David Levering. *When Harlem Was in Vogue.* New York: Alfred A. Knopf, 1981.

Lewis, James R. *Cults in America.* Santa Barbara, CA: ABC-CLIO, 1998.

Lincoln, C. Eric, and Lawrence H. Mamiya. *The Black Church in the African American Experience.* Durham: Duke University Press, 1990.

Link, Arthur. *Woodrow Wilson and the Progressive Era, 1910–1917.* New York: Harper and Brothers, 1954.

Locke, Alain. "Harlem." *Survey Graphic* 6, no. 6 (Mar. 1925): 629–30.

———. *The New Negro: An Interpretation.* New York: Arno Press and New York Times, 1968.

Luker, Ralph. *The Social Gospel in Black and White*. Chapel Hill, NC: University of North Carolina Press, 1991.

Makapela, Alven. *The Problem with Africanity in the Seventh-day Adventist Church*. Lewiston/Queenston/Lampeter: Edwin Mellon Press, 1996.

Manns, J. W. *"Why Free Seventh-day Adventist?"* N.p.: Banner Publishing Association, n.d. The Adventist Heritage Center, Andrews University, Berrien Springs, MI.

Marshall, Norwida A., ed. *A Star Gives Light: Seventh-day Adventist African-American Heritage*. Decatur, GA: Southern Union Conference of Seventh-day Adventists, 1989.

Martin, Tony. *Marcus Garvey, Hero*. Dover, MA: Majority Press, 1983.

———. *Marcus Garvey, Message to the People*. Dover, MA: Majority Press, 1986.

———. *The Pan-African Connection: From Slavery to Garvey and Beyond*. Dover, MA: Majority Press, 1983.

Martin, Walter. *The Kingdom of the Cults*. Minneapolis: Bethany House Publishers, 1997.

———. *The Truth about Seventh-day Adventism*. Grand Rapids, MI: Zondervan Publishing House, 1960.

Massey, Floyd, and Samuel Mc Kinney. *Church Administration in the Black Perspective*. Valley Forge, PA: Judson Press, 1976.

Matthews, Marcia M. *Richard Allen*. Baltimore: Helicon, 1963.

Maxwell, Patricia. *Journey to Freedom*. Boise, ID: Pacific Press Publishing Association, 1987.

McElhany, James Lamar., ed. *Statement Regarding the Present Standing of Elder J. K. Humphrey*. Washington, D.C.: General Conference of Seventh-day Adventists, 1930.

———. "The Greater New York Conference Session." *Advent Review and Sabbath Herald* 107, no. 11 (Mar. 13, 1930): 20.

McElvaine, Robert S. *The Great Depression in America, 1929–1941*. Boston: Beacon Press, 1984.

McKay, Claude. *Home to Harlem*. New York: Harper and Brothers, 1928.

———. *A Long Way from Home: An Autobiography*. New York: Harcourt Brace and World, 1970.

McMahon, Eva M., and Kim Lacy Rogers, eds. *Interactive Oral History Listening*. Hillsdale, NJ: Erlbaum Associates, 1994.

Meier, August. *Negro Thought in America, 1880–1915: Racial Ideologies in the Age of Booker T. Washington*. Ann Arbor, MI: University of Michigan Press, 1966.

Mesar, Joe, and Tom Dybdahl. "The Utopia Park Affair and the Rise of Northern Black Adventists." *Adventist Heritage* 1, no. 1 (Jan. 1974):34–41, 53–54.

Miles, Norman K. "Tension Between the Races." In *The World of Ellen G. White*, ed. Gary Land, 47–60. Washington, D.C.: Review and Herald Publishing Association, 1987.

Morgan, Douglas. *Adventism and the American Republic*. Knoxville, TN: University of Tennessee Press, 2001.

Moses, Wilson Jeremiah. *The Golden Age of Black Nationalism, 1850–1925*. New York: Oxford University Press, 1988.

Nichol, Francis D. *The Midnight Cry*. Washington, D.C.: Review and Herald Publishing Association, 1944.

Osofky, Gilbert. *Harlem: The Making of a Ghetto*. New York: Harper and Row, 1963.

Ottley, Roi. *New World A-Coming*. *New York*: Arno Press and New York Times, 1968.

Ottley, Roi, and William Weatherby. *The Negro in New York*. New York: Oceana, 1967.

Painter, Nell. *Sojourner Truth: A Life, A Symbol*. New York: W.W. Norton and Company, 1995.

Palmer, Ransford W. "In Search of a Better Life: Caribbean Migration to America." In *U.S.-Caribbean Relations: Their Impact on Peoples and Culture*, ed. Ransford W. Palmer, 63–74. Westfort, CT: Praeger, 1998.

———. *Pilgrims from the Sun: West Indian Migration to America*. New York: Twayne Publishers, 1995.

Paris, Peter J. *Black Leaders in Conflict*. New York: Pilgrim Press, 1978.

———. *Black Religious Leaders: Conflict in Unity*. Louisville, KY: Westminster/John Knox Press, 1991.

———. *The Social Teaching of the Black Churches*. Philadelphia: Fortress Press, 1985.

Parrish, Michael. *Anxious Decades: America in Prosperity and Depression*. New Haven, CT: Yale University Press, 1992.

Patterson, Orlando. *Slavery and Social Death: A Comparative Study*. Cambridge, MA: Harvard University Press, 1982.

Pearson, Walter, Jr. "Bound for Glory." *Advent Review* 171, no. 48 (Dec. 1994): 8–10.

Pease, William H., and Jane H. Pease. *Black Utopia: Negro Communal Experiments in America*. Madison, WI: The State Historical Society of Wisconsin, 1963.

Pells, Richard. *Radical Visions and American Dreams: Culture and Social Thought in the Depression Years*. New York: Harper and Row, 1973.

Perks, Robert, and Alistair Thomson, eds. *The Oral History Reader*. New York: Routledge, 1998.

Perrett, Geoffrey. *America in the Twenties*. New York: Simon and Schuster, 1982.

Pinn, Anthony B. *Why, Lord? Suffering and Evil in Black Theology*. New York: Continuum, 1995.

Ponton, M.M. *Life and Times of Henry M. Turner*. New York: Negro Universities Press, 1970.

Powell, Adam Clayton, Jr. *Adam by Adam: The Autobiography of Adam Clayton Powell, Jr.* New York: Dial Press, 1971.

Powell, Adam Clayton, Sr. *Against the Tide: An Autobiography*. New York: Richard R. Smith, 1938.

———. "The Church in Social Work." *Opportunity* 1, no. 1 (Jan. 1923): 15.

Raboteau, Albert J. *African-American Religion*. New York and Oxford: Oxford University Press, 1999.

———. *Canaan Land: A Religious History of African Americans*. New York: Oxford University Press, 2001.

———. *Slave Religion: The "Invisible Institution" in the Antebellum South*. New York and Oxford: Oxford University Press, 1978.

———. "Ricard Allen and the African Church Movement." In *Black Leaders of the Nineteenth Century*, ed. Leon Litwack and August Meier, 1–18. Urbana and Chicago: University of Illinois Press, 1988.

Raphael, Lennox. "The West Indian Syndrome: To Be or Not To Be an American Negro." *Negro Digest* 13, no. 1 (Nov. 1963): 30–34.

———. "West Indians and Afro-Americans." *Freedomways* 4, no. 3 (Summer 1964): 438–45.

Redkey, Edwin S. *Black Exodus: Black Nationalist and Back-to-Africa Movements, 1890–1910.* New Haven, CT: Yale University Press, 1969.

Reid, Ira de Augustine. *The Negro Immigrant: His Background, Characteristics and Social Adjustment, 1899–1937.* New York: Columbia University Press, 1939.

Reynolds, Louis B. *We Have Tomorrow: The Story of American Seventh-day Adventists with an African Heritage.* Washington, D.C.: Review and Herald Publishing Association, 1984.

Roberts, J. Deotis. *Black Theology in Disguise.* Philadelphia: Westminster Press, 1987.

Robeson, Paul. *Here I Stand: An Autobiography.* Boston: Beacon Press, 1958.

Rock, Calvin B. "A Better Way." *Spectrum* (Spring 1970): 21–22

———. *Go On!* Washington, D.C.: Review and Herald Publishing Association, 1994.

———. *Institutional Loyalty versus Racial Freedom: The Dilemma of Black Seventh-day Adventist Leadership.* Nashville: Vanderbilt University, 1984.

Rowe, David L. *Thunder and Trumpets: The Millerite Movement and Apocalyptic Thought in Upstate New York, 1800–1845.* Ph.D. dissertation, University of Virginia, 1974.

Schwarz, R. W. *Light Bearers to the Remnant.* Mountain View, CA: Pacific Press Publishing Association, 1979.

Seventh-day Adventist Encyclopedia. 1976 ed. S.v. "Regional Affairs, Office of, and Regional Conferences."

Singleton, H. D. "Eighty Years of Adventism." In *Telling the Story: An Anthology on the Development of the Black Seventh-day Adventist Work.* Comp. Delbert W. Baker, 4:82–84. Loma Linda, CA: Loma Linda University Press, 1996.

"The Southern Work." *General Conference Bulletin,* Thirty-Fifth Session, 5, no. 13 (Apr. 14, 1903): 202–5.

Sowell, Thomas. *Ethnic America: A History.* New York: Basic Books, 1981.

Spalding, Arthur W. *Origin and History of Seventh-day Adventists.* 3 vols. Washington, D.C.: Review and Herald Publishing Association, 1962.

Spicer, W. A. "New Memorials in Greater New York." *Advent Review and Sabbath Herald* 106, no. 51 (Dec. 19, 1929): 22.

Terkel, Studs. *Hard Times: An Oral History of the Great Depression.* New York: Pantheon Books, 1970.

Thakur, Parsram, Sr. *A Comparison of West Indian and American Undergraduates on Selected Cognitive Factors.* New York: New York University Press, 1975.

Thomas, Bert J. "Historical Functions of Caribbean-American Benevolent/Progressive Associations." *Afro-Americans in New York Life and History* 12, no. 2 (July 1988): 45–58.

Toney, Joyce. "Exporting Culture: Caribbean Americans in New York City." In *U.S.–Caribbean Relations: Their Impact on Peoples and Culture,* ed. Ransford W. Palmer, 87–96. Westport, CT: Greenwood Press, 1998.

Trimview, Darryl M. *Voices of the Silenced: The Responsible Self in a Marginalized Community.* Cleveland, OH: Pilgrim Press, 1993.

Turner, W. Burghardt, and Joyce Moore Turner. *Caribbean Militant in Harlem*. Blooming-
ton, IN: Indiana University Press, 1988.
*Twenty-four Hundred Negro Families in Harlem: An Interpretation of Living Conditions of
Small Wage Earners*. New York: Urban League, 1927.
The Utopia Park Health Benevolent Association, N.p., n.d.
Vanterpool, Donald L. *A Study of Events Concerning the First Harlem Church*. Term paper,
School of Graduate Studies, Andrews University, 1978.
Walter, John C. "Black Immigrants and Political Radicalism in the Harlem Renaissance."
Western Journal of Black Studies 1, no. 2 (June 1977): 131–144.
———. *The Harlem Fox: J. Raymond Jones and Tammany, 1920–1970*. Albany, NY: State
University of New York Press, 1989.
Walter, John C., and Jill Louise Ansheles. "The Role of the Caribbean Immigrant in the Har-
lem Renaissance." *Afro-Americans in New York Life and History* 1, no. 1 (Jan. 1977): 49–64.
Warren, Mervyn. *Oakwood: A Splendid Vision, 1896–1996*. Huntsville, AL: Oakwood Col-
lege, 1996.
Warner, Michael. *American Sermons*. New York: The Library of America, 1999.
Washington, Joseph R. *Black Religion: The Negro and Christianity in the United States*.
Landam, MD: University Press of America, 1964.
———. *Black Sects and Cults*. New York: University Press of America, 1986.
Watkins, T. H. *The Great Depression: America in the 1930s*. New York: Henry Holt, 1993.
Watts, Jill. *God, Harlem, U.S.A.: The Father Divine Story*. New York: Columbia University
Press, 1995.
Weisbrot, Robert. *Father Divine and the Struggle for Racial Equality*. Urbana, Chicago and
London: University of Illinois Press, 1983.
White, Arthur L. *Letter to Mrs. Hedy Jemison*, June 20, 1972. Adventist Research Center,
James White Library, Andrews University, Berrien Springs, MI.
White, Edson, *Letter to Ellen G. White*. Silver Spring, MD: Ellen G. White Estate, General
Conference of Seventh-day Adventists.
White, Ellen. "Lift up Your Eyes and Look on the Field." *Advent Review and Sabbath Herald*
73, no. 4 (Jan. 28, 1896): 49–50.
———. "An Example in History." *Advent Review and Sabbath Herald* 72, no. 51 (Dec. 17,
1895): 801.
———. *The Southern Work*. Hagerstown, MD: Review and Herald Publishing Association,
1966.
———. *Testimonies for the Church*. 9 vols. Mountain View, CA: Pacific Press Publishing
Association, 1948.
White, James. "Developing Black Leadership in White Denominations." In *Metro-
Ministry*, ed. David Frenchak and Sharrel Keyes, 51–57. Elgin, IL: David C. Cook Pub-
lishing Company, 1979.
White, James E. "Report of Southern Missionary Society." *General Conference Bulletin*,
Thirty-Fifth Session, 5, no. 13 (Apr. 14, 1903): 200–1.
Wilmore, Gayraud. *Black and Presbyterian: The Heritage and the Hope*. Philadelphia:
Geneva Press, 1983.

————. *Black Religion and Black Radicalism*. 2nd ed. New York: Orbis Books, 1983.

Wilson, Neal C. "Action Taken to Strengthen Black Work in North America." *North American Informant*, vol. 32, no. 1, January/February 1978.

Wintz, Cary D., ed. *African American Political Thought, 1890–1930: Washington, Du Bois, Garvey, and Randolph*. Armonk, NY: M.E. Sharpe, 1996.

Woodson, Carter Goodwin. *The History of the Negro Church*. Washington, D. C.: Associated Publishers, 1921.

————. *The Negro Professional Man and the Community*. Washington, D.C.: Association for the Study of Negro Life and History, 1934.

Woodward, Vann. *The Strange Career of Jim Crow*. 2nd ed. New York: Oxford University Press, 1966.

Year Book of the Seventh-day Adventist Denomination. Washington, D.C.: Review and Herald Publishing Association, 1922.

Young, Henry J. *Major Black Religious Leaders, 1755–1940*. Nashville: Abingdon, 1977.

Index